WHILE SPRING AND SUMMER SANG: THOMAS BEECHAM AND THE MUSIC OF FREDERICK DELIUS

While Spring and Summer Sang is part of a quotation from Sonnet LIX of Dante Gabriel Rossetti's *House of Life – Youth and Change*, that prefaces the score of Delius's *In a Summer Garden*. These words have long conjured up for the author both the mood of romance inherent in the composer's music and especially in Sir Thomas Beecham's handling of it. It is to the conductor's memory that this book is dedicated, out of gratitude for the intense pleasure that his Delius conducting has given the author for more than fifty years.

While Spring and Summer Sang: Thomas Beecham and the music of Frederick Delius

LYNDON JENKINS

ASHGATE

Published by
Ashgate Publishing Limited
Gower House
Croft Road
Aldershot
Hants GU11 3HR
England

Ashgate Publishing Company
Suite 420
101 Cherry Street
Burlington, VT 05401-4405
USA

Ashgate website: http://www.ashgate.com

British Library Cataloguing in Publication Data
Jenkins, Lyndon
    While spring and summer sang : Thomas Beecham and the music of
    Frederick Delius
    1. Beecham, Thomas, Sir, 1879-1961 – Friends and associates 2. Delius,
    Frederick, 1862-1934 – Friends and associates 3. Conductors (Music) –
    England – Biography 4. Composers – England – Biography 5. Music –
    England – 20th century
    I. Title
    780.9'2

Library of Congress Cataloging-in-Publication Data
Jenkins, Lyndon
    While spring and summer sang : Thomas Beecham and the music of
Frederick Delius / Lyndon Jenkins.
        p. cm.
    Includes bibliographical references.
    Discography: p.
    ISBN 0-7546-0721-6 (alk. paper)
1. Beecham, Thomas, Sir, 1879-1961. 2. Delius, Frederick, 1862-1934. 3.
Conductors (Music)—England—Biography. 4. Composers—England—
Biography. I. Title.

    ML422.B33J45 2005
    780'.92—dc22

                                                                2004027892

ISBN 0 7546 0721 6

Typeset by Express Typesetters Ltd, Farnham, Surrey
Printed and bound in Great Britain by MPG Books Ltd, Bodmin, Cornwall

Contents

List of Illustrations

The author wishes to record his gratitude for various permissions to reproduce the illustrations contained in this book. Those from the Archive of Shirley, Lady Beecham, from EMI or from other sources, are acknowledged separately; the remainder come from the Archive of the Delius Trust or from the author's own collection.

Figures

Plates

Between pages 84 and 85

Preface

In the years since his death in 1961 the reputation of Sir Thomas Beecham – as happens with so many great figures – has undergone something of a reappraisal. From his unquestioned status while he was alive as the only British conductor who could truly take his place on the world stage, his position is now sometimes conveyed by musical writers and commentators (few of whom heard him) as that of a conductor who brought a highly personal style to the classics, had flashes of inspiration among romantic composers, and enjoyed making second-rate music sound rather better than it ought to. Older listeners, and those who experienced him at first hand, will think very differently: among other things, they will remember that in the operatic field alone he commanded a total of 90 operas (including six each by Mozart and Richard Strauss, eight by Verdi and nine by Wagner) and will relish the response with which he once floored an incautious interviewer who thought to suggest that his repertoire was perhaps somewhat narrow – 'I've played five hundred and ninety pieces, if that's what you mean.' The repertoire in question was based on Handel, Haydn, Mozart and Schubert through Mendelssohn, Berlioz, Wagner, Brahms and Tchaikovsky to Strauss, Delius and Sibelius, always spiced by deep explorations of the wider French, Italian and Russian schools, among which Bizet, Rossini and Rimsky-Korsakov were always prominent. Nor should one forget his championing of English composers, particularly in his early years, which goes largely unremarked these days. In fact, Beecham's range was prodigious, and there is no doubt that he understood the language of all those composers, possibly better overall than any of his distinguished contemporaries. From today's standpoint, of course, his arsenal was perhaps deficient in not running to complete traversals of the oeuvres of Mahler and Bruckner, two composers whose music was less esteemed in his day but has in more recent times come to seem indispensable to conductors' reputations. How percipient Frederick Delius was when he spoke about 'vogues' in music: 'Now it's Sibelius,' he would say, 'and when they're tired of him, they'll boost up Mahler and Bruckner.'

Then again, because of Beecham's elegant stylishness and the rapier-like quality of his wit, recent generations have grown up encouraged to think of him as something of a 'character', amusing orchestras and audiences with an endless stream of anecdotes and recollections from his long career. Indeed there may be people who will seize on this book in the expectation of a collection of Beecham 'stories'. They will be disappointed. The public face was only a part of his multi-faceted genius, and can have little real significance in the ultimate assessment of his life's work in music. A vital part of that achievement was without doubt his crusade on behalf of the music of Frederick Delius, and it is by any standards a fascinating tale. Whatever the status of Delius's music in this 21st century, the way in which it was promoted virtually single-handedly to international acceptance during the last through the genius of one executive musician remains unrivalled in the history of music. It is easy to forget that when Delius and Beecham first met in 1907 this music was practically unknown outside Germany. In a sustained campaign over a period exceeding 50 years, by performing it often and everywhere, Beecham propelled it into the wider public arena through his musical gifts and the sheer force of his personality. A string of first performances, operatic stagings and revivals in the early years were succeeded by two magnificent Delius festivals, his own editions of the music, a biography of the composer and the creation of a legacy of recordings of the music that, notwithstanding all that has happened during the last 40 years, continues to stand at the absolute pinnacle of Delius interpretation. In his biography of the composer, Beecham was nothing if not self-effacing concerning his part in this remarkable achievement, and to record it now is the modest aim of this book.

Lyndon Jenkins

Acknowledgements

I am greatly indebted first and foremost to Robert Threlfall, of the Delius Trust, who read my manuscript and made most helpful suggestions and recommendations. It has been invaluable to have the lifetime's experience of the most authoritative living Delian placed at my disposal. Not only have his own publications, produced in parallel with his Herculean labour of seeing into print the collected edition of Delius's works as edited by Beecham, been almost daily sources of reference for me, but it has also been uniquely beneficial to have the sympathetic support of one who saw and heard Sir Thomas conducting Delius's music during three decades from the 1930s onwards. To the Delius Trust and its honorary archivist, Lionel Carley, I am grateful for access to the extensive correspondence held in the Trust's archive, notably that between Frederick and Jelka Delius and Sir Thomas Beecham. Marjorie Dickinson, secretary to the Trust, greatly smoothed my path in this respect. In quoting from this material I have at no point felt it necessary to correct wrong spellings, offer explanations or other simplifications. All the letters are perfectly clear, even if those of Mrs Delius sometimes feature the most delightfully quirky English: but they seem to me to reflect that remarkably single-minded lady in a quite unique way, and an expression such as, 'I objected it to Fred at the time he spoke about it, but he would never hear about it', adds an extra touch of colour to her portrait.

Also invaluable for reference purposes have been the newsletters and journals of the Delius Society of Great Britain produced under successive editors between 1962 and the present day. I should particularly like to thank Jane Armour-Chélu, for locating some rare pieces of print and for other practical helpfulnesses. To old friends of the Sir Thomas Beecham Society, especially Denham Ford, Norman Morrison and Tony Benson, I want to express particular gratitude. The wealth of information yielded by the Society's 30 years of newsletters, quite apart from the estimable volumes begun by Maurice Parker and continued by Tony Benson which list all Sir Thomas's concert and other appearances, has been of enormous assistance, but they have given me help additionally in specialised areas. John Lucas, concurrently engaged in his own study of Beecham, selflessly shared his own research with me, a compliment I fear I was unable to reciprocate in equal measure. Lady Barbirolli kindly allowed me to quote from one of Sir John's letters to her. I also want to acknowledge the help of Malcolm Walker, expert discographer, who was generous enough to look through my own modest effort and offer helpful comments and suggestions, and of Dr David Patmore, who permitted access to a fascinating study of Beecham's dealings with his recording companies.

Finally, I should like to extend my thanks to Shirley, Lady Beecham, and to David Lloyd-Jones, chairman of the Delius Trust, for their encouragement at the start of this project, and also to Professor Stewart Craggs who, although he may not realise it, provided me with the incentive to tackle it in the first place. To Lady Beecham I am also indebted for some of the fascinating photographic material it has been possible to include, and for permission to reprint Sir Thomas's graveside oration at the reburial of Frederick Delius in 1935. The copyright in letters, and extracts therefrom, written by Sir Thomas Beecham remains the property of Sir Thomas's Estate and are herein reproduced with the permission of Shirley, Lady Beecham.

Chapter 1

1907–1919
'I am sure my music has never been played as well by anyone …'*

Thomas Beecham was the grandson of the man who founded the business that became universally famous under the title of Beecham's Pills. Old Thomas (1820–1907) patented the formula he had invented, adopted the neat advertising slogan 'Worth a Guinea a Box', and from small beginnings the business grew into a substantial empire. After he retired in 1895, his son Joseph assumed control, and Beecham's Pills became an international concern, factories overseas being needed to meet the worldwide demand for an estimated ten million pills a day. Young Thomas, the second child and elder boy in Joseph's family of ten children, was born on 29 April 1879 and was musical from the start. He began to take piano lessons at the age of six and, for some years afterwards, during which he travelled widely in Europe and America and listened to music of all kinds and styles, began to see his future as a concert pianist or, more possibly, as a composer of opera. He first stood on a conductor's rostrum at the age of 20, conducting local forces in his home town of St Helens in Lancashire, but less than a month later took charge of a concert by Manchester's famous Hallé Orchestra which his father had hired to celebrate his re-election as mayor of the town. It had not been planned like that, but when the Hallé's conductor Hans Richter declined to be hired along with his players, young Thomas volunteered and his enthusiasm and determination won his father round. More conducting experience was gained when he took his first operatic score along to a London impresario with a view to its performance, and instead ended up directing performances of operas including *Carmen* and *Faust* in suburban London theatres. In 1905, he hired an orchestra to give a concert of his own in London, and the next year announced a series of four concerts to be given under his direction by 40 of the best players in London. Unfortunately his programmes of 18th-century music failed to draw, so he cancelled the last concert and straightaway enlarged the ensemble to symphonic proportions. He and his 'New Symphony Orchestra' then moved operations to London's principal concert venue, Queen's Hall, and in the final months of 1907 were beginning to attract attention.

For Frederick Delius (born Fritz Theodor Albert in 1862 to German parents in Bradford), the whole of 1907 had been a momentous time. After escaping from parental control and the family wool business at the end of the 1880s, he had spent

1

most of his life abroad and, partly because of this, his music was practically unknown in his native country. A concert of his compositions put on at his own expense in London in 1899 had achieved no more than momentary success, and after it he had retired once more to the fastness of his home in the little French hamlet of Grez-sur-Loing near Fontainebleau and concentrated on securing more performances of his works in mainland Europe. In Germany, in particular, he already had supportive and friendly musicians in the persons of the conductors Hans Haym, Alfred Hertz, Max Schillings, Julius Buths and Fritz Cassirer, who had, by this time, been variously responsible for giving first hearings of *Over the Hills and Far Away* (1897), *Paris* (1901), *Lebenstanz*, *Appalachia* and *Koanga* (all 1904) and *Sea Drift* (1906). Cassirer, who was emerging as Delius's foremost champion, in February 1907 had mounted a performance of his latest opera, *A Village Romeo and Juliet*, in Berlin, and was now proposing to bring *Appalachia* to England, for a concert in London at which he would make his English conducting debut.

Delius had meanwhile sent scores of his *Sea Drift*, *Appalachia* and Piano Concerto to the conductor Henry Wood in London, and this initiative had met with a favourable response: Wood was emerging as the first British maestro per se: previously most of the baton-wielders, such as Stanford, Cowen and Sullivan, were really composers who could also conduct, and Wood was establishing himself in London and elsewhere as a concert conductor pure and simple. As well as being connected with most of the provincial musical festivals in England, he had assumed direction of London's Promenade Concerts upon their inception in 1895 and was gaining a reputation there as a promoter of new music. The arrival of Delius's latest scores made him doubly conscious of his unrealised intention to perform the composer's *Lebenstanz* in 1904 and *Paris* in 1905 in London: he immediately informed Delius that he would recommend *Sea Drift* to the authorities of the Sheffield Festival (which he conducted), while the Piano Concerto struck him as 'just the work I should love to do at my popular concerts' (that is, the Promenade Concerts).

Fired by this enthusiastic reaction, Delius travelled to London in the April to make final arrangements with Wood and, rather to his surprise, found himself not merely better known and more highly regarded than he expected, but actually lionised. Invitations to luncheons and dinners proliferated; the composer Cyril Scott found him somewhere to stay; the tenor John Coates (who had been a school friend) wrote welcoming him to England; and Robin Legge, who had known him in the days when Delius was studying at the Leipzig Conservatory between 1886 and 1888 and was soon to become the chief music critic of the *Daily Telegraph*, conveyed greetings from mutual friends then in London: Cassirer, Hertz (who had conducted Delius's 1899 concert) and the American baritone Clarence Whitehill, the *Koanga* of the 1904 première in Elberfeld, who was singing Wagner at the Royal Opera House Covent Garden. The young Ralph Vaughan Williams sought the opportunity to show Delius some of his music, which ended up with him playing the whole of his *Sea Symphony* through on the piano. 'Truly it is not petty' (*mesquin*) was Delius's bemused comment. Best of all, Delius made the acquaintance of Granville Bantock, Balfour Gardiner, Norman O'Neill, Percy Grainger and Frederic Austin, and began friendships with all of them that were to last for the rest of his life.

Wood's promised performance of the Piano Concerto, with Theodore Szántó as soloist, duly materialised on 22 October 1907, and a month later came Cassirer's concert containing *Appalachia*. Originally the London Symphony Orchestra was to have played for Cassirer, but he objected to the additional fees being demanded for the extra rehearsals he needed, and Robin Legge intervened to tell Delius about an orchestra that had been formed in London only recently that he thought might be investigated as an alternative. A letter from Cassirer to Delius on 9 October contains the first mention of the 'Beecham-Orchestra', as the German conductor called it, which, he had discovered, was due to give a concert shortly. 'Perhaps you might go and listen to them?' he suggested to Delius. 'I might decide in favour of these people, because of the money it would save and because of the better opportunities for rehearsal.' The concert was at Queen's Hall on 14 October and Delius did indeed go, finding himself listening to Lalo's Symphony and symphonic poems by D'Indy and Smetana, together with Tchaikovsky's Violin Concerto and Bach's in E major (played by Joseph Szigeti, who was making his London debut at the age of 15). When the concert ended, Delius made his way backstage with the firm intention of meeting the orchestra's young conductor. What happened next is perhaps best told in Beecham's own words:

> At the conclusion of our ... concert a stranger of arresting appearance was brought into the artists' room and introduced to me. It was Frederick Delius, who, arriving from France a few days before, had been struck by the novel look of our programme and had come along to see what was going on. Praising the performance, he told us that the purpose of his visit to England was to investigate the orchestral situation, as a German friend of his, Fritz Cassirer ... wanted to give some concerts in London. An eminent authority whom they had consulted had advised them that there were only two orchestras available, and here to his surprise was a third ... on this he commented in characteristic fashion: 'London is the only town in the world where a first-class band like this can give such a set of concerts without one of its leading musicians being aware of its existence.' A few days later he came to see me again, this time with Cassirer, and engaged the orchestra for a trial concert at which the principal pieces to be played were his *Appalachia* and *Ein Heldenleben* of Strauss.[1]

Later in the course of his account of his first meeting with Delius who, he said, 'had turned up ... like a traveller from distant parts with a trunkful of curiosities', Beecham stated: 'I had dipped only casually into a few of them, but enough to compel the instant recognition of a musical intelligence not only different from but actually antagonistic to any with which I was acquainted.' At this distance one doubts that the shade of Sir Thomas Beecham Bart. CH will be much disturbed if leave is taken to cast mild doubt on the first part of this statement. Unless he had attended Delius's one-man concert in 1899 (which he had not), or had come across a Delius work during his continental travels in the eight years since (in which case one may reason that he might have noticed the music's qualities earlier) he can hardly have heard any of Delius's compositions at all and may not even have heard of their composer. The sole evidence even of the existence of this music available to him at the moment of their meeting was likely to have been the prospect of Henry Wood's forthcoming performance of the Piano Concerto but, although Beecham reported fulsomely on its success, he never actually states anywhere that he was present.

What is in no doubt, however, is that it was Cassirer's concert that proved the instant turning point for Beecham: indeed, it precipitated a conversion as dramatic as that of St Paul on the Damascus road. As Beecham himself put it in *A Mingled Chime*:

> Like every other musician under thirty years of age who was present at the performance of *Appalachia* ... I was startled and electrified. ... Here at last was modern music of native growth in which it was possible with uninhibited sincerity to take pride and delight. I formed the unshakeable resolution to play as much of it as I could lay my hands on whenever I had the opportunity, and at once included in my coming programmes for the New Year, *Paris* and *Appalachia* ...

He was as good as his word. At Delius's home, to which the composer had returned after Cassirer's concert, letters from Beecham soon began to arrive. The first, initiating a correspondence that was to continue on and off for the next 26 years, was dated 1 December 1907:

> Dear Delius
>
> When I looked through 'Paris' a couple of weeks ago, I formed a rather different idea of its difficulties. I thought it was just the sort of thing my fellows would revel in. At the Cassirer concert, the seven best 1st violins were not playing, four regular second violins, and the four principal celli too. So that you can hardly form an idea of their capacities from this particular affair. Personally I think 'Paris' is just the thing for us – I shall have my entire force in January when my own regular season – so to speak – commences.
>
> However I have inserted the 'Dance of Life' in the Programme and may do 'Paris' too – and will you now tell me where I can get hold of the Score and Parts. I shall want to try it over soon. Also I should like the score of 'Paris' and 'Brigg Fair' which I want to rehearse before Christmas as there is such short time after New Year ... If you will look in on Tuesday evening at Queen's Hall, I will show you for approval the sketch Programme of my series –
>
> Kind regards
>
> Yours very sincerely
>
> Thomas Beecham

And on 13 December:

Dear Delius

Could you let me have the scores of – Life's Dance – Norwegian Suite – 'Legende' for Violin – and The Danish songs[2] – ? I shall be able to do all these before Spring. At present I have included in my London series – Brigg Fair and Appallachia – of which I want very much to give another performance (and 'Paris' – provisionally). The Liverpool concert at which I shall be doing 'Paris' is on Jan. 11th – afternoon at the 'Philharmonic Hall'. The final rehearsal for this concert will take place on the morning either of the 9th or 10th – and if possible I should like you to be there as it will be of great help to me. I have got the 'Parts' but cannot have the score for a few days as Cassirer has lent it to someone ...

Very sincerely yours

Thomas Beecham

These letters were followed up by a personal visit by Beecham to Grez-sur-Loing at New Year, when he met Delius's wife, Jelka,[3] for the first time. The hoped-for purpose was to discuss Delius's scores with him so as to obtain a better idea of how they were to be interpreted, but the presence of others at the Delius house on New Year's Eve thwarted this intention. On 9 January 1908, however, Delius was at Beecham's side in London as he rehearsed *Paris* for its first performance in England at Liverpool two days later. That evening Delius wrote to his wife: 'Just a word to say that all is going well – I was at the rehearsal this morning which went very well – Beecham takes good tempi & the orchestra likes the piece – I leave tomorrow for Liverpool – '

After the Liverpool performance on 11 January, Delius was able to report to his wife not merely on that concert but also on a clutch of past and future performances of his works: it demonstrated in a quite startling manner how his musical landscape had altered.

Beecham played 'Paris' very well indeed – It was not quite a finished performance & he was perhaps a bit nervous but in London no doubt they will play it better ... Beecham is giving – Paris – Brigg fair – Appalachia & my Legende – perhaps the Danish songs if he can get the proper singer – ... A Dance of Life was splendidly played by the [London] Symphony Orchestra & admirably conducted by Arbos – first class – better than Haym or Buths. Unfortunately the Albert Hall is so enormous that one could not hear anything – It might have been played in Hyde Park. ... Brigg Fair also went splendidly and Bantock conducted very well ... I conduct Appalachia at Hanley April[4] ... Dec 3 they also give Sea-drift ...

Delius might also have mentioned a performance of *Brigg Fair* in London on 19 February expected from the conductor Landon Ronald, and another due on 6 March from Hans Richter and the Hallé in Bradford, though the latter was abandoned owing to insufficient rehearsal time. Wood's Sheffield festival performance of *Sea Drift*, the first in England, was fixed for 7 October, with Frederic Austin as the baritone soloist. Meanwhile, Bantock, besides conducting the first performance of *Brigg Fair* on 18 January, had been instrumental in

1.1 Delius and Beecham in the early years of their association

suggesting to the singer Olga Wood (Henry Wood's wife) that she should ask Delius to orchestrate some of his songs for her to sing: orchestral versions of *The Violet*, *Twilight Fancies* and *The Bird's Story* resulted, and she sang them under her husband's baton in Liverpool and London on 21 and 25 March.

On Beecham's front, enthusiasm was mounting after his Liverpool and London performances of *Paris* (the latter on 26 February). He now had several other works lined up in addition to the repeat of *Paris* in London on 14 April: *Brigg Fair* was due on 31 March, and *Over the Hills and Far Away* on 16 May (replacing the *Légende* for violin and orchestra: Mischa Elman played concertos by Mendelssohn and Spohr instead). It was London's first hearing of *Brigg Fair* and, though Delius's music was beginning to attract a more sympatheric hearing and reviews, the critic sent by *The Times* chose the occasion to be especially obtuse:

> The ... work was called an 'English Rhapsody', and is written by Mr. Frederick Delius on a very characteristic Lincolnshire tune 'Brigg Fair' which, though never allowed to be heard with what may be called its natural harmonies, supplies most of the thematic material, the remainder being taken from that treasure house of pastoral effects, the Waldweben from 'Siegfried'. The pastoral element at the beginning and end, whatever its source, is the most pleasing part of the composition, which seems to represent English country life as a remarkably sophisticated and decadent thing'.

Next came Beecham's first attempt at *Appalachia* (13 June). Delius was not present, as he was not long back from Munich where *A Mass of Life* had been heard for the first time on 4 June (though not in its entirety), and he wanted to stay at Grez-sur-Loing and work on his latest opera, *Fennimore and Gerda*. Balfour Gardiner reported to him on Beecham's concert: 'I heard your Appallachia yesterday & enjoyed it very greatly: Beecham did it well, & the chorus, though by no means perfect was much better than at Cassirer's concert.' Beecham also wrote, rather more fulsomely and certainly more colourfully, in a letter dated 17 June:

> 'Appalachia' has come and gone – I think it went off pretty well – the public were quite enthusiastic, but the critics nearly all reactionary – except perhaps the faithful Robin [Legge], who has now (and after much obvious mental struggle) arrived at the conclusion that I am a 'musician of genuine capacity' – vide – Daily Telegraph of next day – not a blessed word about the orchestra who blazed away at your work like a gang of navvies. I enlarged the band, doubled the whole brass (in places) and Harps, and we kicked up a rare old shindy. I had the B[irming]ham Choir down and they sang the unaccompanied bit very nicely – better than the Hanley crowd – with more delicacy and expression. They were hardly strong enough for the Finale, but that was perhaps the fault of my 'doublings'. The effect however was quite good. Where we scored was in the funeral March – by aid of the extra Brass, getting a big crescendo up to the – fff – and then diminuendo to the 'Chorale' – I took the whole thing rather easily, especially the 6/8 measures which gained much thereby ... I really enjoyed myself, with the work – thanks to you – and so did the Band, who seemed quite happy and at home ... Have you yet got the Piano copy of the Dowson cycle? Please let me have it as soon as it comes out ...

The reference to the 'Dowson cycle' shows Beecham already enquiring after Delius's as yet unperformed choral work *Songs of Sunset* (1906–07); and his next two letters (3 and 17 July) suggest an even more significant broadening of his horizons: 'I am trying to arrange for the "Mass" [*A Mass of Life*] to be done also in London next season ... I want also to look at "Romeo" [*A Village Romeo and Juliet*] ...'

With the swift expansion of his Delius repertoire Beecham felt it more necessary than ever to consult the composer about how his scores were to be interpreted:

> I was not yet convinced that I was doing the right thing by them. The scores, especially the printed ones, were vilely edited and annotated, and if played in exact accordance with their directions of tempo, phrasing and dynamics could not help being comparatively ineffective and unconvincing ... it seemed that having once got down on paper the mere notes of his creations, he concerned himself hardly at all with how they could be made clear of ambiguity to his interpreters.

So when Delius proposed a walking-tour of Norway during the summer he accepted with alacrity. They met in Oslo at the end of July and spent the whole of August walking in the mountains. The trip was an undoubted success at every level: 'Beecham is enjoying himself immensely,' Delius wrote to his wife, 'and the more I see of him the more I like him ... he is an excellent travelling companion – he does nothing that I do not like.' For his part, Beecham reserved himself to describing Delius as 'a first-rate and tireless walker' and to discussing his literary and other predilections and tastes, though his overall impression at that time was that he

> had never known a keener and brighter spirit than Frederick ... there was nothing in [him] of that vague indetermination associated traditionally with musical genius; in practical affairs he was as hard-headed as any to be found in his native country ... he knew exactly what he wanted and went after it with a simplicity and celerity that were models of direct action.

Since Delius took every opportunity to indulge his keenness for fishing, and would sit peacefully for hours wherever a suitable stream could be found, Beecham seized the opportunity to discuss his compositions with him. How much useful guidance he obtained in this quest, however, is not known, though in later years he tended to count it as little.[5] But it was undoubtedly at this time that he decided once and for all that his future career lay in conducting. It seems strange now to think that he had been contemplating becoming either a composer of operas on a grand scale or a concert pianist. It was the realisation that his talent for composing would probably run only to songs and miniatures that knocked the former on the head, while it was a knock on the wrist (he always maintained) that put paid to his pianistic ambitions. Whatever happened, the way to the rostrum was clear, and Delius was partly responsible, as Beecham acknowledged in *A Mingled Chime*:

It was an agreeable surprise to find strangers from so many different countries hailing me as an orchestral conductor of talent for whom there was a definite future. The encouragement I received was enough to satisfy almost anyone else than myself, but I was still a little reluctant to devote the whole of my energies irrevocably to a single occupation until I could bring myself to believe that I might achieve a success in it that would compensate for my failures elsewhere. That I did take the final plunge was due mainly to the convincing council and constant conviction of Frederick Delius.

Upon their return from Norway, and following a further visit by Beecham to Grez-sur-Loing, his first performances of *Sea Drift* took place on 3 and 4 December in Hanley and Manchester. At Hanley there was the famous incident of Beecham's score mysteriously disappearing between the rehearsal and the performance, forcing him to conduct the work from memory, a circumstance that apparently did not disturb him in the least. Next night, the attendance at Manchester was poor: no doubt at its home base of Hanley the North Staffordshire and District Choral Society and its conductor James Whewell could muster its own solid local support, but in Manchester's Free Trade Hall there were more people on the platform than in the auditorium. Beecham was impervious to such things, of course; he had embarked upon a crusade, and nothing was going to deflect him from his purpose. Two weeks later, Delius, who was present at both the Hanley and Manchester concerts, must have been surprised to hear that Beecham had parted company with the New Symphony Orchestra. There were several reasons for this, mainly that a number of the leading players had declined to travel north from London for the Delius concerts, and the orchestral deputy system,[6] which Beecham despised, was reviving itself within their ranks. When an ultimatum to them did not achieve the result he wanted, he immediately set about forming another orchestra. This was the celebrated band of players that was later to be called the Beecham Symphony Orchestra, although at first it was known as The Thomas Beecham Orchestra. It made its debut with him at Queen's Hall on 22 January 1909; Beecham had already written about it in glowing terms to Delius, naming some of the leading players and concluding: 'I can quite honestly declare that I shall have an orchestra which will simply wipe the floor with all the others combined ...' One month later, at the orchestra's next concert (22 February), he conducted the first London performance of *Sea Drift*, with Frederic Austin, the baritone of all the English performances to date, as soloist. Writing to Delius, he was still evidently intoxicated with his new creation:

'Sea Drift' has come and gone ... Everyone, even the Press, agree about the Band, that it is firstrate. The critic of the 'Times' told Ethel Smyth that it was the finest performance he had ever heard – They certainly played splendidly, I have never heard anything like it before, anywhere – Sea-Drift went stunningly, the Choir were beautifully in tune and quite safe and Austin's tempi were much better. Of course, his voice is very trying, but his share of the work was much better and more elastic – Generally, it was a far and away superior performance to those *you* heard. The Band were frantically enthusiastic, and if you had been there, you would have had a great ovation – They really are a wonderful lot, the richness of tone and delicacy of the wind are remarkable – I am so thankful now that I have got rid of that d——d N.S.O. We shall have a glorious time when the 'Mass' comes off – We shall have a fine 'house' for it – people are coming from everywhere to hear it –

The critics might have been impressed with Beecham's new orchestra, but some were less enthusiastic about Delius's *Sea Drift*; the *Musical Standard*, for example:

> We are afraid that Mr Beecham will scarcely succeed in making Delius' 'Sea Drift' a delight to listen to. The composer would seem to be on the wrong path. We listened attentively to the music ... and there seemed to be no excuse for its dullness and labouredness ... we were very sorry for the vocal soloist [Austin] ... he had abominably monotonous, barbarous and totally ineffective stuff to tackle ... What we strongly object to, apart from the laboured character of the music, is the ugly and meaningless dissonance of 'Sea Drift'. We are scarcely convinced that it is the work of a master-musician of the first rank ...

Such a negative assessment probably caused no more than a ripple in Beecham circles, where Beecham had his hands full with preparations for what was to be the first complete performance anywhere of *A Mass of Life*. Obstacles soon arose, the first of which had been signalled in a somewhat reproachful letter from Beecham to the composer in November 1908: 'I suppose you know that your "Mass" cannot be sung in England at all until it is translated (for the Chorus) into Tonic sol-fa – There is no choir anywhere here that can sing it from the staff notation. You must have a bright publisher – not to have attended to this before – ' Several names of suitable English publishers to produce a sol-fa score were bandied about, and cost estimates considered, before the matter was settled, Beecham urging, 'It is most necessary to have the sol-fa parts soon.' He was no doubt beginning to be concerned about his singers in Hanley, and their chorus-master James Whewall who was to prepare the *Mass* for him.[7] At the end of March he reported favourable progress with the four solo singers who were to take part, but was frustrated that Delius's publishers Harmonie, represented in London by Breitkopf & Härtel, would not sell him a full score of the work: 'They will only let it out on hire. This means I receive a nice clean copy from them to study from, which I must return after the performance with *no* marks, alterations or defacements thereon – Well, you know my method of study, and this is therefore highly absurd.' The eventual resolution of the problem, however, was equally absurd: 'They say they will sell me a Full Score,' marvelled Beecham, 'if I promise not to make use of it for public performance. *Voilà tout!*' In the end Delius sent Beecham his own full score, which was doubly useful as he had found in it and corrected a few mistakes.

A more serious problem concerned the translation of Nietzsche's text to be used in the performance of the *Mass*. Beecham had rejected the English version made by John Bernhoff, which was already printed in the scores, in favour of something that could, as he put it, 'be sung before a British audience without creating either amazement or hilarity', and had asked William Wallace, the Scottish composer and writer, to make him a completely new version: 'He has done it exceedingly well,' he told Delius, who responded with equal enthusiasm: 'Wallace's translation is ripping & reads like an English poem.' The publishers, however, were unhappy at this turn of events, rousing Beecham's ire further and causing him to complain again to Delius:

> B & H are always very disobliging and have already swindled me badly over the hire of parts for Sea-Drift – I must say they are very wearying people – I wish that the whole of the understanding with B & H could be reviewed, as I do not think that the present arrangement furthers your interests at all – I am sure they have no intention of lifting a finger to effect the slightest benefit to any English work – Wallace went to see Kling about this matter of the translation & Kling was quite offensive in his manner – They are nothing but a gang of brigands!

In letters to Delius, Wallace pointed out some of the more obvious flaws in the Bernhoff translation:

> Take the first line: This will be sung – 'O thou my wi-ill'. Page 8; the word 'cleped' is obsolete … Page 14; who will understand what is meant by 'prepared to mine ego', etc. 'That is a dance' is foolish. *Now for a dance* is English. Page 113; 'Rages' has two syllables, not one. Page 180; what singer will have the assurance to get up and declare 'I'm a temulent dulcet lyre' (liar)? … Page 202; that word 'awfuller' gives the text away ... You cannot afford to have your critical taste in English shown up with this sort of thing. Every musician who has seen B[ernhoff]'s text has said it will damn the work …

At length, Harmonie grudgingly gave way. 'As far as I can see, you are allowed to use and to print in the programme my text for THIS performance ONLY,' Wallace informed Delius. 'I think it very important that you should have a clear understanding with "Harmonie" as to what they will allow in the case of other performances of your work after Beecham's', adding a warning that echoed the conductor's words: 'It strikes me that "Harmonie" are not very anxious that your work should have the best possible chance …'

Despite all the setbacks, the performance of *A Mass of Life* came off, as planned, on 7 June 1909. The solo singers were Cicely Gleeson-White (soprano), M.G. Grainger-Kerr (mezzo-soprano), Webster Millar (tenor) and Charles Clark (baritone). Beecham evidently felt the work needed big solo voices: Gleeson-White was later his chosen Brünnhilde and Isolde, and Millar, though not a *heldentenor*, was to take on the roles of Romeo and Faust besides Rodolfo and Turiddu in Beecham's opera companies. Critical reaction ranged from the briefest of mentions in Hazell's *Annual* – 'a brilliant work which won favour' – through 'Nothing was wanting to render the work favourably' in the *Musical News*, to a lengthy and perceptive assessment in the *Standard* which began: 'One of the most striking and original works which have been heard in London for some time was produced last night at Queen's Hall, where Mr Thomas Beecham and his orchestra performed for the first time, "A Mass of Life" by Frederick Delius.' Following a description of the work, the review concluded:

> The work is lofty in conception as it is skillfull in construction. If the music does not always reflect the subtlety of the philosopher ... there is no question as regards the skillfullness of its architecture or the beauty of its design and texture. Considering the difficult and complex nature of the work, great credit is due to Mr. Beecham and his orchestra and to the North Staffordshire Choral Society (especially engaged for the occasion), whose singing was notable for its breadth and precision, and to the soloists ... for the efficient and convincing manner in which they interpreted and performed the by no means easy music.

Beecham seems to have encountered instrumental problems as a result of Delius including a bass oboe in his score.[8] The composer had fallen in love with this recently invented addition to the woodwind family – 'The bass oboe or Heckelphone is simply a lovely instrument,' he enthused to Beecham on 3 May 1909 – and had both written a prominent part for it in the *Mass*, and begun his Dance Rhapsody No. 1 with it. Beecham, no doubt conscious of the fact that Delius was intending to conduct the première of the latter at the Three Choirs Festival later that year at the invitation of Dr G.R. Sinclair, the festival's conductor, offered some helpful advice based on his experiences with the instrument:

> I have arranged about the Bass Oboe for Hereford. I find out however that Sinclair has been writing to another man who plays the 'Heckelphone'. I am told though that this particular instrument is a filthy affair and will not do – The man who played the Bass Oboe in the 'Mass' has overhauled the instrument and got to the bottom of it. He makes it now sound most beautiful and it is quite in tune. I find that it is built to suit either high pitch or low, this being determined by crooks. These latter we did not have for the 'Mass' – hence the weird noises – But now it sounds enchanting, and it is also the only one there is – If I were you I would write to Sinclair and tell him this or else you will be saddled with this other instrument which I am sure you will not like.

What transpired at the eventual performance at Hereford must have discomfited the composer, but it gave rise to one of the best of all Delius 'stories', recounted by Beecham in *A Mingled Chime* in a style and manner that has made it a classic of Delian literature. Although at the beginning wrongly placing the première in Hereford Cathedral (it was the Shire Hall) he soon got into his stride:

> How the piece ever came to be played at all in a sacred [*sic*] edifice remains a mystery ... nothing except possibly the anarchic operations of a swing band would have been less appropriate. Then the composer chose to incorporate into his score an important solo part for an instrument which, like Lucy, there were few to praise and very few to love, the bass oboe. As if these two errors of judgement were not enough, he must needs be persuaded into accepting the services of a young lady of semi-amateur status who had volunteered at short notice to see what she could do with it. Now the bass oboe ... is to be endured only if manipulated with supreme cunning and control; otherwise its presence

in the orchestra is a strain upon the nervous system of conductor and players alike, a danger to the seemly rendering of the piece in hand, and a cause of astonishment and risibility in the audience. A perfect breath control is the essential requisite for keeping it well in order, and this alone can obviate the eruption of sounds that would arouse attention even in a circus. As none of these safety-first precautions had been taken, the public, which had assembled ... in anticipation of some pensive and poetical effort from the most discussed musician of the day, was confounded by the frequent audition of noises that resembled nothing so much as the painful endeavour of an anxious mother-duck to effect the speedy evacuation of an abnormally large-sized egg ...

The summer of 1909 was marked by what Beecham described as 'three events all of capital importance to me'. The first was his performance of *A Mass of Life*, the second the staging under his direction of Ethel Smyth's opera *The Wreckers*, and the third the reconciliation between him and his father after almost a decade of complete estrangement.[9] The effect of the latter was to allow Beecham access to the family wealth and so indulge his plans for the next stage in the development of his artistic career by moving into the realm of grand opera. Since opera had always been one of his father's great enthusiasms, Sir Joseph Beecham reacted immediately and favourably to a scheme proposed by his son to take the Royal Opera House Covent Garden the next year and mount a season of opera there. Apart from Strauss's *Elektra* – which created a sensation and almost eclipsed all the rest – the bill included stalwarts such as *Carmen* and *Tristan and Isolde*. To represent native composers Beecham capitalised on the success of *The Wreckers*, added Sullivan's *Ivanhoe*, and found room for an initial foray into the operas of Delius. Announcing his latest initiative to Delius on 27 November 1909, Beecham again found himself facing up to some of the same practical performing difficulties that had beset his performance of *A Mass of Life*:

> Just a line to ask how you both are, and to tell you that I am producing Romeo & Juliet ... at Covent Garden ... The English text of Romeo will have to be entirely overhauled. I have already mentioned the matter to Wallace – But apparently there is only one Piano copy in existence and that is in my hands, but with no German text. What's to be done? Is it any use asking Breitkopf about it? The last time I was there, they had none – The singers will soon have to be looking at it. I find that Miss Artot de Padilla [Lola Artôt de Padilla, the Vrenchen of the first performances in 1907] is now at the Grand Opera house Berlin – There may be some difficulty about getting her, as I have already engaged so many Berliners, and everyone tells me she is too 'small' for Covent Garden. But I have several possible people on the list. The only person I am concerned about is the Black Fiddler – I have an excellent Tenor – quite splendid and fine appearance –

> P.S. Do you think in the Prologue that the parts of Vrenchen & Sali should be sung by two girls, both of very small stature, one a mezzo-soprano & dressed as a boy? I think myself this would be much more natural – They have very little to do – only a few lines –

The 'excellent tenor' referred to was Walter Hyde, who duly took the part of Sali opposite Ruth Vincent as Vreli: she was evidently one of the 'possibles' on

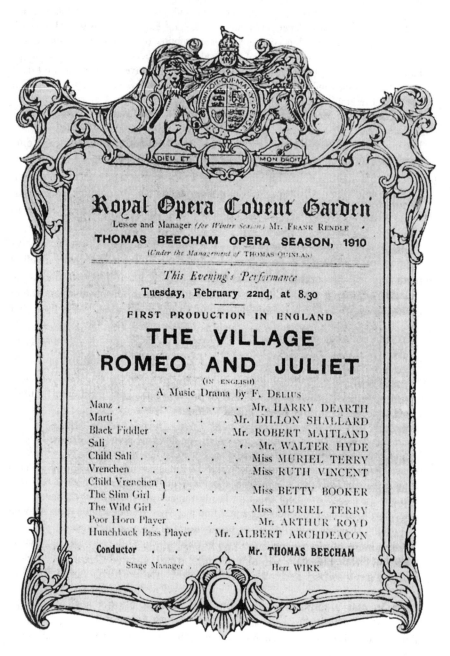

1.2 *A Village Romeo and Juliet*: **programme of 1910 performance**

Beecham's list of replacements for Lola Artôt de Padilla and proved to be a good choice, coming in for much praise. Robert Maitland sang the Dark Fiddler, and the part of Manz, Sali's father, was taken by Harry Dearth. It is a tribute to the versatility of singers such as Dearth and Hyde that they could make the transition to the opera house in such a production when most of their stage experience around that time had been gained in the rather different world of the Savoy Operas. The soprano Carrie Tubb, too, who took a minor role, had for the previous two years been singing in a concert party at Margate. Doubtless they all felt the change less keenly when Beecham, who had specially hired a merry-go-round for the Fair Scene, introduced a lighter note to the proceedings by insisting on climbing on to one of the wooden horses and giving himself a ride. The opera took the Covent Garden stage for two performances, on 22 and 25 January 1910. Delius was present at the rehearsals but, judging by his subsequent censorious comments – 'a miserable failure – inefficiency and inexperience bursting from every crack ... the only good point was the splendid orchestra and Beecham's conducting' – he was either powerless or unable to effect any improvements. Though not finding fault with the performance and praising the performers, most of the critics were unimpressed by the opera as a whole and thought the libretto weak. Predictably, it was pronounced undramatic, though those who took that line were effectively trounced by W.J. Turner in *Musical Life*:

> How ridiculous it is to complain that this story is not dramatic. One might as well complain of burgundy for not sparkling! The fact is, our operatic public has got so used to fat tenors brandishing cardboard swords, and to daggers, poison, and revolvers, and to abductions, seductions and desertions, that they do not know what to make of such a strange, inert, flowerless passion as that of Sali and Vrenchen.

No sooner was *A Village Romeo and Juliet* out of the way than Beecham was thirsting after another of Delius's operas to perform in his next season. 'As you will see by the enclosed circular I have included Koanga,' he told Delius in a letter dated 18 August, 'but if you have anything else you would prefer to have done and of which the material is available *and performable* (!) please let me know. I should like to know as soon as possible, so could you let me have a reply within a day or two – also information about Koanga itself.' Within a week, however, he was proposing *A Village Romeo and Juliet* again, 'unless you have any objection. I am personally very anxious to repeat the work, as I am convinced the more it is heard the more it will be appreciated, and I can see my way to giving a very much more adequate representation of the work than what you heard here last February.' He went on: 'I propose, subject to your approval, to retain in the cast the two principal characters, namely Miss Ruth Vincent, Vrenchen and Mr Walter Hyde, Sali, also the Wild Girl, Miss Muriel Terry. I can find fresh artists more suitable for the other roles.' This all sounded very promising, but the performance did not materialise. Beecham wrote early the next year to explain (15 January 1911):

I should have written long ago but until the end of the season I was overwhelmed with work ... From a public point of view the last opera season has been a failure, the audiences being absurdly inadequate – that is really the reason why I decided against reviving 'The Village Romeo' this autumn: I feel most strongly that a work like that needs everything in its favour for success – proper time for production and sympathetic audience. I think during the present year things will look up a little: all during the last, everything was under the shadow of old Edward's decease. [King Edward VII had died on 6 May 1910.]

I am delighted to hear 'Fennimore' is now finished and that you have dedicated it to me – it is very kind of you, old man, and I fully appreciate it. We will produce it here during this coming season – de luxe – with the real cast of singers for the job – I am picking these up by degrees – Whitehill I find to be excellent and I have a wonderful little soprano with a lovely voice, prefect style (and a splendid musician) who sings everything, your music included, at sight – Maggie Teyte[10] – she was formerly at the Opera Comique, Paris. I gave 'Brigg Fair' twice at my concerts this Autumn and the Piano Concerto. [He might have added *Paris*, given at his debut concert for the Royal Philharmonic Society on 7 December 1910.] In the Spring, I am doing the Mass of Life again, the Dowson Cycle and some of the other works I have already played ... It is possible that in April I may go to Paris with my orchestra – you should hear the beggars play *now* – the other day I did 'Heldenleben' of Strauss and at the first rehearsal they read the whole thing from beginning to end without a stop or any palpable slip whatsoever. They make 'Brigg Fair' sound quite divine ...

The performance of *A Mass of Life* did not take place either – 'I cannot get hold of the right singers,' Beecham told Delius on 19 May; instead, he announced a concert devoted entirely to his music and including what would be the first performance anywhere of *Songs of Sunset* and his own of Dance Rhapsody No. 1. He had been talking to Delius about the vocal work since the earliest days of their association and now its performance was possible: 'To sing the Solo Voices in the Dowson Cycle, I have got Julia Culp and Von Warlich (a most excellent singer) ... Do come over as there will be a good audience.' In the event, the English baritone Thorpe Bates replaced Reinhold von Warlich, and the complete programme, given on 16 June, became *Appalachia*, *Songs of Sunset*, *Paris* and the Dance Rhapsody No. 1. The *Daily News* devoted a lengthy review mostly to discussing how Delius's style had developed during the previous decade, and failed to mention either *Paris* or the Dance Rhapsody in the context of the concert. About the new work the writer seemed equivocal:

> With regard to Delius's 'Songs of Sunset', the words of which ... Madame Julia Culp and Mr Thorpe Bates sang so well in conjunction with the Edward Mason Choir, frankly they must be heard again. A first hearing seems to show that the songs are not all upon the same lofty level as that beginning 'Exceeding Sorrow', but we are glad to have made the acquaintance of a work that is of immense sincerity and truth ... Mr Beecham fully earned the applause that greeted him not only for his enterprise, but also for the wholly admirable manner in which he had carried it to a highly successful issue.

Both Delius and his wife attended the concert, which also became an occasion for meeting up with friends and supporters who were present, including Granville Bantock and Balfour Gardiner. During the concert interval a young British music enthusiast, Philip Heseltine,[11] made himself known to Delius, afterwards writing most effusively (he was only 17 and studying at Eton) about the music and Beecham's conducting of it, and seizing upon Delius's suggestions for further meetings, even one proposed at Grez-sur-Loing. Heseltine became an ardent admirer of Delius, and would in due course be of considerable assistance to Beecham in his promotion of Delius's compositions.

During the next few years Beecham's international travels as a conductor began, giving him a first opportunity to broaden the extent of his self-imposed task to preach the Delian gospel as widely as possible. In December 1912 he took his orchestra to Berlin for a pair of concerts at which *Brigg Fair*, Dance Rhapsody No. 1 and *The Walk to the Paradise Garden* were played, and in June 1913 he guest-conducted *Appalachia* in Paris at a concert given under the auspices of the Société des Grandes Auditions Musicales de France. He reported enthusiastically to Delius on the reception that he and his orchestra (and the music) had received in Berlin, but in Paris, where the composer was present, he faced a new orchestra unfamiliar with the music as part of a huge programme of contemporary music involving two other conductors besides him; the concert overran and had to be curtailed. Since France was one country in which his music had made no headway whatsoever, Delius's disappointment was understandable: 'The Orchestra was 2nd rate & the Chorus awful & Beecham seemed to be entirely out of his water and made nothing of Orchestra or Chorus,' he told Philip Heseltine.

Back at home, Beecham was turning his attention increasingly to the provinces. During 1907–08 he had been in charge of the concerts of the Birmingham Festival Choral Society, but had managed to interpolate into his programmes *Paris*, *The Walk to the Paradise Garden* and the Piano Concerto (with Arthur Cooke, who repeated it with him in London). But the whole experience, he told Delius in a letter dated 17 June 1908, had been unfortunate and he much regretted ever having gone there. Matters had seemingly come to a head over his initial performance of *Appalachia*:

> for which, as you know, I hauled the Choir up to London, who brought along with them (to boom and write them up) a doddering old idiot, Buckley by name, who has been put up as a sort of rival critic to [Ernest] Newman in B'ham. This damned old fool wrote a column of praise on the Choir's performance and lustily trounced both myself and the orchestra, asserting that the performance of Appalachia was very mediocre and altogether wanting in mastery and finish. I am sure you will not think I am overstating the case when I say that not only did the orchestra not make one technical slip, but they played with the utmost enthusiasm, finish and splendour of tone. It was far and away the best performance we have given of a work of yours – Paris not excepted – and everyone thought the work was magnificent ...

But if his experiences in Birmingham proved both short-lived and disappointing, he now struck up associations with Liverpool's Philharmonic Orchestra and Manchester's Hallé which were to be much longer lasting. Both his debut programmes in those cities featured Delius works – *Brigg Fair* in Liverpool and the Dance Rhapsody No. 1 in Manchester. And there were other musical centres he had identified for attention. Early in 1912, Percy Grainger appeared for the first time at a Beecham concert, although it was two years before they collaborated over Delius's Piano Concerto. This was at the last of the Torquay Music Festivals to be arranged by the resort's musical director Basil Cameron (then calling himself Basil Hindenberg[12]) before the 1914–18 war ended them. Beecham contributed some Delius works to the programmes, afterwards reporting to the composer in a letter dated 20 April 1914:

> I have just come back from Torquay where we all had great fun and wished unanimously for you to be with us. Nearly every English composer in the land was there, the weather was ideal, a circumstance which appeared to affect favourably their usual condition of native spleen, and many agreeable people motored in from the country houses round about ... Percy Grainger played your Piano Concerto and it went fairly well in performance, and most successfully with the Public. Percy was good in the 'forte' passages, but made far too much noise in the quieter bits, rather to the poetic detriment of the work. The 'Dance Rhapsody' was also an immense favourite with the Public, who greeted most of the novelties with the stoniest silence ... I have given your two little pieces ([I] The Cuckoo and [2] On the River) once or twice lately at private concerts ... They are concerts from which I exclude both Public and Press, and for which only invitations are sent. The last was at Howard de Walden's house, on which occasion we gave your pieces, which everyone liked immensely ...[13]

This letter contains the first mention in the Beecham record of Delius performances of the 'Two Pieces for Small Orchestra' (*On hearing the First Cuckoo in Spring* and *Summer Night on the River*), which had been premièred in Leipzig in October 1913 under the baton of Artur Nikisch and introduced in London for the Royal Philharmonic Society in January 1914 by Willem Mengelberg. Interestingly, Percy Grainger liked to think that he had been responsible for Delius composing these two pieces: he had made such a request 'around 1910', he said, and had reason to believe that subsequently Delius had acted upon it. When in March 1913 he renewed his appeal for something 'for not *too big* orchestra' he was evidently unaware that the *First Cuckoo* and *Summer Night on the River* were virtually already in existence. Grainger's letter to Delius of 5 March 1913 is more interesting for what it had to say about Beecham):

> I rejoice to see that Beecham is giving your 'Mass of Life' on March 10, but at the same time gnash my teeth, as I am in Switzerland on that date playing ... Beecham has done many thrilling & perfect performances of your lofty and adorable things of late, & I have been there and relished. It is a great joy to follow the progress of your works in this country *within the last year*. You are written of & spoken of in quite another tone now,

& *tower* above the other British composers more & more *in all sorts of people's minds.* Folk in this country want hammering away at, & the much that dear Beecham & little old Balfour [Gardiner] has done in the last year have together got home. Of course things move slowly, but by all I can see, as far as I can judge you will not lack *appreciation on the broadest possible lines* in this country if things go on as at present ... It fills us all with joy to see your power here growing in this steady way, & all who adore your work must feel ever so much love & thankfulness for the way Beecham has performed you here, both as to *oftenness* and as to the *touching glory* of the excellence of his performances. He is a ripping genius ...

The performance of *A Mass of Life* that Grainger mentioned was the one deferred from 1911. This has often been held to be a failure, and it is easy to see that it did not take place under exactly favourable circumstances. Again Beecham went for big solo voices: Anna Gura-Hemmel was a Brünnhilde, Herman Weil a Hans Sachs, Doris Woodall a future Carmen and Frederick Blamey a future Don José. The intention seems to have been that they would use the German text, though this was thwarted when Weil had to be replaced by Charles Clark, the singer at the 1909 performance, who could only sing it in English. The result was that he and the Chorus sang in English, while the other soloists stuck to the German. All four were placed uncomfortably out in front of Beecham and within a few feet of the front row of the audience, because even the large Covent Garden stage had difficulty in accommodating 250 singers and an orchestra of 90. The main criticism, however, seems to have been levelled at Beecham's favourite chorus from Hanley, which did not acquit itself so brilliantly as it had done on the earlier occasion. The reasons for this are easy to understand too. To begin with, James Whewall had died in 1909, and his standards had not been maintained. Then, from a purely practical point of view, the singers had travelled most of the day by train from Hanley, getting to London just in time for their one and only rehearsal with the orchestra at 4 pm prior to the performance at 8.30 pm. This was hardly the best preparation for an extended, intricate and taxing work, and it was perhaps significant that Herbert Whittaker, Whewall's successor, did not take a bow. In his book on Delius, Philip Heseltine dismissed the whole performance as 'not merely mediocre but appalling', borrowing a neat phrase from Sir Thomas Browne: 'A work of this nature is not to be performed upon one leg'. On the other hand, Delius, who could be outspokenly critical, seemed happy with at least the instrumental portion of it. He had heard every performance of the *Mass* and so could make comparisons. Jelka Delius recorded that 'Fred said that, apart from the singers, in this performance his orchestra was for the first time just as he had conceived it, & Munich & Elberfeld so bad that he had had doubts about the quality of the work' and the *Daily News* supported this assessment: 'The Beecham Symphony Orchestra came well through their appointed task ... and Mr Beecham, who conducted with complete authority, received at the close tributes of the warmest.'

1914 was to prove to be an unsettling year for the Deliuses, though it began quietly enough. No sooner was Beecham back in London from the Torquay

Festival than he was contemplating another all-Delius concert. The programme as originally planned was outstandingly interesting for the intended inclusion of first performances of *North Country Sketches* and *An Arabesque*, and Beecham's first attempt at *In a Summer Garden*. For various reasons, only the last of these was heard. There was a mix-up over *An Arabesque*, whose première Delius's publishers had apparently promised to Henry Wood, and Wood's message waiving this right never reached Delius; in the case of *North Country Sketches*, it seems that the orchestral material was not available in time. Ultimately, besides *In a Summer Garden*, the programme as performed on 8 July 1914 was made up of *Brigg Fair*, the *First Cuckoo*, *Summer Night on the River*, Dance Rhapsody No. 1, three songs, and Scenes 5 and 6 from *A Village Romeo and Juliet*. Delius, who received a warm reception from the audience, shrugged off any disappointment he may have felt at the loss of the original scheme, writing to his wife: 'I never heard Beecham play my things so wonderfully, and indeed, I am sure, my music has never been played as well by anyone ... Beecham has real genius, he feels every bar of my music like no one else.' When the autumn season began, Beecham introduced the *First Cuckoo* and *Summer Night on the River* in Bradford and Liverpool, conducted *Paris* in Sheffield (all with the Hallé Orchestra) and included the Dance Rhapsody No. 1 at a musical festival in Brighton. In November, he renewed his association with the Royal Philharmonic Society when he was engaged for several concerts in their 1914–15 season: one of them (24 November) contained excerpts from *A Village Romeo and Juliet*, and another (13 April 1915) was notable for the first appearance in a Beecham programme of anything from *Koanga*: labelled 'Epilogue' it was evidently the passage that became familiar later under the title 'Closing Scene'. Passages from *A Village Romeo and Juliet*, variously described as 'Selection from ...', 'Scenes from ...' and so on, were to become a feature of Beecham's concerts during the next few years, possibly to make up for the absence of any Delius on the stage, though nothing more from *Koanga* was heard until he staged the whole opera in 1935.

The outbreak of war in September 1914, and the early advance into France of the German Army, caused the Deliuses to leave their home. They reached Orleans, but when better news was received there they retraced their steps to find Grez-sur-Loing 'as quiet and peaceful as ever' (Delius told Percy Grainger). Grainger was urging them to leave for the complete safety of the USA, but it was Beecham, in a letter dated 25 October, who offered a more acceptable as well as practical solution to the uncertainties facing them:

> Now I will tell you what is the best thing for you to do – You ought to come to England in about three weeks time – I am taking a beautiful little place in the country about sixteen miles from London where you can settle yourselves, and write and paint at your complete convenience. When you wish to go to London, you can both stay at 8a Hobart Place [Beecham's London house], which will also be kept going through the winter – you will thus be spared the expense of any household cares, and I can arrange for one or two musical societies to pay you fees for the performances of your works that I shall give,

that will keep the 'pot-a-boiling' for some months to come. I am sure you will understand that in making these suggestions I am doing so only by reason of the stringent nature of the times ... I think it would be a great pity for you to interrupt your work in order to go to America or take up professional work. But if you come over here, as I suggest, and continue your work quietly and without outside worries, I shall have no trouble in arranging for fees with different societies, but of course you would have to be present at each concert, *not* necessarily to conduct, but simply in evidence as an 'English' composer! Only you ought to come here without much further delay – please do not leave it until too late ...

With his letter Beecham enclosed a description of the 'beautiful little house' in the country mentioned in his letter. It must have been an enticing prospect for the Deliuses: they accepted, and came to London in mid-November, staying at first with Beecham in London while there were concerts to attend, and then moving out to Watford on 5 December to take up residence in Grove Mill House; there they stayed until July 1915. No sooner had they arrived there than Beecham whisked Delius off to be present at a concert in Manchester which, as it included some of the music from *A Village Romeo and Juliet*, would earn the composer a fee. It was on this trip that the composer met two young English instrumentalists, May and Beatrice Harrison, who were the soloists in Brahms's Concerto for violin and cello in the same concert. Much taken with their playing, Delius announced that he would write a 'double concerto' of his own for them.[14]

Beecham's activities during the years 1913–16 were divided equally between opera, ballet and the concert hall. In his opera seasons either at Covent Garden, His Majesty's or Drury Lane, *Die Meistersinger* and *Tristan and Isolde* rubbed shoulders with Strauss's *Der Rosenkavalier* and *Ariadne auf Naxos*, and he even took a *Ring* cycle on tour to Manchester, Edinburgh and Leeds. The Russian Ballet and Opera Company he and his father had brought over proved a huge success – the London public 'has gone mad' over them, he told Delius – and in the orchestral field he was dividing his time between the Hallé Orchestra in Manchester and the Royal Philharmonic Society (which had its own orchestra) in London. The Beecham Symphony Orchestra had faded from the scene at the end of 1914: when he needed an orchestra in London now he had a replacement vehicle in the London Symphony Orchestra, which was shortly to elect him as its principal conductor. Not that their relationship was as smooth as had been the case with the Beecham Symphony: the LSO was a self-governing, seasoned band, and while its directors doubtless welcomed the financial support that Beecham's wealth could give them, the players as individuals were at first perhaps not so easily won over. Beecham, for his part, was already used to having his own way with orchestras, and in such circumstances disagreements and tussles were inevitable. At a rehearsal of Delius's Piano Concerto early in 1915 the pianist Benno Moiseiwitsch was witness to one:

Beecham had two or three contretemps with a woodwind player, a rather elderly musician and set in his habits but a good solid performer. He had been in the orchestra for so long that he did not relish repeated criticism in front of junior members of the team. So the next time Beecham criticised him he put down his instrument and said: 'Mr Beecham, this is the way I have always played it. This is the way the other conductors have accepted my performance. This is the way the audiences have always liked it. And in any case, I'm so old and set in my ways that I simply can't play it any other way.' Beecham nodded. 'Very well, then. Let me put the alternatives to you. Let me put the alternatives to all you gentlemen. Either I sink to your level or raise you to mine. Now which is it to be? Am I to go down to yours? By God, gentlemen, no. If it kills me I shall raise you up, if I have to do it to you individually and bodily, each in turn, with a crane or without.'

In the event Beecham only dallied with the LSO for a year or so, but what is perhaps surprising is that he persevered with it at all, especially as a vehicle for playing Delius's music, with its heavy dependency – at least in his hands – on delicacy of nuance and plasticity of phrasing. And there was plenty of Delius about then: *Sea Drift*, *In a Summer Garden* and several performances of the Piano Concerto were in sight, not to mention an important first performance, that of *North Country Sketches* (on 10 May). Philip Heseltine who, for all his youth, was becoming an outspoken critic, reported that the latter 'failed to do justice to some of the loveliest pages that Delius has ever written', which suggests that Beecham was still not getting his own way with the orchestra. It might have been that, while he was also appearing regularly at this time with several other orchestras in London (and visiting the Hallé in Manchester with increasing frequency), he felt that to have just one of these in regular contact with Delius's music was most likely to pay dividends. Looked at another way, Beecham was sufficiently busy just then so that he may simply not have had the time to consider the question properly and look for a better solution. He gave some idea of his workload during the 1915–16 season in a letter to Delius on 14 August 1916: 'I have given forty consecutive weeks of opera ... and have directly or indirectly been responsible for over eighty concerts.' Among a plethora of international operas he managed three performances of Joseph Holbrooke's *Dylan*, but there was no sign of the piece that Delius had dedicated to him, *Fennimore and Gerda*, despite his declared intention of performing it.[15]

His enthusiasm for Delius's music in general, however, never flagged for a moment. During 1915 he gave twenty-five performances of ten widely ranging works in Manchester, Edinburgh and Birmingham besides London. *Paris* was heard three times, *Sea Drift* and *In a Summer Garden* twice each, and the Piano Concerto no fewer than six times. Benno Moiseiwitsch was the soloist in three performances,[16] Evlyn Howard-Jones in two, all in London, while Manchester heard it from Robert (R.J.) Forbes. At least one of Evlyn Howard-Jones's performances was attended by Delius, who afterwards regarded the pianist as its most successful interpreter. Among the rest, on 24 January Beecham had selected a passage from the score of the incidental music that Delius had composed in 1897 for a production in Oslo of Gunnar Heiberg's dramatic satire *Folkeraadet*. This was one of the scores, referred to under the title 'Norwegian Suite', that he had asked about in his earliest correspondence with Delius in 1907; he now gave it in a concert with the LSO. The very next day, at a miscellaneous concert with small orchestra in the Music Club series at London's Grafton Galleries, he included Delius's settings of three poems by Verlaine (*Il pleure dans mon Coeur*; *Le ciel est, par-dessus le toit*; *La lune blanche*) together with the *Légende* for violin and orchestra. The songs, sung by Jean Waterston, were heard in orchestrations made by Philip Heseltine, while Beecham's leader Albert Sammons was the soloist in the *Légende*.

Although safely settled in England, Delius's finances were beginning to worry him more and more, as his income and royalties from performances in mainland Europe since the beginning of the war were drying up. America, where Percy Grainger was taking every opportunity to play his works and promote them with conductors such as Leopold Stokowski and Frederick Stock, was a new option and Delius was severely disappointed to discover that most of his music was unobtainable there. Even worse, it was becoming unavailable in England, since wartime restrictions prevented its importation from his German publishers. Something had to be done to enable him and his wife to survive: once again, Beecham came to the rescue (29 April 1915):

> In case I do not see you tonight I write to remind you of the conversation we had at the Devonshire Club on the subject of your works. My offer is to buy from you –
>
> | (1) The Violin Sonata | £300 |
> |---|---|
> | (2) The Legende | £150 |
> | (3) North Country Sketches | £250 |
> | (4) Three Songs | £200 |
>
> The total amount payable to you would be therefore £900 to be disbursed by me over a period of three years – an equal payment for each year, amounting to £300 per annum. After the expenses of publication are cleared off, I will hand you over the copyright of these works, to be your own property. I am enclosing a cheque for £50 on account of this agreement, which we can complete in a few days.

A simple agreement to give effect to this executed between him and Delius the following month must have relieved the Deliuses considerably, and they were soon enjoying a restful holiday in Norway away from all war danger. Apparently they had been more than usually anxious to leave London, despite the compositional work that Delius had been able to achieve while there: the contrast between London and his normal tranquil life in France must have been considerable, and he told Heseltine that the whole period had been 'a nightmare'. After Norway they returned home in November to Grez-sur-Loing, determined to sit out the rest of the war there.

The next month Beecham had a novel – for him – experience with a Delius work. He was in Rome, breaking new international ground through a pair of concerts with the Santa Cecilia Orchestra and had programmed, besides works by Mozart, Borodin and Rimsky-Korsakov, some native pieces by Ethel Smyth, Elgar

and Grainger besides Delius's *Paris*. Unfortunately, he knew very little about the
state of local musical culture, as he admitted in *A Mingled Chime*:

> and had I been better informed about it I should have proceeded even more
> conservatively ... things went smoothly enough until we reached *Paris* ... the public of
> the Augusteo, dumbfounded by the tone-picture of a city of which their acquaintance
> probably did not extend much beyond the Avenue des Champs Elysées, the Ritz tea-room
> and the cabarets of Montmartre, endured it in silence for about ten minutes, and then
> began to shuffle their feet and break into conversation. A few serious listeners
> endeavoured to silence the chatter but succeeded only in increasing it. Presently a few
> bolder spirits began to whistle; the opposition responded with furious cries and gestures
> of protest, and from that moment on the rest of the work was inaudible. I did not attempt
> to finish it, but waited for a likely place to stop and walked off the platform. The
> unexpected cessation of the music had the instant effect of quieting the uproar, and I
> returned to play the little overture of Paisiello's *Nina o la pazza d'amore*, whose artful
> simplicity enchanted both sides of the house and saved the situation.

1916 brought Beecham a knighthood but, other than that, it was a year that
plunged him into an unexpected and completely unlooked-for situation, not of his
making, which was to have far-reaching ramifications. Since early 1914 his father
had been involved in a project to buy and sell the huge Covent Garden Estate in
London, but now Treasury wartime restrictions on capital issues were bedevilling
the whole affair and all the parties involved were forced to a solution whereby a
'standstill' agreement was necessary to put the matter on hold until after the war.
During the night before the date the agreement was to be signed (23 October 1916)
Sir Joseph Beecham died, effectively nullifying the 'standstill' agreement and
plunging the whole Covent Garden affair into chaos. His eldest son's financial
position was never the same again. Even before his father's death the war was
having an adverse effect on the Beechams' business, and the newly ennobled Sir
Thomas wrote to Delius on 14 August 1916 that he was unsure as to whether he
was destined for 'a state of temporary pauperdom' on account of the disruption that
it was causing. His letter gives a rare glimpse of Beecham the businessman, the
more fascinating for its unexpectedness:

> You have rightly imagined that there have been lively times over here and for over three
> months my interests hung badly in the balance. On March 31st last the Government
> forbad the importation of certain articles – parts of machinery, manufactured wooden
> goods and other things that are vitally necessary for the carrying on of our various
> businesses including the one at St. Helens. Indeed had I not obtained special concessions
> (only a week ago) we could not have gone on after Xmas next. Our big motor industry
> in which I hold the controlling share, would have had to close down next month. Luckily
> I have been able to obtain favoured treatment so that everything is now flourishing as
> before ... I have paid two instalments for you into the Bank which takes us up to the New
> Year, and your publications are going apace. The 'Legende' is out and the others are on
> the point of appearing. So that from now on you need not have the smallest worry about
> material matters ...

This last statement was to prove premature, because in the new situation that was about to be created by his father's death Beecham was not going to be able to honour the promised payments on the music. That was in the future, however; for the next few years he managed to keep his musical activities going, albeit on a gradually diminishing scale, before having to retire altogether in 1920 to give more time to restoring the Beecham family's business fortunes. So far as Delius's music was concerned during these four years, most of the regular works were repeated, with *Sea Drift*, *Brigg Fair*, *Paris* and the Piano Concerto (two performances by William Murdoch) still prominent at Beecham concerts. In January 1916 there was a flurry of activity over the early *Légende*, when Beecham gave it at a Hallé concert in Manchester, accompanying the Hallé leader Arthur Catterall at the piano. The piece evidently found favour, as it was encored: so they repeated it at the Hallé's Pension Fund concert shortly afterwards, when it was encored again. Possibly the fact that it had been published that year in Manchester by the local firm of Forsyth Bros. Ltd had some bearing on its success, besides which Catterall had given the first performance the previous year of Delius's first Violin Sonata, another Forsyth publication. Early in 1917, when Catterall was again the soloist at a Hallé concert, the *Légende* made yet another appearance. Back in London on 29 January to conduct a Royal Philharmonic Society concert, and perhaps looking for another novelty or at least something unfamiliar with which to celebrate Delius's birthday on that day, Beecham turned for a second time to the *Folkeraadet* music.

But as his conducting activities began to reduce, the remainder of the decade inevitably saw a gradual falling off also in Delius performances: the twenty-five works played in 1915 fell to eight in 1916, seven in 1917, four in 1918 and three in 1919. This was partly attributable to the fact that Beecham had by now given most of his personal first performances, and, although there were new works coming along and others that he had not done (*Eventyr* in the former category, and *An Arabesque* and *The Song of the High Hills* in the latter), the financial and business problems which were besetting him meant that the time was not favourable. The première of *An Arabesque* was secured for a musical festival in Newport, Wales and took place on 28 May 1920. Henry Wood introduced *Eventyr* in London on 11 January 1919, and later the same month the Violin Concerto, completed in 1916, was conducted by promising newcomer Adrian Boult (30 January). Both these first performances Delius was able to hear, as he and his wife had been in London since September 1918.[17] The soloist in the Violin Concerto for the Royal Philharmonic Society was Albert Sammons, originally introduced to Delius as leader of the Beecham Symphony Orchestra and now the Concerto's happy dedicatee. Of the Beecham Symphony Orchestra's founder, however, there was now no sign: his last Philharmonic Concert – for the moment – had taken place on 15 April 1918.

Notes

* Letter from Delius to his wife after a Beecham concert on 8 July 1914.
1 Thomas Beecham, *A Mingled Chime* (Hutchinson & Co. Ltd, 1944).
2 In an interview in 1974, despite being 98 years old, the soprano Carrie Tubb (1876–1976) retained a clear memory of rehearsing what she recalled as 'Five Songs with Orchestra' with Beecham, in Delius's presence, for a Music Club concert in London in 1911. These songs would almost certainly have been the group to Danish texts which had been first performed at Delius's one-man concert in 1899: *Through long, long years*; *Let springtime come*; *Irmelin Rose*; *On the Seashore*; *Wine Roses*. (Later, with the addition of *Silken Shoes* and *In the Seraglio Gardens*, first performed in Paris in 1901, the five became *Seven Danish Songs*.) No trace has been found, however, of a Music Club concert in 1911 at which Beecham conducted, so one concludes that the rehearsal was either a run-through, perhaps to enable him to assess the songs for inclusion in a future programme, or possibly that Miss Tubb sang the songs under somebody else's direction.
3 Delius's wife Jelka was known by the diminutive of her first name: she was born Helene Sophie Emilie Rosen in 1868 (in Belgrade where her diplomat father was then serving at the German Embassy). Her mother was a daughter of the pianist and composer Ignaz Moscheles (1794–1870). It was while she was studying painting in Paris in 1896 that Jelka Rosen met Delius and they married in 1903, by which time she was already the owner of the property at Grez-sur-Loing that was to be their home for the rest of their lives. It was also at the time of their marriage that Delius renounced his first name, Fritz, by which he had been known up to that time, in favour of Frederick.
4 Delius's own attempts at conducting his own music in public were restricted to just three occasions: the second performance in England of *Appalachia* (2 April 1908 at Hanley); the first performance of *In A Summer Garden* (in its first version: 11 December 1908 in London for the Royal Philharmonic Society); and the first performance of Dance Rhapsody No. 1 (8 September 1909 at the Three Choirs Festival at Hereford). Beecham, attending the *Appalachia* performance, noted Delius's apparent inability even to beat time correctly in a straightforward four-in-a-bar: 'He contrived, I never knew how, to beat five-to-the-bar throughout.' Granville Bantock, another witness, also tried to discourage the composer from conducting and, upon hearing that he was determined to undertake the première of *In A Summer Garden*, gave him a friendly warning 'not to beat 4 in a 6/8 measure'. The composer Ethel Smyth (1858–1944) described Delius as 'an amusingly helpless conductor'. She was present at the rehearsal of *In a Summer Garden* and was delighted by his response when she suggested that the orchestra had perhaps been dragging his music: 'Dragging it?' he replied: 'I should think they were! But what can you do if they will go on playing slower and slower?' Delius's final attempt to conduct his own music (Ethel Smyth, *Beecham and Pharaoh*, Chapman & Hall Ltd, 1935) is described on pp.12–13.
5 At the time of the publication of his biography of Delius (*Frederick Delius*, Hutchinson, 1959) Beecham was interviewed by Edmund Tracey for the BBC TV programme *Monitor*. At one point Tracey was exploring the 'special understanding' that Beecham apparently had for Delius's music, but when he supposed that this came from Beecham often discussing his scores with the composer, the conductor replied that he had never done so: 'Why should I? He couldn't tell me anything about them! ... What occasionally happened was that I would say to him, "Now, Frederick, I want to ask you what you want done here": and he would say, "Well, I can't remember now, so do anything you

like with it" ... Then when he heard them on the radio or in the concert-room he'd say; "That's the way I want it ... Don't change that" ...'

6   The Deputy System in British orchestras, which was rife in the early part of the 20th century and lingered on into the 1930s, has been summarised like this: Player A, whom you want, attends the first rehearsal; he sends Player B, whom you don't mind, to the second rehearsal; he sends to play at the concert Player C, whom you would have paid to stay away.

7   Possibly Beecham was mindful of the ill-fated première in 1900 of Elgar's *The Dream of Gerontius*, which failed to make its impact because the music arrived too late for the chorus to rehearse and absorb adequately. One of the consequences was its labelling as 'difficult', and Beecham must have been relieved that the North Staffordshire and District Choral Society had recently mastered Elgar's work and performed it under James Whewall. It shared the programme of the concert in Hanley on 2 April 1908 at which Delius conducted *Appalachia*, so Beecham is likely to have heard it and been reassured.

8   The heckelphone (used by Richard Strauss in *Salome*, *Elektra* and the *Alpine Symphony*) is not the same as the bass oboe. Beecham was well aware of the difference between the two instruments, though Delius was apparently not so at first. (Some of his manuscripts indicate one, some the other, but all six of his relevant published scores call for the bass oboe.)

9   Beecham's father, Sir Joseph, had in the late 1890s had his wife placed in an asylum on grounds of doubtful legality. In 1900, Thomas and his sister Emily, Joseph's eldest son and daughter, began moves to have their mother released. They were successful, to the fury of their father, who promptly disinherited them both.

10 The English soprano Maggie Teyte (1888–1976), born in Wolverhampton, achieved early fame as a result of studying the role of Mélisande with Debussy himself in 1908. She was a most versatile artist, equally at home in opera, operetta and musical plays, and had a long career, during which she became a superb interpreter of French *chanson*.

11 Philip Heseltine (1894–1930) was the real name of the composer Peter Warlock. Despite their age gap he became an intimate of Delius almost from their first meeting, and they corresponded regularly over a long period. In 1921–22 he composed his *Serenade for Frederick Delius on his 60th birthday* and the following year published a book on Delius (*Frederick Delius*, 1923). Afterwards his first enthusiasm seemed to wane, although it revived to help Beecham with the 1929 Delius Festival. In 1930 Heseltine committed suicide.

12 The English conductor Basil Cameron (1884–1975) was the son of a German father and a Scottish mother. His real name was George Basil Hindenburg, but for almost the whole of his career he adopted his mother's maiden-name of Cameron. He gained his early conducting experience in Torquay, beginning in 1912, and before that engagement was ended abruptly by the 1914–18 war managed to mount a centenary Wagner season and ambitious programmes that included pieces by Stravinsky and Richard Strauss. For such concerts his regular Torquay Municipal Orchestra was augmented to 70 players, and he conducted as Basil Hindenburg because he believed an English name to be a barrier to musical progress. He soon realised that this was an error of judgement, and in later years would ruefully recall Beecham's pointed greeting on one occasion: 'Hello, Basil. What alias are you trading under these days?'

13 Beecham's letter goes on to tell Delius of a recent 'highly comical' occurrence: 'On Saturday I went to see Mrs Hunter [Ethel Smyth's sister] in the country ... She informed me that she had a selection arranged for the "Pianola" from your "Village

Romeo & Juliet" which she was in the habit of playing to everyone who came to the house, and that this piece was most popular with all, and had won for you no end of admirers. On my expressing some curiosity to know which portion of the Opera it was, I was told that it was the "Entr'acte" between the Final scenes which I have myself played many times on the Orchestra, and they proceeded to demonstrate how beautifully it was reproduced on the "Pianola". You may imagine my astonishment when I heard issuing from this "Automaton" the unfamiliar sounds of a merry little "Rigadoon" or hornpipe, played at terrific speed and with tremendous gaiety by some very brilliant pianist. Everyone was enchanted, and *I* sat rooted to my chair as if paralysed. After it was over, I examined the different rolls of music and discovered the truth. It seems that into the box bearing the name of your work had been placed by mistake a piano piece of "Moskowski" and that this had for months past been performed to countless visitors as a choice example of your style –'

14   The Harrison sisters were the violinist May (1891–1959) and cellist Beatrice (1892–1965). A third sister, Margaret, was also a violinist and a fourth, Monica, studied singing. Delius dedicated his third Violin Sonata to May, and his Cello Sonata and *Caprice and Elegy* to Beatrice. His Double Concerto he dedicated to them both.

15   It is possible that Beecham's ultimate disappointment in the opera had crystallised as early as this. In *Frederick Delius* (1959) he gives a trenchant account of its shortcomings as he saw them: 'None of the characters … makes a sympathetic appeal to us. Only towards the end, when it is almost too late, does the piece take on any really dramatic character, as if to remind itself that some sort of action is desirable as well as requisite upon the stage. Although there is no fault to find with the orchestral portion of the score, which is in Frederick's ripest and most sumptuous manner, its attractions do not entirely avail to gloss over the predicament of three dreary people who have nothing to sing.' Beecham never performed the opera either on the stage or in concert, though he did include Scenes 10 and 11 in the 1929 Festival and later twice recorded the two purely orchestral interludes, arranged with Delius's approval, which became known as the Intermezzo from *Fennimore and Gerda*.

16   In the October 1978 issue of the magazine *Hi-Fi News* a curious account appeared of Benno Moiseiwitsch's experiences with Beecham over the performance of Delius's Piano Concerto: 'Sir Thomas Beecham had planned to introduce the work to London audiences and the soloist whom he had engaged for the performance became indisposed no more than a week before the concert. He tried desperately to find a replacement and it was suggested to him that Moiseiwitsch, with whom he had never worked, was outstanding in his ability to learn new scores. He contacted Benno, who agreed to tackle it. Moiseiwitsch's wife, the outstanding Australian violinist Daisy Kennedy, quickly learned the orchestral part on a second piano and the two worked relentlessly on the piece during every waking hour for a week. On the day of the concert, the Concerto was memorised and the rehearsal began. It did not go well. Beecham had strong and uncompromising views on how he wanted the work performed, and Benno had equally assertive views on how he was going to play it. Tempers flared, heels were dug in, and few of the problems resolved. The performance was inevitably a tug-of-war and at the Concerto's conclusion Benno was off his seat and off the platform almost before the work's conclusion, leaving an enraged Beecham to take the applause by himself. They never spoke again throughout their lives, and if Benno's name appeared on a series of Beecham concerts, a guest conductor was engaged in his place.'

The facts are that Moiseiwitsch played the Concerto three times under Beecham's baton at this time (on 8 and 14 February, and 2 April 1915). It was not the first time that London had heard it, as Beecham had himself already conducted it twice, and it had been given twice more at the Proms since its première there in 1907. Hazell's *Annual* for 1915 recorded the Moiseiwitsch-Beecham performances as 'notable'; more significantly, the first of them was reviewed next day in the *Daily Mail* by Philip Heseltine (9 February): 'The feature of the London Symphony Orchestra's concert in Queen's Hall last night was the performance of Frederick Delius's Piano Concerto. The neglect of this magnificent work is inexplicable, in view of the tremendous applause with which it is always greeted ... yesterday's revival of the work was solely due to Mr Thomas Beecham ... Mr Moiseivitsch's rendering of the piano part was as good as taking trouble could make it; the great technical difficulties were all overcome in a masterly manner ...' According to Maurice Moiseiwitsch, his uncle's opinion of Beecham was that 'he had very great distinction and superlative taste' (Maurice Moiseiwitsch, *Moiseiwitsch*, Frederick Muller Ltd, 1965). It is also not true that the pianist and conductor never collaborated again, though it did happen only once: in Houston in 1955, when Beecham was guest-conductor of the Houston Symphony Orchestra, they played Rachmaninov's second Concerto together. Houston's publicity claimed that 'the world renowned pianist had appeared with Sir Thomas many times', which was certainly inaccurate. Probably it was the pianist's repertoire, with its heavy dependence on works that almost never appeared in Beecham programmes, which meant their paths had tended not to cross.

Delius's Concerto remained in Moiseiwitsch's repertoire: as well as the three Beecham-conducted performances in 1915 he played it that year at the Proms with Sir Henry Wood and was still playing it 40 years later when he appeared in it again in the 1955 Proms season, with Sir Malcolm Sargent conducting. Most important of all, in August 1946 he made the first-ever recording of it, with the Philharmonia Orchestra conducted by Constant Lambert. This was only very shortly before Sir Thomas and Lady Beecham made their recording subsequent to the 1946 Delius Festival, and one surmises that the producer of Moiseiwitsch's recording, Beecham's former confidant Walter Legge, would not have been too popular with the Beechams for stealing a march on them, and even less so when the critics generally preferred the Moiseiwitsch-Lambert version to theirs.

17 The Deliuses had decided to leave mainland Europe until the war came to an end. (Partly this was because upon returning to Grez-sur-Loing after spending the summer of 1918 in Biarritz they found that their house had been ill-used so badly during their absence – not by the invading Germans but by French officers who had requisitioned it – that Delius contemplated selling it. They did, however, return to it in October 1919, and were to remain there for the rest of their lives.) Arriving in London in September 1918 they lived briefly at a house let to them by Henry Wood in St John's Wood, before moving to 44 Belsize Park Gardens, where a plaque now records their residence between October 1918 and July 1919.

Chapter 2

1920–1929
'This Festival has been the time of my life.'*

One of the last Delius projects to be undertaken before Beecham's temporary disappearance from the musical scene in 1920 was his revival of *A Village Romeo and Juliet*. This had been intended for the autumn of 1919 but there was evidently some sort of misunderstanding between conductor and composer over various aspects of the production, and then other differences of a practical nature arose. On 12 November 1919 Beecham wrote to Delius:

(1) I told you last Summer … that I was giving your Opera this winter: that I was inserting the tableau scene we had discussed a long time ago, and in consideration of this substantial alteration in the presentation of the work I have felt justified in announcing it as a 'revised version'. This is the only revision that has been made, not a note or bar of your music having been altered.

(2) With regard to the financial arrangements, I leave those to the business management. The latter have approached every publisher in London and apparently none of them either have material of your opera or are authorized to deal with us for it. You may have forgotten, but you undertook last Summer to see that fresh material was sent over to London from wherever your German publisher is, but up to the present nothing has arrived. I think you had better authorize some responsible person here to go into these matters with us without further delay, as otherwise the production of the opera may be jeopardised.

(3) I have advertised two performances only, because firstly, the present season is short with a large repertoire, and secondly because the work is given in the second half of the season. If successful it will of course take it's [*sic*] place in the current repertoire and be played again next February. It will also be taken to Manchester for the Winter Season there in January.

(4) The rehearsals have been going on for some time in sectional form. Full rehearsals will begin in a few days time as soon as Parsifal is out of the way. I hope this information will satisfy you. I am sorry you should have been worried about the affair, evidently without much cause.

In the event the revival was postponed to the following year. In a letter dated 5 December to a friend of theirs, Marie Clews, Jelka suggested that her husband had been largely responsible for the decision to delay: 'We were summoned to London as Beecham intended giving the Village Romeo and Juliet – and Fred thought it necessary to be on the spot, and actually postponed the performance – it was all too hurried and they could not get the music over in time – so it was a good thing we went ...' Probably the fact that the orchestral material was not available was the more likely reason for the postponement to the following year, but then three performances were given at the Royal Opera House Covent Garden (19 and 25 March, and 6 April 1920).[1] Miriam Licette took the part of Vreli and Percy Heming that of the Dark Fiddler, while Walter Hyde reprised the role of Sali that he had taken at Beecham's 1910 staging. The somewhat world-weary tone of Beecham's patient explanation to Delius doubtless reflects the strain he was under by November 1919. He probably realised that some of the assurances he was giving the composer might not be fulfilled; and indeed, while there was one more season of opera at Covent Garden – though no Delius – the winter season in Manchester never took place at all. But, so far as *A Village Romeo and Juliet* was concerned, Delius was mollified and travelled to London in February 1920 in order to attend, in addition to the opera's first night, the first performances of his Concerto for violin, cello and orchestra, given by its dedicatees May and Beatrice Harrison conducted by Sir Henry Wood (21 February), and of *The Song of the High Hills* under Albert Coates (26 February). 'The Concerto went wonderfully well,' he reported to his wife, 'the girls played superbly and Wood surpassed himself – It was enthusiastically received – The Hall was crowded – the best of the season ...' He was not so pleased over *The Song of the High Hills*: 'Coates evidently did not quite know what to do with my music,' he wrote to the composer Charles Orr. 'It was unfamiliar to him and I am afraid he had not occupied himself sufficiently with the score ...'

The same letter contained his impressions of the performance he attended of *A Village Romeo and Juliet*. 'It went off as well as expected and much better than 10 years ago,' he told Orr. 'Beecham and his orchestra were perfectly splendid ... Hyde unimpassioned as usual – The black fiddler was good – Vrenchen – fairly good – Manz and Marti good – the two children also good – Scenery by Allinson not particularly good – The last scene was very good ...' There was an important sequel to these performances. The London theatrical producer Basil Dean had since 1919 been looking for someone to compose incidental music for a production he intended to stage of James Elroy Flecker's play *Hassan*. Several approaches, including one to Maurice Ravel, were coming to nothing when he and his designer, George Harris, dropped in one evening to hear *A Village Romeo and Juliet*. There and then Dean decided that Delius was the man for him and, within a few months, had travelled to Grez-sur-Loing and secured Delius's agreement (15 July 1920). Alerted to the possibility of Delius's involvement, Flecker's widow, Hellé, also visited the composer at his home, quickly signalling to Dean her support for his initiative: 'I think Mr Delius is anxious to do the music for the play and judging from his appearance – a bundle of quivering and spasmodic nerves – he is probably a good musician,' she wrote on 27 July. In the August Delius signed a contract to compose the music for *Hassan*.[2]

2.1 *A Village Romeo and Juliet:* **programme of 1920 performance**

By this time Beecham had withdrawn from the musical scene: for the next few years Delius would have to rely on others to perform his music. But he and the Deliuses met in London during the spring of the next year (1921), when the composer and his wife attended a performance, conducted by Albert Coates, of *Appalachia*. Jelka reported to Marie Clews (31 July):

> T.B we also met again in London. I had not seen him since 1915 and we fairly hugged one another on meeting again. He had no side on whatever and was really delightful – he and Fred and I sitting on a big Sopha in an upstairs room at Lady C[unard]'s[3] who was receiving her habitual tributees downstairs. Then he came to dine with us up in Hampstead and was most awfully nice too.

The following March saw the first performance of Delius's *Requiem* at a Royal Philharmonic Society concert, again conducted by Albert Coates (23 March). The Deliuses, who were by that time pursuing health cures in Germany following a sudden deterioration in Delius's health, had to forgo it, but they caught a second performance by local forces under the baton of a new Delius conductor, Oskar von Pander, in Frankfurt on 1 May. Jelka told his publishers that 'the enthusiasm and the emotion of the audience was quite touching', but Delius was more matter-of-fact: 'The performance of the Requiem was very good, orchestrally, it could have been better still with more rehearsals, but the choir was excellent.' On 31 January 1923, the Cello Concerto was heard for the first time, when the Russian cellist Alexandre Barjansky introduced it in Vienna with Ferdinand Löwe conducting.[4]

During the winter of 1922–23, Beecham paid a visit to the Deliuses at Grez-sur-Loing. This was the first time he had seen Delius for over a year and he was disconcerted by the composer's physical appearance. 'I questioned his wife, who admitted that he was having trouble with his eyes and a general lassitude in his limbs,' he wrote in *A Mingled Chime*; and continued:

> As I scrutinized him, I recalled the vigorous athletic figure that had climbed mountains with me only fourteen years before. He was not yet sixty, and had no business to be looking like that. I begged them to call in a specialist, as they were employing a homeopathic doctor, and they promised to do so. I did not see him again for some years, when I learned that my advice had not been followed, that the malady which then had been in an incipient stage had taken a firm grip of him, and that it was almost too late to avert disaster. I made one more effort by bringing over from London an authority on such cases, who prescribed what it was ascertained afterwards was the only course of treatment likely to be effective. But once again the blind belief in homeopathy prevailed and nothing came of it. The disease took precisely the course my expert had predicted, and Delius, although surviving another eight years, spent the last six of them in total blindness and paralysis.[5]

Beecham was already preparing for his 'official' return to the musical scene. The conclusion of his financial and business worries were summed up in a few words at the end of *A Mingled Chime*:

Thus ended the troubled and anxious period which began with the death of my father in October 1916 and ended that May morning of 1924 in the High Court of England. The long ordeal was a thing of the past. I could now resume my career or take up another. Anyway, I was free once more to do as I liked.

The words suggesting contemplation of an alternative career were written long after the event, and can be discounted: Beecham had already returned to conducting more than a year before 'that May morning of 1924'. The first two concerts announcing his return to the rostrum took place in Manchester and London (15 March and 8 April 1923 respectively, with different orchestras). Though both programmes included *The Walk to the Paradise Garden*, over the next few years nothing like the wholesale promotion of Delius's music that had characterised earlier times was evident. Instead, isolated performances – *Paris* in 1925, and again the next year with *In a Summer Garden*, together with *Summer Night on the River* – were the sum total until he took the London Symphony Orchestra on a tour of England, Scotland and Ireland in 1926 when the *First Cuckoo* figured in nearly every one of the 25 programmes. In May that year a plan for the LSO and Kennedy Scott's Philharmonic Choir to give some concerts in Paris with Beecham and Scott conducting had to be abandoned on account of the General Strike in Britain. Delius and his wife were disappointed, since one of the works was to have been *The Song of the High Hills*, which Delius had not heard since Coates's première in 1920. During a second UK tour by Beecham and the LSO in the November and December of the same year, the *First Cuckoo* was given frequently as an encore.

The *First Cuckoo* – though not conducted by Beecham – was probably the first piece of his own music that Delius heard via the radio, when it was broadcast from the Three Choirs Festival in 1925 at Gloucester: Delius was able to go to a neighbour's house to listen. The Deliuses had no electricity, and so no radio of their own. It was the first-ever transmission of a concert from the Three Choirs Festival, and the first time that Delius's music had been heard at one since he had taken charge of his Dance Rhapsody No. 1 in 1909 at Hereford. (Although the Cello Concerto was given in 1927, only five Delius works were played at the festivals between the two world wars. Beecham never conducted at a Three Choirs Festival.) Early in 1926, the Deliuses listened in again when the Cello Sonata was played by John Barbirolli and, later that year, with their house now wired for electricity, they acquired their own radio. The increasing number of Delius performances in Europe was to give them much interest and intermittent pleasure over the next few years. For Jelka Delius, perhaps understandably, there was never enough of her husband's music broadcast, and she was soon describing the programmes they were able to receive from Germany and Spain as 'abject'; but it was better than nothing while they awaited the return to the field of Delius's real champion.

It was 1927, however, before Delius's music resumed something of its former significance in Beecham's programming. In January that year he was again abroad, conducting opera in Vienna and Budapest, but an isolated concert with the Czech

Philharmonic Orchestra in Prague on the way gave him the chance to introduce *The Walk to the Paradise Garden* there; of greater significance, a concert with the Vienna Symphony Orchestra in February included *Paris*. Possibly remembering his Roman experience of a decade earlier, when the protesting Augusteo audience had caused the abandonment of his performance of the work, he rearranged the order of the programme without any announcement or warning. As the programme contained also Elgar's *Cockaigne* Overture and Lord Berners's *Fugue*, with which the Viennese audience in the Konzerthaus was unlikely to be familiar, no doubt the subterfuge worked. Unhappily for the Deliuses *Paris* was not broadcast; nor was a performance of *Sea Drift* that Beecham gave upon his return to London in April. More performances of the *Paradise Garden* and *First Cuckoo* were varied by one of *Eventyr* in October, but the most significant event of the year came right at its end. The world of the gramophone had been revitalised in 1925 by the advent of electrical recording in place of the old acoustic system, and Beecham was giving more and more time to making records under the new process.[6] He had never attempted to record anything of Delius's before, but evidently was now satisfied that justice could be done to the composer's elusive sound-world; on two days in December, he made the first of his long series of recordings of Delius's music. These were *On hearing the First Cuckoo in Spring* and *The Walk to the Paradise Garden*. The orchestra was the pick-up group of freelance musicians that played for the concerts of the Royal Philharmonic Society and consequently assumed on record labels the dignifying title of Royal Philharmonic Orchestra. 'The Orchestra of the Royal Philharmonic Society' would have been the more accurate description, but there is no denying the glamorous implication and effect of the one they used. Beecham would have known these particular players well, through his association with the Philharmonic Society since 1910.

1927 was also enlivened for the Deliuses by several visits from Beecham to Grez-sur-Loing. It was on one of these that he brought with him the London specialist whose recommendation for dealing with Delius's condition was a prolonged period of treatment in a sanatorium. Jelka effectively vetoed that as she thought it would make Delius miserable, but she and her husband did act upon a recommendation to consult a doctor in Paris. This brought no positive result either, since his view was that to risk any kind of drastic treatment that might make Delius's condition worse would be a mistake. 'That is my feeling too,' Jelka wrote to Percy Grainger. 'Let us make him as happy as possible and not ruin him with Medicine-poisoning etc.' So nothing was done, and Delius's infirmity was left to run its course. Beecham was right to draw the inference he did in *A Mingled Chime*, but in the Deliuses' defence it should be said that their lives ever since Delius's condition began to show signs of deterioration had been an endless round of medical treatments in several countries with only moderate, and always temporary, success to show for it. In the circumstances, it is perhaps not surprising that after six years they were thoroughly disillusioned with the medical profession and by what little it had been able to achieve for them.

2.2   Delius and Beecham in the 1920s

Now that they could no longer travel to performances, the gramophone they had acquired in 1925 brought them some consolation. At first their collection of Delius discs was necessarily small, consisting mainly of the few orchestral works of his that had been recorded up to that time by the acoustic process: these included versions by Eugene Goossens of *Brigg Fair* and the *First Cuckoo*, recorded for HMV in December 1923 and January 1924 respectively, and Henry Wood's 1923 discs for Columbia of the Dance Rhapsody No. 1. Either Albert Sammons or Evlyn Howard-Jones would have seen to it that their 1924 recording of the Violin Sonata No. 2 would have found its way to Grez-sur-Loing, and equally certainly HMV would have sent Delius their two discs of music from *Hassan* played by His Majesty's Theatre Orchestra conducted by Percy Fletcher as a souvenir of the rehearsals and performances there that he had attended in 1923. With electrical recording came the Cello Sonata played by Beatrice Harrison and Harold Craxton, and the song *To Daffodils* sung by Muriel Brunskill: 'a contralto-dragoon!' Jelka wrote scornfully to Philip Heseltine. She had, however, heard of a new record of *Twilight Fancies* and *Venevil*, but she wanted Heseltine to listen to it: 'If it is no better than Daffodils it is no pleasure for Fred to hear it,' she wrote in her forthright way.[7]

Fortunately for the Deliuses, Beecham's new records would soon arrive, and these were to give them unalloyed pleasure for the rest of Delius's life. Writing to Percy Grainger in May 1928, Jelka described them as 'so fluid and balanced and suave'; and when another disc came along Delius wrote to Beecham: 'I am quite delighted with your last record "Summernight on the River" ... it is lovely and so delicate. The three best records of my work are your Cuckoo, Summernight and Walk to the Paradise garden.' More recording was to follow in 1928, with attempts by Beecham on *Brigg Fair* in July and *Sea Drift* in November. Both were unsuccessful, but *Brigg Fair* was returned to and eventually all was well. It is a measure of the pains that he took that one complete version of the work should be rejected, and a total of 11 waxes expended on the first side alone of its successor before he was satisfied that the standards he set himself in Delius's music had been achieved. That *Sea Drift* did not come up to expectations was not altogether surprising: on the day that it was recorded Beecham and the same performers – Dennis Noble, the Manchester Beecham Opera Chorus and the LSO – somehow contrived to give a public performance of it in the afternoon at the Royal Albert Hall.

Beecham's international travelling was continuing, notably in the USA where, early in 1928, he made his debut with the New York Philharmonic, Boston Symphony and Philadelphia Orchestras. *The Walk to the Paradise Garden* featured in all the programmes, changed in favour of *Paris* and the *First Cuckoo* for the last of three concerts with the NYPO in Carnegie Hall. A total of eleven performances of *The Walk to the Paradise Garden* and two of *On hearing the First Cuckoo in Spring* (together with *Paris*) made an effective springboard from which to launch a Delian assault on the USA (where he was conducting for the first time), besides providing excellent publicity for the recordings of both of the smaller works that he had just made in London which were about to be released there. Percy Grainger was present at (at least) one of these American concerts and duly reported upon it to Grez-sur-Loing. 'It was lovely that you heard Beecham conduct,' Jelka responded, 'he must have done the Delius beautifully, judging from 2 Gramophone records he made for Columbia, and which are just out ... He gave 2 concerts in Paris and did the Interlude [*Paradise Garden*] in the first one, but it was very severe weather and we could not go there.'

Stimulated by the news of the success of his music in the USA under Beecham's baton, Delius wrote on 11 February to his publishers to tell them of it and to suggest that *The Walk to the Paradise Garden* should be extracted from the opera and published separately, not only for orchestra but in a piano arrangement as well. This was a theme that he had been pursuing for several years, without success, though this time he had a surprise: although Universal demurred on the grounds that the music was scored for too big an orchestra to secure sufficient performances, they were thinking instead about an arrangement for a smaller, salon orchestra. Delius, normally extremely quick to jump on any suggestion of his music being altered, amended or arranged by anybody, hesitated before sending his insistence that the music should be published as it stood. But Universal had gone ahead and commissioned the new version, effectively wrong-footing him. He appealed to Beecham on 10 March:

> Keith Douglas has made an arrangement [of the *Paradise Garden*] for a rather smaller orchestra, 2s and 3s of Brass and woodwind. He sent it straight to my publisher's, the Universal-Edition-Vienna and they seem to have accepted it. But I am telling them to send you a copy of the score *at once*, and I beg you to look at it. Of course I do not want this version to be played when a bigger orchestra is available.

At Delius's insistence, Universal eventually sent the score to Beecham but publication was delayed for several years.[8]

In June 1928, Delius received a letter from an unknown young Yorkshireman, Eric Fenby,[9] who wrote to express his gratitude for the loveliness that the composer's music had brought him. At first this was treated as being in the nature of a 'fan' letter and replied to accordingly, but Fenby's sensitive nature subsequently became completely consumed by the plight of this distant composer whose physical condition was preventing him from finishing his music. After wrestling for several weeks with the seeming enormity of an idea that had formed in his mind, he followed up his first letter with an offer to work as amanuensis in an attempt to help Delius complete his manuscripts. This offer was accepted, and Fenby arrived in Grez-sur-Loing on 10 October: for the next six years he was to be an integral part of the Delius household, his whole life inextricably linked with Delius's. Within a day he was able to observe the composer's reaction to his own music, first when Mrs Delius put Beecham's record of the *First Cuckoo* on their gramophone, and later during a Beecham-led performance of *Brigg Fair* broadcast from a BBC concert in London (12 October). 'Splendid, Thomas!' Delius called out as the sounds from the radio died away. 'That is how I want my music to be played. Beecham is the only conductor who has got the hang of it! That was a beautiful performance ...' During the *First Cuckoo*, Fenby recalled, 'a curious other-worldliness possessed him. With his head thrown back, and swaying slightly to the rhythm, he seemed to be seeing with those now wide-open yet unseeing eyes, and his spirit ebbed and flowed with the rise and fall of his music.'

1928 was the year that Beecham's programmes began fully to reflect the old commitment to Delius's music. It might have been the success of his American season, or stimulation from making the first gramophone records of the music, but from this time onwards Delius's music was firmly back in Beecham's repertoire, where it remained for the rest of the conductor's life. Not only did he begin to play it with greater frequency, but it must have been at this time that a plan for some sort of celebration of Delius's music was beginning to develop in his mind. In October, the Leeds Festival provided him with the opportunity to give *Sea Drift*, which he repeated in London the next month; then came *Brigg Fair* for the BBC (referred to above) and, three nights after that, *North Country Sketches* – or at least parts of it; the concluding movement, *The March of Spring*, was not played. Beecham turned to the audience in Queen's Hall with the explanation that the orchestral material, which was still in manuscript, had been found to be full of errors, so that complete rehearsal had been impossible. In these circumstances he felt sure that 'the most critical audience in London would rather hear three of the movements and wait for the fourth another time'. One cannot help wondering why, if this was the same manuscript material that had been used at the only previous performance of *North Country Sketches*, its première in 1915, it was still full of errors.

The following year (1929) began optimistically, with Delius being created a Companion of Honour in the New Year Honours. Beecham had begun to lobby as early as 1927 for some sort of recognition for him from his native country when, in a carefully reasoned and persuasive article in the London *Evening Standard* of 13 January, he had suggested the award of the Order of Merit. Possibly he was influenced by the fact that Elgar had been a recipient of this award (in 1911), though Beecham naturally did not mention it in his article. Delius was quick to acknowledge Beecham's intervention: 'For this distinction they have bestowed on me I owe all thanks *to you*, dear friend.' Jelka was less impressed: 'It has made us have a terrible lot of correspondence, and old friends and ancient schoolfellows have turned up or written,' she told Marie Clews, adding sourly: 'When the people of the world sit near him gushing they look like horrid caricatures and so much older, pleated and yellow than he does that I am amazed at their courage, talking nonsense to him.' Delius's condition meant he had to decline the invitation to attend the investiture by the Prince of Wales in London on 26 March, so instead the British Minister Plenipotentiary in Paris, Nevile Henderson, visited him at Grez-sur-Loing on 21 July to perform the ceremony.

Beecham must have calculated that the award of an honour, if and when it came, would create an upsurge of interest in Delius and his music. He had already been talking openly of some sort of Delius celebration being planned – as early as the previous November Jelka, in a letter to May Harrison, had spoken of her determination to take Delius to London 'if as is so repeatedly proposed there will be a Delius concert or festival in spring' – and now the award gave him the final impetus he needed. 'Frederick, in journalistic jargon, became news,' he wrote in *Frederick Delius*. Thus:

> It seemed not only timely but fitting that some weighty demonstration should be forthcoming, to enable the man in the street to become better acquainted with both the personality and the music of one of the few truly original geniuses the country had produced during the past hundred years. And as some individual has always to start anything of the sort, I took it upon myself to organize a festival of his music, to be heard in London at six concerts during the coming autumn.

In Grez-sur-Loing, Eric Fenby noted that Delius's immediate reaction was to wag his head and say that it sounded 'too good to be true', though his response to Beecham, as dictated to Jelka, was suitably positive: 'I was overjoyed by your letter about the proposed Festival, etc. What good news! What life & enterprise you have and what would musical England do without you?' A month earlier Beecham had conducted in London an all-Delius concert that had served to give them an exciting foretaste of what might be to come. Jelka's enthusiasm knew no bounds; on 9 February she wrote to Beecham:

> Dear Thomas,
>
> It was too glorious last night! It came through so well. At once with 'Paris' you took us to another world. The 'Cuckoo' was so touchingly tender and beautiful, and then the delicate 'Summernight' – even the pianissimos were quite audible … The second Dance Rhapsody was too lovely. Oh, could you only have seen our beloved Fred looking so serene and happy and as the piece unrolled itself looking transfigured with delight … Delius said: 'He is a genius! *How* he interprets it!' The songs sounded beautiful too. The wonderful purity and tenderness in Miss Labettes singing! The end of the cradle song was divine. And then the Walk to the Paradise Garden with all its tenderness and sadness. Nobody will ever play it like you! Never! 'Eventyr' was delightful – a great contrast. And all the witty and amusing things you said – we heard them all! …
>
> Yours devotedly
>
> Jelka Delius

One of the 'witty and amusing things' concerned the Dance Rhapsody No. 2. As noted down by Fenby, they heard Beecham say to the audience in Kingsway Hall:

> Ladies and Gentlemen, the next piece we are going to play is the least known of Delius's orchestral works, his second Dance Rhapsody. This is not strange, for, though this unfortunate work had been given on several occasions, it has not yet been heard at all. You will now hear the first performance.[10]

Three of the songs in the concert – *The Violet*, *The Bird's Story* and *Cradle Song* – were heard for the first time in orchestral versions made by Henry Gibson, Beecham's musical secretary (although *The Times* in its report of 11 February spoke of them having been scored 'by Sir Thomas Beecham for Miss Dora Labbette'). The newspaper's critic thought them less successful than the originals:

> because so much gain is won at the expense of something else ... the piano is the perfect medium of accompaniment, since the minutest shades lie under the player's fingers in a way that no orchestral conductor can hope to attain ... the orchestra sacrifices in subtlety more than it gains in delicacy of colour.

Preparations for the festival quickly got under way. All his life Beecham had understood the essential nature of publicity, and now a 'Preliminary Announcement', clearly framed by him, fired off the first shot:

> It is now more than thirty years since the name of Frederick Delius was first made known to the London public by means of a concert of his works which was given at the old St. James's Hall in the spring of 1899. His music was applauded by the public, and the critics were unanimous in acclaiming Delius as a mature and strikingly original personality. The musical profession was slow to welcome him, and for the next eight years no more was heard of him in this country; but during this period of neglect, he composed a number of works which compelled the discerning few who heard and studied them to regard him as one of the most important of living musicians. He has never courted publicity, but he has not lacked enthusiastic champions, here and in Germany; and slowly his reputation has spread from his disciples to their fellow-musicians, and thence, more slowly still, to the general music-loving public.
>
> The Committee of the present Festival desires to give the public an opportunity of appreciating the fact that in Frederick Delius England has produced not merely a great British composer but one of the greatest composers of all time. A proper estimate of his stature cannot be formed from the sporadic performances of individual works with which the public have had, hitherto, to content themselves. It is therefore proposed to hold a Festival in his honour in London during October next, consisting of six concerts at which practically all his most important Choral, Orchestral, and Chamber compositions will be performed. Such an event is without parallel in the history of music in England: no such extensive recognition has ever before been accorded to any living composer, British or foreign, in this country. The scope and variety of Delius's compositions will surprise many who know him only through one or two familiar works. There will be few actual novelties: ill-health has, unfortunately, put a stop to his creative activity in recent years. The majority of the works to be performed have long been known and admired by musicians; and amid the desert of post-war sensationalism and experiment, the music of Delius will seem to those whose ears are surfeited with strident expressions of the spirit of the present age, an oasis of pure and ageless beauty ...

The Press was quick to pick up on the organisers' 'belief that a proper estimate of his stature cannot be formed from sporadic performances of individual works', and gave the event extensive coverage. *The Times* happily agreed that the project was 'without exact parallel in the history of British music', and the *Daily Post* hailed it as 'a very handsome gesture to the composer's genius, which was neglected for years until Sir Thomas persuaded the public to realise the musical stature of this Yorkshireman'.[11]

Beecham enlisted the aid of, among others, Philip Heseltine, particularly to act as link between himself and the Deliuses, which was essential as he had a full diary of engagements that was taking him all over England and to Ireland. The concerts he conducted during this period frequently included Delius's music; mostly these were the shorter pieces but on one occasion (21 March) *Appalachia* made its appearance and on another the Double Concerto (14 June, with the Harrison sisters). The Concerto he was possibly trying out to see whether to include it in the festival: he had not conducted it before.[12] In June and July he went into the recording studio to accompany Dora Labbette at the piano in half-a-dozen songs – *Irmelin*, *The Violet*, *Le ciel est, par-dessus le toit*, *Twilight Fancies*, *Cradle Song* and *The Nightingale* for Columbia – though only the last three were published.[13] He also asked Fenby to explore whether Delius had any unperformed works that the festival could present as novelties, and this resulted in the unearthing at Grez-sur-Loing of *A Late Lark* and *Cynara*: the former had been not quite complete in 1925 when Delius's sight had finally failed; the latter dated back to 1908 when it was conceived as part of *Songs of Sunset*, but not finally included in the cycle. Fenby's assistance enabled Delius to put the finishing touches to both these items, and Beecham had his novelties.

At the end of April Heseltine visited the Deliuses as Beecham's emissary: he too was pursuing the quest for novelties, and sounded Delius out about some of his early pieces. But the composer was not keen for them to be included, at least not while there were mature works such as *An Arabesque* which he had never even heard. There was more discussion over which songs were to be included in the festival. Delius specified three that he did not want performed – *The Nightingale*, *Spielleute* and *Verborg'ne Liebe* – though Jelka contradicted this: 'If it upsets Beecham's plans, let them be sung.' They were. Beecham would have wanted *The Nightingale*, in particular, to be heard as he and Dora Labbette had just recorded it; the other two were perhaps the choice of the respective singers, Olga Haley and John Goss. Next, Delius was puzzled by an announcement of a forthcoming performance of his three Verlaine songs at a Promenade Concert to be conducted by Sir Henry Wood on 5 September: 'Who has orchestrated them?' Jelka wanted to know. 'Delius does not remember having done so.' Heseltine reminded them that he had, for a Beecham concert in 1915. 'Fred really thinks them better with piano', was the blunt verdict after the Deliuses had listened to the broadcast.

All this time Delius was extremely pessimistic as to whether he should be able to undertake the journey to London to attend the festival, even though he was being urged on every side to make the effort. For her part Jelka concentrated on keeping up the pressure on Beecham: 'It is all too wonderful about the Festival and I can not tell you how much it means to us,' she wrote on 14 August ' – and then your delightful and generous invitation to stay so comfortably at the Langham! And then all those glorious Gramophone records the Columbia is bringing out! Then there is your great idea about the Delius-Edition!! ... Our hearts are ever with you!' Delius's Paris doctor came regularly, and on 26 August gave his opinion that the journey should be attempted, 'if all is done for Fred's comfort regardless of expense' (Jelka told Grainger). This last point had been answered already by Beecham, who had offered a motor ambulance for the journey from Grez-sur-Loing to Boulogne and from Folkestone to London where he had arranged for the Deliuses to stay at the Langham Hotel (opposite Queen's Hall). Fenby played his part in the urging: 'Delius, you have not heard the sound of the orchestra for all these years. Think of the thrill you will get when you hear your music in the concert-room again. Isn't that enough temptation to risk it?' But Delius still hesitated: 'Yes, yes, lad, I know. But I haven't the strength, and when I die I want to die in Grez.' It was Beecham himself who finally secured Delius's agreement to attend the festival, one day in the August, when he came over from Fontainebleau where he had been staying briefly on his way back to London after a holiday spent memorising the scores for the festival.[14] Fenby's first-hand account catches the occasion with graphic sureness:

> It was just such another sweltering day as we had endured on the arrival of Percy Grainger when Sir Thomas, immaculately dressed, hat in hand, carrying an armful of scores and smoking an enormous cigar, stepped briskly into the courtyard, but, unlike his colonial friend, he took the very first opportunity of divesting himself of as much apparel as the laws of decency would admit, and permitted his taxi to wait nine hours for him at the door with all the disregard for triviality of the true *grand seigneur*. He soon settled the matter with dignity and calm, so that Delius had not a word to say. His mission achieved, he sparkled with his wine, and was gay and light-hearted as only he can be, poking fun at everything and everybody in music, himself included ... He explained that he had been advised to drink but little, and, on Delius's insisting, 'Do have another glass, Thomas,' he stood up, tested his foot carefully, and, pondering for a moment, as he fingered his beard, decided that it might stand another drop!

The Deliuses set out on 6 October 1929 and reached London without incident on the 9th. Beecham withdrew from an operatic engagement in Manchester and was in London for their arrival: two nights earlier, in Cardiff, as part of the preparation for the festival, he and Evlyn Howard-Jones had collaborated over the Piano Concerto, which they had not performed together since 1915. Fenby had left Grez-sur-Loing a few weeks before the Deliuses, ostensibly to take a holiday before the festival, but soon found himself sucked into Beecham's organisational machine, assisting particularly with the marking of the orchestral parts:

> Sir Thomas would come out from rehearsal and announce his intention of editing some score. Often he would mark it in the train on his way to conduct in the provinces, and send it back with the guard on the next train so that we could get to work without delay ... I knew very little in those days about those blue-pencilled markings that covered every page, but it was not long before I was to realise that in effect they made all the

difference between a good performance and a bad one. There was scarcely an expression mark ... that he had not altered or modified. I saw that his energy and industry were alike prodigious, and when ... he was playing *Songs of Sunset* from a vocal score and calling out all the orchestration to me as I sat beside him with the full score on my knee, I marvelled at the accuracy with which he retained the orchestral detail in his head.

Fenby was naturally apprehensive about the work he had done with Delius, especially on *Cynara*, for he was clear that its success would be crucial to the future development of their relationship. Delius was evidently more confident, for when he set out for London he had three five pound notes ready, 'for Eric, if it comes off well.' Fenby got his fivers: 'There was a moment in the green-room at Queen's Hall when, suddenly coming in from the noise of the street, I heard the distant sounds of its (*Cynara*'s) quietly ascending introduction for divided strings as it was being rehearsed, and there seemed no fairer music in the world than this,' he later recalled. He must also have been gratified when Delius turned to him immediately after the festival's opening work, *Brigg Fair*, to say: 'You were right, Eric. How wonderful the orchestra sounds to me after all these years! I am so glad I came.'

The full programme comprised the following:

THE DELIUS FESTIVAL

October–November 1929

Conductor and Organiser: Sir Thomas Beecham, Bart.

Programmes

12 October 3 pm Orchestra of the Columbia Graphophone Company
Brigg Fair
A Late Lark (first performance) – Heddle Nash
Dance Rhapsody No. 2
Sea Drift – Dennis Noble, London Select Choir
In a Summer Garden
A Village Romeo and Juliet – Scenes 5 and 6
     Pauline Maunder, Heddle Nash, London Select Choir

16 October 8.30 pm Small Orchestra
A Song before Sunrise
Seven Songs sung by Olga Haley accompanied by Evlyn Howard-Jones
     Heimkehr; Verborg'ne Liebe; Beim Sonnenuntergang; Sehnsucht;
     Le ciel est, par-dessus le toit; In the Seraglio Garden; Eine Vogelweise
Sonata for violoncello and piano – Beatrice Harrison, Evlyn Howard-Jones
Summer Night on the River
Air and Dance (first performance)

Six songs sung by John Goss accompanied by Evlyn Howard-Jones
  Black Roses; Chanson d'automne; Silken Shoes; I-brasîl; Das Veilchen;
  Spielmann
Nine Pieces for piano played by Evlyn Howard-Jones
  Three Preludes; Dance (originally for harpsichord); Five Pieces
Six Songs sung by John Armstrong accompanied by Evlyn Howard-Jones
  Irmelin; To Daffodils; The Nightingale has a Lyre of Gold; Il pleure dans mon
  Coeur; So white, so soft, so sweet is she; Let Springtime come then
On hearing the First Cuckoo in Spring

18 October 8 pm BBC Orchestra
Eventyr
Cynara (first performance) – John Goss
Piano Concerto – Evlyn Howard-Jones
An Arabesque – John Goss, London Select Choir
Appalachia – John Goss, Royal College Choral Class and BBC National Chorus

23 October 8.30 pm
Three Unaccompanied Choruses sung by the London Select Choir
  The Splendour Falls; On Craig Ddu; Midsummer Song
Four Songs sung by Dora Labbette accompanied by Evlyn Howard-Jones
  The Nightingale; Autumn; La lune blanche; Klein Venevil
Sonata No. 1 for violin and piano – Arthur Catterall, Evlyn Howard-Jones
Three Songs sung by Heddle Nash accompanied by Evlyn Howard-Jones
  Indian Love Song; Love's Philosophy; To the Queen of my Heart
Two Unaccompanied Choruses 'To be sung of a summer night on the water'
  Heddle Nash, London Select Choir
Four Songs sung by Dora Labbette accompanied by Evlyn Howard-Jones
  Twilight Fancies; Am schönsten Sommerabend war's; Margaret's Lullaby;
  Spring, the sweet Spring
String Quartet – Virtuoso String Quartet (Marjorie Hayward, Edwin Virgo,
  Raymond Jeremy, Cedric Sharpe)

24 October 8 pm Orchestra of the Royal Philharmonic Society
Dance Rhapsody No. 1
Songs of Sunset – Olga Haley, John Goss, London Select Choir
Violin Concerto – Albert Sammons
Fennimore and Gerda – Scenes 10 and 11
  Pauline Maunder, John Goss, London Select Choir
North Country Sketches

1 November 8 pm BBC Orchestra
A Mass of Life – Miriam Licette, Astra Desmond, Tudor Davies, Roy Henderson,
  Philharmonic Choir

DELIUS FESTIVAL

Conductor and Organiser - SIR THOMAS BEECHAM, Bart.

REMAINING CONCERTS

✧c⟩✧✧c⟩✧✧c⟩✧✧c⟩✧✧c⟩✧✧c⟩✧✧c⟩✧✧c⟩✧✧c⟩✧✧c⟩✧✧c⟩✧✧c⟩✧✧c⟩✧

(1) ÆOLIAN HALL Wednesday Evening, October 16th at 8.30

Sir Thomas Beecham will conduct a specially selected Orchestra of 30 performers.
THE FIRST CUCKOO—SUMMER NIGHT—AIR AND DANCE (first performance)—
SONG BEFORE SUNRISE—'CELLO SONATA—SONGS AND PIANO PIECES
The soloists will include Miss Beatrice Harrison ('Cello), Mr. Evlyn Howard-Jones
(Pianoforte), Miss Olga Haley (Mezzo-Soprano), Mr. John Armstrong (Tenor) and
Mr. John Goss (Baritone).

(2) QUEEN'S HALL Friday Evening, October 18th at 8
(Sole Lessees—Messrs. Chappell & Co. Ltd.)

*Choral and Orchestral Concert, given by the British Broadcasting
Corporation*
EVENTYR—ARABESK (first performance)—PIANO CONCERTO—CYNARA (first per-
formance)—APPALACHIA
Sir Thomas Beecham will conduct the London Select Choir and the British
Broadcasting Orchestra. The soloists will be Mr. John Goss (Baritone) and Mr.
Evlyn Howard-Jones (Pianoforte).

(3) ÆOLIAN HALL Wednesday Evening, October 23rd at 8.30

STRING QUARTET—VIOLIN SONATA (No. 1)—SONGS and PART-SONGS
The London Select Choir, The Virtuoso String Quartet, Mr. Arthur Catterall
(Violin) Mr. Evlyn Howard-Jones (Pianoforte), Miss Dora Labbette (Soprano) and
Mr. Heddle Nash (Tenor).

(4) QUEEN'S HALL Thursday Evening, October 24th at 8
(Sole Lessees—Messrs. Chappell & Co. Ltd.)

Choral and Orchestral Concert, given by the Royal Philharmonic Society
NORTH-COUNTRY SKETCHES—SONGS OF SUNSET—VIOLIN CONCERTO—DANCE
RHAPSODY (No I)—GERDA (first performance in England)
Sir Thomas Beecham will conduct the London Select Choir and the Royal
Philharmonic Orchestra. The soloists will include Miss Olga Haley (Mezzo-
Soprano), Miss Pauline Maunder (Soprano), Mr. Leyland White (Baritone) and
Mr. Albert Sammons (Violin).

(5) QUEEN'S HALL Friday Evening, November 1st at 8
(Sole Lessees— Messrs. Chappell & Co. Ltd.)

*Choral and Orchestral Concert, given by the British Broadcasting
Corporation*
" A MASS OF LIFE "
Sir Thomas Beecham will conduct the Philharmonic Choir and the British Broad-
casting Orchestra. The soloists will include Miss Miriam Licette (Soprano), Miss
Astra Desmond (Contralto). Mr. Tudor Davies (Tenor) and Mr. Roy Henderson
(Baritone).

Reserved Seats : **12/-, 8/6, 5/9.** Unreserved : 3/6 and 2/4. Prices include tax.
Tickets for any or all of the Concerts may be obtained from Messrs. Chappell's Box Office,
Queen's Hall, Langham Place, W. 1 or from the Box Office, Aeolian Hall, New Bond
Street, W. 1.

32

2.3 A page from the 1929 Delius Festival programme

All the choral and orchestral concerts were given in Queen's Hall, the two smaller ones (16 and 23 October) at the Aeolian Hall in New Bond Street. As can be seen, several orchestras were involved: the one that played at the opening concert given under the auspices of the Columbia Graphophone Co. Ltd. was described as 'Specially Selected'; the Royal Philharmonic Orchestra was the Orchestra of the Royal Philharmonic Society, which sponsored the concert on 24 October; and the BBC Orchestra was the forerunner of the BBC Symphony Orchestra (the latter's debut did not occur until 22 October 1930). Both of the concerts involving its orchestra that the BBC sponsored it also broadcast. The small orchestra ('30 performers') which played the four orchestral miniatures under Beecham's baton in the Aeolian Hall on 16 October was again 'specially selected' and was doubtless drawn from the ranks of the larger organisations: leading it was Charles Woodhouse (leader of the interim BBC Orchestra 1929–30) who also led Columbia's orchestra at the opening concert. Except for the BBC Orchestra, the others consisted mostly of freelancers, and Beecham would have been familiar with their make-up and well acquainted with the individual players.

The two new vocal works – *Cynara* and *A Late Lark* – duly appeared, but a third novelty was the *Air and Dance* for string orchestra which was receiving its first public performance. (Beecham had given it at a private concert in 1915, the year of its composition; later, Delius dedicated it to the National Institute for the Blind, a fact referred to in an advertisement in the festival programmes in which the Institute made an appeal for funds on its own behalf.) The tiny *Dance for Harpsichord* composed in 1919 for the harpsichordist Violet Gordon Woodhouse, which Evlyn Howard-Jones played (on the piano) was also perhaps being heard for the first time in London, although he had given it as early as January 1922 in Paris. For Howard-Jones it must have been an exceptionally onerous festival: not only was he the soloist in the Piano Concerto at the second orchestral concert, but at the two smaller events in the Aeolian Hall he took the piano parts in the violin and cello sonatas, played most of Delius's mature piano pieces (some dedicated to him), and accompanied all five singers in every one of their songs, a total of 30 vocal items.[15] Beatrice Harrison played the Cello Sonata dedicated to her and which she had premièred in 1918, and Arthur Catterall, whom Beecham had known for many years as leader of the Hallé Orchestra, played the Violin Sonata of which he had given the first performance in 1915. All the principal singers, notably Dora Labbette, Heddle Nash and Dennis Noble, were Beecham 'familiars': Noble, in particular, had sung in several recent performances of *Sea Drift* including in Beecham's first attempt at recording it.[16] The programme-books were lavish affairs, each containing a lengthy essay by Philip Heseltine on the composer, photographs and extensive notes on each of the works performed. In the case of *Sea Drift*, the whole of Walt Whitman's text was reproduced, with the passages Delius had set indicated by means of brackets. It was sung by the 65-strong London Select Choir, which had performed *Appalachia* with Beecham shortly before.

The presence of Delius naturally added an enormous extra dimension to the interest in the Festival, and helped to sell every seat at all the performances. He was made a great fuss of, and no pains were spared to ensure his comfort. The Royal Philharmonic Society's management committee met on 19 September to lay plans to convert Block A of the Grand Circle in Queen's Hall into a box to accommodate the composer and those with him: there he was to sit with Heseltine, along with Jelka and Delius's manservant, and also Fenby. A portrait by Ernest Procter was executed here, and Augustus John drew him in his room at the Langham Hotel. Souvenir postcards – a set of six photographs of Delius taken in 1874, 1882, 1914 and 1929 – were on sale. Advertisements for Columbia's latest recordings, notably Beecham's of *Brigg Fair*, appeared everywhere, with Beecham reciprocating by describing Columbia as 'one of our greatest musical organisations'. At each concert Delius received a rapturous welcome, and afterwards hundreds of people queued in corridors to file past him and pay their respects, sometimes shaking his hand as their names were announced. Albert Sammons' son-in-law, Lionel Hill, attended every concert: waiting in the Aeolian Hall for one to begin, he was disconcerted when the whole audience suddenly rose to its feet to applaud while apparently staring straight at him; he looked round to see Delius's carriage being manoeuvred into position across the gangway. During the concert Hill managed to steal a furtive glance or two at Delius: 'Tears were running down his pitiably sunken cheeks, and I distinctly heard him murmur, "Beautiful, beautiful".'

At the conclusion of *A Mass of Life* at the final concert on 1 November, Beecham made a speech in which he jocularly suggested that Delius had been so touched by the warmth of his reception in London that 'he is contemplating stopping here'. The *Times* report said that, in expressing his own thanks for the enthusiastic public support shown to the festival, 'Sir Thomas Beecham reaffirmed his belief that Mr Delius had written a greater quantity of beautiful music than any other living composer, and said he wished to correct any notion that this festival had exhausted the store of works from Mr Delius's great workshop; on the contrary, he could supply more than enough for another festival next week'. Then, to everyone's surprise, Delius himself spoke: 'Ladies and Gentlemen, thank you for the very fine reception you have given me. It was wholly unexpected. I also wish to thank Sir Thomas Beecham for the inspired manner in which he has played my music. This Festival has been the time of my life. Again, I thank you.' The Deliuses stayed on for a few days, writing letters of thanks to artists who had taken part and to Delius's publishers: 'The whole festival has been a fabulous success,' Jelka told Universal. As the boat left England Delius asked for his chair to be turned so that he could face its fading shores. Among the last to see him before his departure was Eric Fenby:

> I left Delius, after the Festival, full of praise for Sir Thomas Beecham's masterly interpretations of his music ... in some of his purely orchestral works it had seemed that Delius had been listening to them for the very first time, so perfectly had their inner meaning been grasped and realised in performance. That was the way he wanted his music to be played – Beecham's way – and he hoped that the Festival would do one thing

above all else, and that, to establish a tradition by which his music should live. If there was to be a future for his music – and, despite his habitual egotism, there were moments when he was curiously humble about his work – it could only live in the tradition which Beecham had been at such pains to create.

Notes

*   Delius to the audience at the close of the 1929 Delius Festival.

1   The third performance replaced *The Magic Flute*, which had been advertised as recently as the previous day (5 April) with Eugene Goossens (1893–1962) as conductor. On 6 April, however, when the announcement was made that 'owing to unforeseen circumstances' Delius's opera would be given that evening instead of it, Beecham's name was given as conductor and also appeared in the programme. On the face of it, therefore, there is no reason to think other than that he conducted all three performances of Delius's opera, though Goossens, in *Overture and Beginners* (Methuen & Co., 1945) tells a different story:

> That Drury Lane [*sic*] season carried a memory of other incidents, both potentially disastrous, in which I played an embarrassing part. *A Village Romeo and Juliet*, the beautiful and in some ways un-operatic masterpiece of Delius, was having its second performance, and we had reached the last act, in which the lovers write *finis* to earthly suffering by scuttling their boat in the middle of the lake. This effect was extremely realistically achieved at Covent Garden by the simple process of lowering a portion of the stage, with the boat on it, at a given musical cue. The procedure had to be accomplished in order to give the lovers ample time to sing the concluding part of their final duet while the boat was going under. I promised Beecham, who was conducting, that I would give the stage-manager the cue at the right moment, whereupon the vessel would slowly start disappearing from view. It did, but four pages of score too soon, owing to my mistaking an identical phrase occurring earlier for the real stage-cue. Moreover, it seemed that once the process of lowering the hydraulic stage-bridge had started, there was no possibility of arresting it. It also seemed that never before had the bridge moved so quickly, so that, to the dismay of everyone concerned, the lovers were compelled to sing at least two pages of their duet from the submarine depths of the lake. This episode earned me a peppery rebuke from T.B., who, incensed by other mishaps – principally musical – during the performance, said, 'Next time, you conduct the damn thing yourself.' I did, and someone else gave the stage cues. Out of excessive caution, however, that person gave the fatal cue much too late, with the result that the boat started sinking only with the final curtain. I'm not at all sure but that my way wasn't dramatically the more effective! ...

2   The London production of *Hassan* opened at His Majesty's Theatre on 20 September 1923 and was an immediate success, eventually running for 281 performances. Delius attended the dress rehearsals and two performances. Eugene Goossens conducted the première, handing over to the Theatre's musical director Percy Fletcher (1879–1932) for the rest of the run. Fletcher subsequently made a recording of some of the music on two acoustic 78rpm discs for HMV (C1134/5). Throughout his long life, Basil Dean (1888–1978) often recalled with affection his association with *Hassan* and Delius's part in it, not only in his autobiography (*Seven Ages 1888–1927*, Hutchinson, 1927) but in radio interviews. Even as late as 1973, appearing as a 'castaway' on the BBC's long-running radio programme *Desert Island Discs* he chose both the Serenade from *Hassan*

and *The Walk to the Paradise Garden* among his eight records to take to the mythical island, and nominated the *Hassan* excerpt as his selection if he could take only one of the eight.

3 American-born Maud Burke (1872–1948) became Lady Cunard when she married Sir Bache Cunard, a member of the shipping line family. A notable hostess in social circles, she had known the Deliuses since 1911 when Beecham had introduced them, and had entertained the composer and his wife frequently in London and abroad.

4 In *Portraits with Backgrounds* (Geoffrey Bles, London 1947), Catherine Barjansky, wife of the cellist Alexandre Barjansky (1883–1961), states erroneously that the première was given on 30 January 1923 in Frankfurt in Delius's presence. The January première was in Vienna and the Frankfurt performance took place on 1 March 1923 when the conductor was Paul Klenau (1883–1946). This latter performance was the one attended by Delius, along with Percy Grainger, when both met Barjansky for the first time.

5 The cause of Delius's illness has long been attributed to tertiary syphilis, contracted during his youthful years in Paris. In his biography of the composer, Sir Thomas Beecham executed a characteristically graceful pirouette around the subject by referring to Delius having suffered 'a heavy blow in the defection of his favourite goddess Aphrodite Pandemos who had returned his devotions with an affliction which, though temporarily alleviated, was to break out again incurably some 25 years later'. In the years since Delius's death the syphilis theory has been questioned at various times, but no alternative diagnosis has been proved with certainty.

6 Beecham had been making recordings under the old acoustic process since 1910, but even at the time of the changeover to the electrical method in 1925 was inclined to disparage the whole process: 'Improvement in the gramophone is so imperceptible that it will take quite 5,000 years to make it any good,' he was quoted as saying. Astonishing, then, to see how quickly he embraced the possibilities of the new medium, soon producing Mozart and Beethoven symphonies as well as larger-scale works. Chief among these was Handel's *Messiah* which featured a young English singer, Dora Labbette (1898–1984), as the soprano soloist. In December 1927, a week before his initial Delius recordings, he conducted (anonymously so far as the record's label was concerned) a small orchestra when she made a record of two of Grieg's songs, 'The Nightingale' Op. 48 No. 4 and 'The Emigrant' Op. 58 No. 5, for Columbia. Beecham was soon to use her in Delius's vocal works, and she became a great favourite of the Deliuses, who liked to refer to her as 'The Nightingale' after Grieg's song. (Delius and Grieg had been friends for 20 years, from 1887 until the older composer's death in 1907.) In 1935, Dora Labbette perpetrated an excellent joke on the musical establishment when she launched a new operatic career as an 'unknown' under the pseudonym of Lisa Perli. This was a diversion into which Beecham entered with relish, and she was still appearing with him under this name as late as 1940.

7 *Twilight Fancies* and *Venevil* had been recorded on 29 January 1926 by the Welsh mezzo-soprano Leila Megane (HMV E430; *Twilight Fancies* was subsequently included in HMV's double-LP album 'A Treasury of English Song' [EX2909113, issued in 1986]).

8 In 1933 the matter resurfaced, when Jelka took it up again in a letter to Beecham. The Douglas arrangement had been quite forgotten about, she said, but now Universal Edition had sent Delius proofs corrected and ready for publication. 'After you have given so generously your time and your genius in marking and editing all Fred's works we feel we cannot allow this to go into print without your consent,' she wrote on 29 August. Beecham agreed to look at Universal's score, and Jelka forwarded it to him in

London. Two weeks later the publishers were writing 'most pressingly' for the score, and she begged him to release it to them, but he failed to do so and they published Douglas's arrangement as it stood. Beecham's own arrangement of *The Walk to the Paradise Garden*, 'made in order to bring the work within the scope of smaller orchestras', was not published until 1940. The previous year Universal had published an arrangement by Keith Douglas of the 'Waltz' (that is, The Fairground Music) from the opera, in which the arranger acknowledged Beecham's 'advice and help' in its preparation.

9   Eric Fenby (1906–97) was born in Scarborough, Yorkshire. His six years as Delius's amanuensis from 1928 to 1934 are described in his book *Delius as I Knew Him* (London, G. Bell & Sons Ltd, 1937 and subsequent reprints). In later years he was Artistic Director of the 1962 Delius Centenary Festival at Bradford and President of the Delius Society from its inception in 1962 until his death.

10 The first performance of Dance Rhapsody No. 2 had taken place on 20 October 1923 under Sir Henry Wood. Delius's disappointment at Wood's conducting – 'he took all the wrong tempi' – had doubtless been communicated to Beecham, whose relationship with Wood was, in any case, never easy and occasionally broke out into open warfare.

11 The views of one reporter, presumably not entirely smitten with Delius's music, ran somewhat counter to the prevailing mood of rejoicing: 'Would that Sir Thomas were able to extend his interest to some other native-born composer with equal liberality.' This view found at least an echo in a conversation between two ladies at one of the concerts which was overheard by a friend of Beecham's and reported to him: 'This is really a remarkable festival, isn't it?' said one. 'Just look at all those people who seem to like it, or are they pretending to?' 'I have no idea,' replied her companion, 'but I am quite certain that I don't, and what I have been wondering for the best part of an hour is why they have not been playing the music of some other composer.'

12 An earlier Beecham performance, with Albert Sammons and Felix Salmond as soloists, had been announced for 14 March 1921, but in the event Albert Coates took over the concert, substituting Brahms's Concerto Op. 102 for the Delius. Following Beecham's conducting it for the Harrison sisters in June 1929, Percy Grainger sent a glowing report to Delius: 'It is perfection ... Beecham conducted like a god ... he is finer than ever.' The *Musical Times* reviewer agreed, saying that the concerto had 'probably never had so sympathetic a performance'. But it was not included in the festival, and Beecham conducted it again only once, in an all-Delius programme on 10 March 1935 with Paul Beard and Anthony Pini as soloists. It was included in the 1946 festival, with the same players, though Richard Austin conducted.

13 Beecham was not the only one recording Delius at this time. For HMV, Columbia's rival company, Geoffrey Toye (1889–1942) made discs of *Brigg Fair, In a Summer Garden* and *On hearing the First Cuckoo in Spring* in January 1928. The conductor must have been gratified by Delius's reaction: 'Dear Toye, The records are splendid and I am delighted with the way you conducted them, all three. Your interpretation of these works is most poetical and understood entirely; I am very grateful to you for having made these records. Please thank the orchestra for me for having played so beautifully.' Delius also wrote to HMV: 'The records have arrived and I have heard them several times. They are most satisfactory. Mr Toye has thoroughly understood the works and he has given a most poetical rendering. All three, *Brigg Fair, Summer Garden* and *On hearing the cuckoo*, are excellent, and I shall be glad to have them sold as authorised by me.' (In this letter he was careful to request that the older versions of

Brigg Fair and the *First Cuckoo* conducted by Eugene Goossens should be withdrawn from HMV's catalogue.)

It was only to be expected that HMV would make the most of such good publicity, particularly as its rival Columbia was directly associated with the Festival and was even sponsoring the orchestra at the opening concert. 'It is amusing how HMV come out with their advertisement *now*!!' observed a vexed Jelka to Heseltine. Columbia became alarmed, and on 28 August 1929 sent an emissary to secure an encomium from Delius for its own records. The result appeared in the company's advertisements of new records and in the festival programmes, in the latter case under the heading 'A Letter from Mr Frederick Delius, Grez-sur-loing, 28.9.29: I want to say that all of my works as recorded by Sir Thomas Beecham by the Columbia Graphophone Company are most beautiful and delicate and in every way satisfactory. They are the most beautiful records that I have heard.' Columbia went further in the lead-up to the festival, recording Beecham accompanying Dora Labbette in some of the songs and taking down a selection of Delius's piano music played by Evlyn Howard-Jones, as well as the violist Lionel Tertis in his transcriptions of the Violin Sonata No. 2 and the Serenade from *Hassan*.

The Decca Record Company also entered the fray with new recordings of *Sea Drift* and *North Country Sketches* made in London in 1929 (they also intended to record, and indeed announced, the *Air and Dance*, but in the event this was not done). Anthony Bernard (1891–1963) was the conductor and Roy Henderson sang in *Sea Drift*. Only *Sea Drift*, recorded on 29 May 1929, was published (Decca S10010-2). Eric Fenby wrote to his parents: 'The gramophone records of "Sea-Drift" were very poor indeed. A bad orchestra, a miserable little chorus and faulty singing by Roy Henderson, the soloist, and a poor reading by the conductor, Anthony Bernard. Delius did not recognize much of it.' Jelka Delius was presumably being especially tactful when she told Heseltine, who had brought Bernard to Grez-sur-Loing only a month or so earlier, that the records had been 'greatly enjoyed'.

14   Beecham paid several visits to Delius that summer (1929) whilst staying at Fontainebleau. 'On one occasion, at tea in the garden,' Eric Fenby recalled, 'Delius mentioned that he had been too unwell to dictate an article on the state of modern music which he had promised to a Polish newspaper. Whereupon Sir Thomas lit a cigar [and] delivered himself brilliantly upon the subject. It emerged as a piece of brilliant prose, lucid, apposite and authoritative. Having asked me to read it aloud – to frequent nods of approval from Delius – it was decided that not one word should be changed. The article appeared under Delius's name, much to Sir Thomas's relish.' (Eric Fenby, *Delius as I Knew Him*; in Appendix II of the revised edition published by Faber & Faber, London, 1981)

15   Evlyn Howard-Jones (1877–1951) was devoted to Delius. He and his violinist wife Grace often visited Grez-sur-Loing to play his music to the composer, entering into the enclosed Delius world with wholehearted enthusiasm. According to Eric Fenby, Howard-Jones played with 'all the classical control and restraint of a fine teacher', though his outlook and Delius's frequently clashed. 'Once when there had been some heated remarks about Beethoven's pianoforte sonatas, Howard-Jones had declared the Op. 110 in A flat to be "great music". Delius challenged him: "Well, play it then!" ... all through the sonata the old man was restless, and frowned as he followed the music, "Listen – listen," he kept on saying and pointing excitedly with his finger the while (he could only do this when aroused). "Listen – banal – banal – listen – listen, my boy – fillings – fillings!" When the music had ceased, and Howard-Jones had come beaming

down the stairs to receive his bouquet, all he got for his pains was, "Evlyn, why do you waste your time practising such rubbish?"'

16 This was the recording made on 11 November 1928, the day that the same performers gave a public performance of *Sea Drift* at the Royal Albert Hall; it was not approved at the time and went unpublished until 2001, when it was released on compact disc.

Chapter 3

1930–1939
'The clue, to my mind, lies in Beecham's temperament ...'*

At the beginning of the 1930s Beecham suffered a setback. During 1927–28 he had guest-conducted the New York Philharmonic, Philadelphia, Boston Symphony, Czech Philharmonic and Paris Conservatoire Orchestras, and he had returned to England determined to create an orchestra that would be their equal. He found that the BBC, having become fired by the same idea, was actively seeking his cooperation and so, for the next two years, he and the Corporation worked in a desultory sort of way towards the same end. It was a strange union, for Beecham had always been ambivalent about the BBC, whose whole ethos of control and strict organisation ran counter to his essentially free spirit. At times he had been an extremely outspoken critic of broadcast music: 'The most abominable row that ever stunned and cursed the human ear, a horrible gibbering, chortling and shrieking of devils and goblins', was one of his more colourful descriptions, while a newspaper article by him blandly entitled 'Why I dislike the wireless' was hardly calculated to endear him to the men of Savoy Hill. Even while the collaboration was proceeding he treated the BBC with a characteristic combination of disdain and raillery, but he had his supporters within the Corporation who recognised his conducting genius, and it suited him to involve himself in case things ran his way.

They did not: it hardly requires hindsight to see that they never would have done. The BBC wanted a flagship ensemble, of better quality than it had previously maintained, which it would administer and in which it would have a controlling interest. Beecham, on the other hand, saw himself at the head of a first-class orchestra which, under his direction, would make music of a quality to rival anything to be heard anywhere in the world. There the two aims met and the fundamental differences in approach were never likely to be reconciled. Beecham's interest in the partnership lapsed, and the BBC went ahead on its own. His cherished intention, however, remained. During much of 1930–31 he was again abroad, guest-conducting the Vienna and Berlin Philharmonics, the Gewandhaus in Leipzig and the Santa Cecilia in Rome, and fulfilling engagements at the opera houses of Cologne, Hamburg and Wiesbaden; these experiences only served to stiffen his ambitions for London.

Beecham's promotion of Delius's music continued in the wake of the Delius Festival with as much enthusiasm as ever. Scarcely a programme failed to include something, especially in provincial centres such as Brighton, Bristol and Cardiff. Liverpool seemed almost targeted, with a mini-festival that took in the Violin Concerto (Sammons), *Sea Drift* (Dennis Noble) and a selection of the songs in the course of three concerts spread over a month; in the last Beecham accompanied Dora Labbette at the piano, affording excellent publicity for the new disc of the songs they had recently made together. The Leeds Festival of 1931 created the opportunity for another performance of *A Mass of Life*, with a team of soloists – Lilian Stiles-Allen, Muriel Brunskill, Francis Russell and Roy Henderson – which was to remain practically unchanged throughout the 1930s. The following year began with a visit to The Hague to conduct the Concertgebouw Chamber Orchestra (29 January 1932): this arose because the oboist Léon Goossens had been engaged to play the Concerto his brother Eugene had composed for him, and the orchestra's management, seeking a conductor, were inspired to wonder to Goossens if 'Sir Beecham' might be available. The oboist acted as intermediary and, as it happened, Beecham was; but they got *A Song before Sunrise*, the *First Cuckoo* and *Summer Night on the River* as part of the bargain. Two nights later, back in London, Beecham had Katharine Goodson as his soloist in the Piano Concerto (the first of five performances they were to give together during the 1930s); though she had played it as early as 1923 under Albert Coates's baton for the Royal Philharmonic Society, this was a first time with Beecham. A few weeks earlier, at another of his LSO concerts, Beecham had conducted an isolated performance of *In a Summer Garden*, and he even managed to insinuate *The Walk to the Paradise Garden* into a programme marking the Haydn bicentenary (where it must have made odd company with a Bach violin concerto played by Fritz Kreisler and two of the master's symphonies).

Always intent on gaining international audiences for Delius's music, in Rome Beecham conducted *The Walk to the Paradise Garden*, in Leipzig and Munich *Brigg Fair* and in Berlin *Eventyr*. 'Beecham gave a splendid concert at the Gewandhaus in Leipsic,' Jelka told Percy Grainger, 'and we managed to hear it here fairly well, exceptionally well *really* for so distant a station. He gave a heavenly performance of Brigg Fair. It came after the Hebrides Overture, which he gave in a most lively fashion. Then this heavenly calm of the Brigg Fair opening, and a quite celestial quality and roundness of tone, which, Fred thought, was due to the wonderful Gewandhaus-Accoustic.' The folksong melody of *Brigg Fair* was launched by the Gewandhaus Orchestra's youthful principal oboist Rudolf Kempe, then just 20. He and Beecham were not to meet again for almost 30 years, by which time Kempe had become an admired conductor himself and Beecham was looking to appoint him as his associate conductor.[1]

The year 1932 was also notable for another performance of *A Mass of Life*, this time for the Royal Philharmonic Society (28 April), with the same soloists as in the Leeds Festival performance the previous October. Jelka thought that it was a great triumph that there were 8,000 (*sic*) people in the Albert Hall – 'it gives Fred a new and much larger public and that may have been T.B.'s idea,' she observed to Eric Fenby. Equally notable was a studio broadcast for the BBC on 20 May of *A Village Romeo and Juliet* in which the principal performers were Dora Labbette as Vreli, Jan van der Gucht as Sali, and Dennis Noble, who sang not only the Dark Fiddler but Manz and the first Bargee as well.[2] This took place in the midst of a Wagner Festival at Covent Garden; only the previous night Beecham had conducted *Götterdämmerung*. He was just back from the USA, where a total of 25 concerts with the New York Philharmonic in March and April had included *Brigg Fair* besides the *First Cuckoo* and *Summer Night on the River*. At an additional concert at the Metropolitan Opera House in New York he had conducted 200 unemployed musicians in a huge programme that included Berlioz's *Carnaval Romain*, José Iturbi in concertos by Bach and Liszt, Borodin's Polovtsian Dances – and Delius's Dance Rhapsody No. 1.[3]

Once back in Britain, Beecham considered his options on the orchestral front in the wake of the collapse of the BBC negotiations. At that time the best of the established ensembles was the self-governing London Symphony Orchestra, founded in 1904. He had mostly used the LSO for his concerts and some recordings since 1923, and had had a good opportunity to assess its current form at the recent Leeds Festival in a series of his favourite works including, besides *A Mass of Life*, Berlioz's *Grande Messe des Morts* and Strauss's *Don Quixote*. Evidently satisfied, he now set about seeing whether it would meet his permanent ambitions. Changes in personnel that he considered necessary were agreed in principle by members of the LSO's board but, as negotiations progressed, they became increasingly uneasy at the amount of weeding-out being insisted upon. This was hardly surprising, since some of the orchestra's directors were on Beecham's list of those to be dropped. In July 1932, these negotiations, too, collapsed, and Beecham had no option but to contemplate going it alone. By this time, however, he could be confident of success. He had acquired the regular concert series of the Royal Philharmonic Society and arranged a lucrative recording contract with Columbia; moreover, he was negotiating to take over the artistic direction of the Royal Opera House, Covent Garden, so that his new ensemble could become resident there and his players would enjoy permanent employment all the year round. But the orchestra still needed more regular work, and it was at this point that Malcolm Sargent (1895–1967) stepped in fortuitously with the suggestion that the new orchestra might play at three concert series – the Royal Choral Society, the Courtauld-Sargent Concerts and the Robert Mayer Children's Concerts – which he conducted. This was exactly what Beecham needed to take the final decision: he quickly accepted the offer and invited Sargent to join him as associate conductor.

As soon as the decision to proceed was made events moved quickly. Beecham had already identified in his own mind key players he wanted and he had been

3.1 A Beecham orchestration of a Delius song

Daf-fo-dills we weep to see you haste-a-way so soon;

dropping clear hints about his intentions to some of them (such as Léon Goossens) for some time. Goossens and others were easily signed up by his administrators, and indeed appeared at a Folkestone Festival concert on 22 September as part of an 'augmented' Municipal Orchestra: no doubt the augmentation was a nucleus of players Beecham had already engaged for the new orchestra. Filling the string ranks took longer. Most provincial players, after their six-month winter season at home, spent their summers at the seaside in theatre orchestras and pier bands. The players Beecham particularly wanted were contacted by telegram. One was Paul Beard, the 31-year-old principal violin of the City of Birmingham Orchestra, who was summering at Llandudno. Beecham's offer of the leader's position came completely out of the blue, but Beard's telegraphed response was unhesitating: 'Accept with pleasure. Am packing my bags.' Twelve rehearsals were arranged to begin in the last week in September, and Beecham's new orchestra, which he named the London Philharmonic, made its first appearance at the opening concert of the Royal Philharmonic Society's 1932 season in Queen's Hall on 7 October.

It was an outstanding success. If part of Beecham's intention had been to shake up the British orchestral scene, he certainly succeeded. Critical and public reaction was immediate and unanimous. In the hall, as the overture ended, excited concert-goers stood on their seats to cheer, and they greeted each new piece with torrents of applause. When the players returned to the platform after the interval, Beecham's reappearance was the signal for an ovation that went on for several minutes. Ernest Newman, senior among London critics, writing in the *Sunday Times*, spoke for everyone:

> Sir Thomas Beecham's new orchestra began its operations on Friday night ... Berlioz's *Carnaval Romain* overture had an air about it of 'You Londoners want to hear what an orchestra should sound like? Well, just listen to this.' The demonstration was certainly complete enough. Nothing so electrifying has been heard in a London concert-room for years. The tone was magnificent, the precision perfect, the reading a miracle of fire and beauty.

Only the orchestra's name worried Newman: 'A plain "The London Orchestra" would have been far better,' he declared. 'For one thing, that is evidently what the new orchestra is going to be.'

All this must have made uncomfortable reading for the BBC, whose own orchestra's launch two years before had attracted a welcome which, if neither so fulsome nor excited, had at least been respectful. But now cooler estimates were being voiced, and attendance at BBC concerts was declining. Matters were exacerbated when their orchestra's account of Strauss's *Ein Heldenleben* under Sir Henry Wood a few weeks later was compared most unfavourably with that of Beecham and the LPO at their debut concert. Worse still, when Beecham made his own first appearance with the BBC Orchestra (on 22 November 1933, in a programme that included *Eventyr*) not only was it a huge success, but it drew the blunt comment from the *News Chronicle* that, 'One thing only can prevent this occasion standing out like a mountain on a vast desert plain; that is, many more appearances of the same conductor with this orchestra.'

Beecham now took the LPO on a tour of England and Scotland, and the new orchestra's fame was soon sweeping the country. His programmes were chosen judiciously to provide just the variety his listeners wanted, and the concerts everywhere were outstanding successes. Delius's music was well to the fore. After *Brigg Fair* in the orchestra's debut concert, *Paris* was the next major work to make its appearance (on 24 November); a few of the miniatures were heard in subsequent programmes and then, in March 1933, Beecham mounted an all-Delius concert consisting of *Appalachia*, *Songs of Sunset*, Dance Rhapsody No. 2 and some of the *Hassan* music. In discussing the music, the London critics spoke of 'the lasting mystery of how Sir Thomas Beecham comes to have his astonishing intuitive sympathy with it'. *A Mass of Life* followed six days later (on 11 March), and another performance of *Songs of Sunset* later in the year. Clearly Beecham was intent on giving Delius's music a higher concert profile than ever before, and it soon became evident that he was laying plans for its systematic recording as well, though this would not begin for another year: arrangements had to be put in place so that the records he would make, instead of being sold individually, could be offered to the public in albums on a subscription basis.

This was to be done through the Delius Society, which had been founded in 1932 and was quietly gaining strength. Beecham was president, Granville Bantock and Henry Wood were vice-presidents, and Jean Michaud, the London representative of Delius's publishers Universal Music Agencies, was chairman of the committee. On 5 September 1933, Michaud reported progress to Eric Fenby: 'Up to now, we have 161 subscriptions of 2 guineas each to hand ... received from Australia, New Zealand, Canada, Mexico, Cyprus, China and some from the continent. We require at least 500 and are aiming at 1,000.' Keith Douglas, who had become the society's honorary secretary, was a great admirer of Delius, considering him to be 'the greatest musical genius since Wagner'. He was also honorary secretary of the Royal Philharmonic Society and had doubtless helped Beecham in his negotiations to secure the Society's concerts for the LPO. Now he threw his energies into the plans that Beecham was developing to record Delius's music for Columbia. By the end of 1933 the composer was aware of Beecham's intentions and, in the wake of a recent BBC broadcast to which he had listened, he sent him a heartfelt plea:

> Your superb performance of Eventyr gave me another great thrill. Luckily there was no crackling and it came through wonderfully. I have a new Gramophone E.M.G. & derive great pleasure from your records of my works. When am I to have the records? I am just longing to be able to put them on my gramophone. This is now my only pleasure. Do not wait too long, dear friend, or it will be too late for me to enjoy them.

By the early months of 1934 it was evident to Keith Douglas that progress on the administrative side was not being made speedily enough: despite persistent lobbying, Columbia was dragging its feet. In an inspired move, he suggested that

Delius should write independently to the record company. The composer was happy to declare that the project was 'the greatest interest I have in life – that those who admire my music shall have good records of my works conducted by Beecham'. (These words were used, understandably enough, in the record company's subsequent publicity.) The strategy paid off: 'I must tell you that your letter to Columbia has worked wonders,' Douglas wrote to Delius on 21 March; '[they] approached us and offered to sponsor the Society. They are also ready to start recording as soon as Sir Thomas and ourselves are ready.' Whether it was simply Delius's intervention that brought about the fundamental change in the arrangements between the Delius Society and Columbia or the general dissatisfaction at lack of progress evinced by Keith Douglas (doubtless prompted by Beecham) is unclear, but the following announcement which appeared in *The Gramophone* in October 1934 under the heading 'Columbia takes over the Delius Society' would tend to suggest the latter:

> As ... forecast last month, the negotiations between the Committee of the Delius Society and Columbia, which began in April, have at last been completed. The original Committee of the Delius Society has resigned and now and henceforward this enterprise will be run under the auspices of Columbia, although, as everyone will be pleased to hear, Sir Thomas Beecham remains President and Artistic Advisor. The change-over has resulted in a considerable improvement in the contents of the first album. Instead of the songs that were first announced in company with 'Paris', it has been decided to record 'Eventyr', the final scene from the unpublished opera, 'Koanga', and the Serenade and Finale from 'Hassan' [*sic*]. Columbia ... hope that their enterprise will be rewarded by a great influx of subscriptions. Sir Thomas has written a special message to the British musical public asking for more support, to the tune of 750 new subscribers, and this message has been incorporated in a new prospectus that is now obtainable from all Columbia dealers.

Evidently the question of repertoire for the initial volume of records had taken time to settle. The first suggestion from the Delius Society was prudent: the third Violin Sonata and a selection of the songs, with only *Paris* involving orchestral forces. When he heard about it Delius had been 'overjoyed' at the thought of *Paris*, but inclined to prefer some of his newest compositions – *Cynara* and *A Song of Summer*, both results of his collaboration with Fenby – together with the Dance Rhapsody No. 2, for the remaining discs. At this point Beecham took a hand: he was unenthusiastic about *A Song of Summer* (he was never to conduct it) and evidently felt that neither *Cynara* nor the Dance Rhapsody No. 2 was strong enough. As could be read into the announcement in *The Gramophone*, his views had prevailed, and *Paris* and *Eventyr*, together with excerpts from *Koanga* and *Hassan* and some of the songs, were settled upon to fill the 14 78rpm sides.

While these plans were evolving, Delius's health had been slowly deteriorating: in Grez-sur-Loing Jelka was nearing her wits' end as to how to keep the fragile Delian ship-of-state afloat. Delius had been very unwell, she reported to Beecham on 21 January 1934, and the strict diets necessary had depressed him as well:

I feel an enormous responsability and I feel that above all things he needs agreable impressions, and it is his hearts greatest desire to hear your Delius concert in Manchester. We are so afraid that thro' Michaud's shortsighted obstinacy Appalachia may not be given and the whole concert fall through. Please, dearest Thomas, do not allow that to happen. We have listened to two heart-rending performances: Song of the H. Hills, and Fantastic Dance. Simply murderous; and Fred must have something to counteract this and to look forward to.

The reference to Beecham's Manchester concert kept on the boil a furious row with Delius's publishers which had erupted a month earlier when they wanted to charge the Hallé Concerts Society a performing fee of 8 guineas for Beecham to give *Appalachia* in his all-Delius programme scheduled for 1 March 1934. The Hallé Society had countered with an offer of half that figure, which had been declined. So far as Delius was concerned, it was just the latest in the long-running battle with his publishers whose high performance fees militated against the works being heard at all. Jelka was typically forthright: 'As regards Fred he has always been swindled by publishers and is accustomed to it,' her letter to Beecham went on. 'What is much more serious for him is that performances are made rare if not impossible by their manouvres.'

3.2 Beecham in 1934

3.3 Dora Labbette, who sang Delius's songs to him and recorded several of them with Beecham

At this point Beecham decided to enter the fray. Delius's differences with his publishers were one thing, but when they affected him and his plans it was quite another. He got Michaud of Universal in his sights, and went in with all guns blazing on 16 December:

> Sir, I have just seen the letter dated Dec.14th which you have sent to Mr R B Hesselgrave [the secretary of the Hallé Concerts Society] in which you say that you have heard from my secretary that I do not wish to pay the performing fee for 'Appalachia' and consequently will remove the work from the programme. You go on to say that you will inform Mr. Delius that I wish to make use of his compositions while denying him the right to receive proper remuneration as a composer.
>
> As a mixture of humbug and inaccuracy your letter would take a lot of beating. In other words, it is an example of that deplorable and mendacious insolence which characterizes the communications of the publishers of this unfortunate composer. What are the true facts? On March 5th of this year you charged me £2.17.6 for playing 'Appalachia' at my own concert, and you charged Mr Keith Douglas, of Bradford and the Royal Philharmonic Society £4.4.0 for the same work. You have asked the Hallé Concerts £8.8.0 also for 'Appalachia' in a concert programme made up entirely of the works of Delius and including 'Eventyr', 'Songs of Sunset', and the Intermezzo from 'A Village Romeo'. It is with difficulty that I have convinced an impecunious society in the most impoverished town in England of the necessity of giving an all-Delius concert of this kind, with all the considerable expense of extra rehearsals requisite for model performances of such works as 'Eventyr' and 'Songs of Sunset', which have never been heard in Manchester. The average sane human being would think that under these circumstances those responsible for the advancement of Mr Delius's reputation and business interests would take the opportunity of doing all in their power to facilitate the success of this event, but Mr Delius's agents and publishers are not to be included in the category of normal-minded creatures; they are a parcel of the most crack-brained fools ever inflicted upon a suffering artistic world by a grimly ironical providence.
>
> It is not I who have refused to pay the £8.8.0 you have demanded on this occasion, but the Hallé Concerts Society, with whose administration I have no concern. You will kindly understand that the question at issue is not the simple one of withdrawing 'Appalachia' from an ordinary programme but the far more important one of whether Manchester is to hear this all-Delius concert or not. The programme I have selected is designed to present the genius of the composer in its most varied and favourable light. Therefore, if 'Appalachia' is not performed neither will be the other works of Delius, and for this disaster your grasping irrationality will be alone responsible.
>
> It is now 26 years since I first began to play the works of Delius, and on no single occasion within my recollection have I declined to pay the fees rightfully due to this composer. Accordingly, your suggestion that at this time of day I am taking such a step is both an outrageous piece of impudence and a gross libel upon myself. I am sending copies of all correspondence pertaining to this matter to the composer so that he may judge for himself how indifferently he is served by his representatives in the country which, in spite of its limitations of opportunity, always does its best to do him honour. Yours faithfully, Thomas Beecham

In a response to Delius, Universal put up a measured defence of their business practices. They stoutly defended their employee – 'We are of the opinion that you will find no better representative of your interests than Mr Michaud' – and pointed out that a portion of the fee they were asking they were obliged to seek on behalf of the Performing Right Society: the fee due to the PRS amounted to £5.5.0 so that Universal were asking only £3.3.0 as hire fee for the material. In writing to Delius, as their client, they were clearly anxious to avoid direct confrontation with Beecham, though they were also keen to try to secure better relations between him and them through Michaud: 'We would be especially delighted if we could eliminate certain differences between him and Mr Beecham.' The concert, made up of *Eventyr*, *Songs of Sunset*, *Appalachia* and *The Walk to the Paradise Garden*, took place as planned. A relieved Jelka Delius wrote about it to Eric Fenby:

> Did you hear Beecham's concert? Eventyr, Fred thought was quite amazing, wonderful; he had never heard it like that. Songs of Sunset was lovely too, especially Olga Haley – Dennis Noble less good, a little stilted. But the suavity of the whole and the exquisiteness of the orchestra ... that 'Exceeding Sorrow' was really moving ... The 'Walk' was glorious too, rather more strong and passionate than our record ... Oh, I enjoyed it immensely and it was so lovely to see Fred nodding so elatedly his head to the music ...

Fortunately, Delius was enjoying better relations with the publishers of his most recent works, Boosey & Hawkes, and all the titles he had produced since 1929 working with Eric Fenby had been both published and performed without any difficulty. With only one of the works in this group, however, did Beecham choose to involve himself. This was the last of them, the *Idyll* for soprano, baritone and orchestra composed in 1932 to words by Walt Whitman, selected by Robert Nichols, to music from Delius's unperformed opera *Margot la Rouge*. Jelka told Beecham: 'All that lovely music is freed from the beastly subject for which it was always too good and refined. All the knife and murder bits are eliminated, and the music ... an exhalted love poem.' The new piece evidently interested Beecham to the extent that, although Sir Henry Wood had secured the première for his BBC Promenade Concert on 3 October 1933 with Dora Labbette (replacing Olga Haley), Roy Henderson and the BBC Symphony Orchestra, he held a preliminary run-through of his own with the singers before Wood's performance. Shortly afterwards he conducted the piece himself with Dora Labbette and Dennis Noble at the Mayfair Hotel (12 November). A letter to him from Jelka Delius dated 14 September 1933 makes clear that he had also offered to edit the work.

The other major fruit of Fenby's work was *Songs of Farewell* for chorus and orchestra, about which Beecham seemed at first enthusiastic. It had taken most of the second half of 1930 to compose, and immediately it was finished Delius wanted Beecham's opinion of it. 'Beautiful!' he declared after Fenby played him the first of its five numbers in London early in 1931, and 'Lovely!' after the second. When he had heard them all his typically Beechamesque compliment to Fenby, upon his skill in getting such a complex work down on paper under such extraordinarily difficult circumstances, was, 'I think you ought to be a cabinet minister!' The première of the new work, however, was secured for the

Courtauld-Sargent concert series, when Samuel Courtauld's wife Elizabeth visited Delius at Grez-sur-Loing in March 1931. Bruno Walter, the Courtaulds' co-conductor with Malcolm Sargent, was to have conducted, but found he could not manage the date, so Sargent stepped in. The Deliuses then had second thoughts. They seemed to think that Beecham would be offended by not being given the première, though Mrs Courtauld discounted that impression by reporting to them that Beecham had told Sargent he had no prior claim on the work and was quite happy for the Courtaulds to be presenting it. Then the possibility of a Beecham performance in Liverpool arose, but this came to nothing because the only available date would have preceded the already announced first performance. 'A great pity,' the Deliuses wrote to Fenby; they thought Sargent 'dashy and tempestuous', though they were mollified when it was arranged for Fenby to attend his rehearsals for the première. Neither of the first performances (there were two, on 21 and 23 March 1932, by the Philharmonic Choir and the LSO) was broadcast, but the Deliuses were gratified to hear good reports of them, and of a subsequent Sargent performance in Bradford, from both Robert Nichols and Eric Fenby.

With all his compositions finished, Delius's hopes were now pinned on the long-awaited Delius Society discs. Beecham's commitments, however, made it impossible for him to begin on them until April 1934: his practice was first to try out in the concert hall works which he planned to record, and at the LPO's early concerts Delius's music had to take its turn in a huge repertoire which he was exploring while his new orchestra established itself. But, with recording sessions for the Delius Society looming, *Paris* was found a place in the Queen's Hall concert on 25 February; then, so as to key his players up to a further pitch of readiness, Beecham arranged another performance 'by special request' on 8 April, the day before the first recording session. (Doubtless the 'special request' was his own: after all, not only was the orchestra his but so was the Beecham Sunday Concerts series; he could do as he liked.) After a second session on 22 April to remake the second of the six sides, the test-pressings of *Paris* were quickly processed by his recording producer Walter Legge[4] and despatched to Grez-sur-Loing on 21 May with a letter inviting Delius's reaction: 'If you feel as enthusiastic about them as Sir Thomas and I do,' suggested Legge, 'perhaps you will also be so kind as to write me a letter expressing your pleasure and approval of them, couched in terms that we can use for advertising purposes.' Alas for Legge's hopes: bureaucracy intervened, and the records were held up in customs at Calais while officials puzzled over whether they were for sale or not. Eric Fenby sent desperate letters and telegrams from Grez-sur-Loing explaining the true circumstances, but his attempts to secure their release were unavailing: when at last they did arrive, it was too late.

Delius's final weeks had coincided with his wife's collapse: she was found to be suffering from cancer and on 16 May was taken into hospital in Fontainebleau for an operation. Fenby rushed from England to be with Delius, and did all he could to distract the dying composer, reading to him and playing him the long-familiar recordings of his music. As the end drew near, Jelka was brought home to be with the man to whom she had devoted her life. Delius was aware of her heroic effort, and was comforted by it, but he gradually lapsed into unconsciousness and died in the early hours of Sunday, 10 June 1934. That evening the BBC's announcement of his passing was followed by part of Beecham's record of *The Walk to the Paradise Garden*. Jelka and Fenby heard it together; they were coping as best they could with their dramatically changed circumstances. An inevitable consequence of Delius's death was that his private world became public overnight: the next morning, Fenby recalled, 'there were more people in his garden than in all the years during which I had shared his seclusion'. One of those who arrived was Dora Labbette, sent by Beecham to see if she might be of help. Fenby recalled her pausing in the doorway, 'a lovely reminder of another world that seemed so distant from the household, as she gazed down tearfully at the body of Delius lying on the studio couch'. Two days later the composer's remains were laid to rest in the village churchyard pending a decision about his final resting-place.

*   *   *

> With the death of Delius there has died a world the corresponding loveliness to which it will be a long time before humanity can create for itself again. It may be that, as some think, we are now in the first hour before a new dawn in music. But that hour is grey and chilly: and those of us who have been drunk with the beauty and the glory of the sunset of civilisation as we knew it must find our consolation in the melting colours of the cloud-shapes of the music of this last great representative of that old dead world.

So ended Ernest Newman's thoughtful valedictory reflections on the loss of Frederick Delius, a week after the composer's death. In England, the musical establishment's tributes were headed by Walford Davies, Master of the King's Musick, who thought that Delius's 'rich contribution to the harmonic texture of music will live, especially in view of the fact that he orchestrated so beautifully'. Tributes from overseas were led by Richard Strauss, who described Delius's death as 'a profound loss to music; his melody was a great gift to the world'. For his part, Beecham contented himself with a few dignified sentences: 'What I have to say of this great man cannot be expressed in a few words, or moments. He and I were friends for a great number of years, and the sense of loss is now too painful ...'

In London, memorial concerts were planned. *A Mass of Life* with Beecham conducting BBC forces opened the corporation's 1934–35 season on 24 October. The intended presence of Jelka Delius may have prompted him to decide to use the German text (for the first time in a performance in England), and he arranged for Hermann Nissen from the Bavarian State Opera, who had sung in his *Ring* cycle at Covent Garden the previous May and at the Leeds Festival with him on 3 October in Verdi's *Requiem*, to be engaged as the baritone soloist. Four days before the performance, however, illness forced Nissen to cry off, and the BBC turned to Roy

Henderson as replacement. He accepted, but could only offer the English text, which he knew by heart. Beecham appealed to him to learn the German, but Henderson could not do so in the time available. The conductor next proposed a postponement of the performance, which the BBC refused to consider, whereupon he threatened not to conduct. Unfortunately for him, the BBC held the trump card: if he withdrew, they would simply get their music director, Adrian Boult, to conduct instead. Faced with an impasse Beecham conducted, and *A Mass of Life* was once more heard in English. Jelka Delius did attend, and on arrival in the hall was greeted by the Philharmonic Choir with flowers and cheering.

The Royal Philharmonic Society's own tribute to its distinguished member (Delius had been awarded the society's Gold Medal in 1925) followed on 8 November and was a happier affair. With his own LPO Beecham programmed *Paris*, *Eventyr*, *Sea Drift*, *Cynara* and excerpts from *Koanga* and *Hassan*. In a touching letter to him next day, Jelka Delius said she found it

> impossible to say in words what I feel about the heavenly concert last night. It was all so exquisite and I realized so intensely what your genius and devotion means to the Delius Music, how everything you touch you bring up to its most perfect expression. Why, Paris was miraculous and Seadrift, that touchingly beautiful work had never been quite so lovely ... and Fred's beloved Eventyr, it was grand. And the Road to Samarkand ending in that unearthly ppp; just what he always desired. I was also astonished how charming the closing scene of Koanga is. I last heard it when the Opera was given just 30 years ago at Elberfeld. Oh, what great satisfaction it must be to you to be able to electrify all those Masses of Musicians, to give their very utmost, and to attain such unheard of beauties!
>
> I must tear myself away on Monday; alas! and live on my memories.
>
> Your ever devoted Jelka

She would surely also have been impressed to read in the concert's programme 'A Message from Sir Thomas Beecham' headed by an exhortation to 'JOIN THE DELIUS SOCIETY!' Then came a signed appeal from him:

> Five years ago I had the idea of organizing in London a festival of the work of Frederick Delius. I talked the matter over with a few admirers of the composer and I was surprised at their disbelief in the chances of success. Their argument was, 'You and I and a few others know this music to be the finest written in our time, but there is as yet no public for it such as there is for certain other modern composers.' I ventured to question the accuracy of this view and went on, to the astonishment and dismay of my friends, to embark upon a festival of six concerts, of which four were devoted to orchestral works and two to songs and chamber music. Each concert was sold out, and at the conclusion of the festival I told the public that I could easily have given another six concerts of Delius's music hardly inferior in quality to the series just completed.
>
> For my part, I have no hesitation in declaring the life and work of Delius to be the greatest and most far-reaching incident in music during the last fifty years. The Delius Society proposes in the first years of its life to record those works which, from my long association with the composer, I know he would have sanctioned for priority of

ROYAL PHILHARMONIC SOCIETY

123rd SEASON   1934-35

THIRD CONCERT

1st SERIES

Thursday, November 8th

QUEEN'S HALL, 8.15 p.m.

Programme

DELIUS MEMORIAL CONCERT

Suite, " Hassan "   -   -   -   -   ⎫
" Eventyr "   -   -   -   -   -   ⎪
" Sea Drift " -   -   -   -   -   -   ⎬ *Delius*
              INTERVAL   ⎪
" Paris " -   -   -   -   -   -   ⎪
" Cynara "   -   -   -   -   ⎪
Final Scene, " Koanga "   -   -   -   ⎭

Conductor   SIR THOMAS BEECHAM

THE LONDON SELECT CHOIR

(Conductor - ARNOLD FULTON)

WILLIAM PARSONS

LONDON PHILHARMONIC ORCHESTRA

Seven

3.4 **Beecham's memorial concert for Delius**

appearance. At the moment we have about 400 members, and at least 600 more are required if the intended programme is to be carried out efficiently. I appeal to all who love this music to assist in the worthy task of perpetuating the life labour of a great master by joining the Society at the earliest possible date.

The previous month at the Leeds Festival Beecham had conducted *Songs of Sunset* as well as reviving *An Arabesque* (which had not been heard since the 1929 festival). Both works were recorded by Columbia during rehearsals, possibly for inclusion in a future volume of Delius Society issues, though they were not published. (Recording on location was still considered a hazardous business, although Beecham's records of the Polovtsian Dances from Borodin's *Prince Igor*, also made at Leeds that year, were hugely successful and became one of the jewels of Columbia's catalogue in the 1930s.) For years afterwards a few sets of test-pressings of the Delius works which circulated privately confirmed that parts of *Songs of Sunset* as sung on that occasion by Olga Haley and Roy Henderson at Leeds were not surpassed in either of Beecham's later recordings.[5]

By this time Beecham had the Delius bit between his teeth, both on record and in the concert hall. During 1934 alone, in addition to conducting *A Mass of Life* and the two all-Delius concerts in London and Manchester, he programmed six performances of *Paris* and two of the Piano Concerto besides isolated accounts of *North Country Sketches* (the first time he had conducted it since the 1929 festival) and *In a Summer Garden*. Some of the songs sung by Dora Labbette in orchestral arrangements by Beecham or Heseltine and the *First Cuckoo* were also heard, resulting in a total of more than 30 Delius works for the year. All in all, one is not entirely surprised to learn that LPO leaders sometimes begged to be let off Delius rehearsals for fear the music would go stale on them. Doubly fortunate, then, that a major Beecham-Delius enterprise which had long been arranged for June 1934 did not involve them but an orchestra all agog and straining at the leash to play under Beecham's baton. For a few years he had found time to conduct an opera annually at the Royal College of Music, London, at the behest of his old friend Sir Hugh Allen, the college principal; in 1934 the choice had fallen upon *A Village Romeo and Juliet*, and three performances were to be given. The prospect had naturally delighted Delius, who declared that, if Beecham were to stage the opera he had not heard since 1920, he might make a second supreme effort to travel to England.

The composer's death 17 days before the first night gave the whole project extra significance and purpose. The opera had been prepared by the college's Head of Opera, Hermann Grünebaum, assisted by Constant Lambert, and a team of professors led by Hugh Allen himself together with a small army of students worked against the clock to transfer Beecham's phrasings and other markings from his score into the orchestral parts. The list of performers ran to 141 (all but 17 were students at the College) and included some names that were destined to become well-known: Peter Pears and Frederick Sharp (who sang in Beecham's later recording of the opera) were just two of the voices, while in the student orchestra were the oboist Evelyn Rothwell, clarinettists Stephen Waters and Bernard Walton (the last Beecham snapped up a few years later for the LPO), and the horn players John Denison and Francis Probyn; Michael Mudie, later a Sadler's Wells conductor, was the timpanist and many of the string players became familiar faces in London orchestras for decades afterwards.

All these people waited for Beecham to arrive for the first rehearsal in various stages of excitement or nervous apprehension, heightened when he sat outside in his chauffeur-driven Rolls-Royce for some time finishing his cigar. After that, though, he quickly got down to business, winning over the nervous young string players of the college orchestra with an approach that had the effect not only of putting them at their ease but of making them feel as if they were complete professionals alongside him. 'That marvellously elegant way of talking to you made you feel you were "up there" with him, that you and he were working *together* on this thing,' recalled the orchestra's young leader, Ralph Nicholson, who was seated so close to Beecham's rostrum that at one point the conductor's baton knocked his bow off the strings of his violin.[6] In the audience was Albert Sammons, who had led the orchestra at Beecham's earlier performances, as well as Delius's sister, Clare Black. Before the curtain went up on the first night, Beecham paid a memorial tribute to Delius, described by Richard Capell in the *Daily Telegraph* as 'most felicitous and graceful in its phrasing and moving in its seriousness'. 'How little, my soul, thou needest to be happy', from the text of *A Mass of Life*, was its keynote, because of its extreme suitability to Delius, said Beecham:

> A garden in France, a summer holiday in Norway – this was all he asked of life ... He chose a life of simplicity, and the simplicity of that life, and of Delius's pleasures – the sight of sunlight on his flower-beds, and the sound of wind in the leaves – was in his music, 'a music,' in the Wordsworthian phrase, 'born of murmuring sounds.'

The three stagings (27, 28 and 29 June) were a triumph for everyone involved and made a great impression. 'This is the most heartbreaking music in the world,' Hugh Allen observed to Beecham at one point. According to an unattributed report in the *Liverpool Daily Post*, Beecham himself considered them 'far finer than his earlier performances at Covent Garden in 1910 and 1920'.

Volume I of the Delius Society recordings appeared at the end of 1934. It consisted of *Paris*, *Eventyr*, the Closing Scene from *Koanga* and the 'Intermezzo and Serenade' from *Hassan* (in Beecham's own arrangement), together with two songs ('To the Queen of my Heart' and 'Love's Philosophy') sung by Heddle Nash accompanied by Gerald Moore. Handsomely packaged in stout albums, the seven 78rpm discs had a specially designed label depicting Delius's head and boldly advertising '*THE DELIUS SOCIETY – Artistic Director Sir Thomas Beecham Bart.*' Inside each album was a booklet containing analytical notes with copious musical examples, and an essay by the writer and critic A.K. Holland. Acting well in advance of Columbia's own publicity for its new venture, Beecham had rallied influential friends. Ernest Newman had already devoted a sizeable portion of his *Sunday Times* review of Beecham's BBC performance of *A Mass of Life* to a direct appeal for support. After praising 'the abundant lovelinesses that Sir Thomas Beecham drew from the BBC Orchestra', he plunged straight in:

> I would urge every admirer of Delius who can afford it to join the Delius Society at once, and so make possible a series of authoritative gramophone records of this and other works under the only conductor who both possesses the secret of Delius and has the ability to make it visible to others. One shudders at the thought of what will happen to Delius's music in the future at the hands of the ordinary conductor unless the only authentic interpretations of his works are established for all time, as those of Elgar's works have been by the composer himself.

Beecham himself then seized the opportunity provided by the Royal Philharmonic Society's memorial concert on 8 November to make a speech of his own concerning the forthcoming discs. 'Competent critics,' he declared loftily, 'consider my recording of *Paris* to be the best orchestral records ever produced.' As soon as the records appeared, he kept public interest up by arranging another all-Delius concert in London on 10 March 1935 at which, as *Paris* had been heard quite frequently, he singled out the other major work on the records, *Eventyr*, for prominence instead. He did, however, include *Paris* in provincial guest-conducting engagements early in 1935 in Birmingham and Manchester, and planned to take it more widely: Berlin was scheduled to hear it at a Philharmonic Concert in the April (though this was cancelled) and in June he conducted it in Brussels when he took the LPO there for two concerts at the Palais des Beaux-Arts. The following January *Eventyr* as well as *Paris* featured in concerts with the New York Philharmonic in Carnegie Hall and later in 1936 he conducted *Brigg Fair* in Stockholm and Oslo. At other concerts where these larger works were not practicable, shorter pieces were substituted. One such miniature, *Summer Night on the River*, he went on to record in 1935, and this was issued on its own on a 10-inch 78rpm disc (a format that excluded it from the Society albums which all contained 12-inch discs). The disc helped to keep up interest in the gaps between the issue of the Delius Society volumes, which, with good commercial acumen, had been carefully planned to appear at two-yearly intervals in order to allow sufficient time between the release to the public of each volume.

A decision about Delius's final resting-place had now been reached. It was to be Limpsfield in Surrey, near the home of the Harrison family at Foyle Riding, Oxted. Delius had apparently once remarked to Mrs Harrison that he wished to be buried in England, a point over which Jelka was insistent to May Harrison during a visit the violinist made to Grez-sur-Loing in the months after Delius's death. Mrs Harrison was herself now dead, but no doubt the composer had been influenced by her assurances that the younger members of the Harrison family would be on hand to look after the grave for the foreseeable future. Some people, including Beecham and Jelka herself, thought this a mistake. Writing to Eric Fenby five weeks after

Delius's death, Jelka said: 'I think Beecham is right about Fred being buried in Yorkshire and I objected it to Fred at the time he spoke about it, but he would never hear about it.' Despite her misgivings, early in 1935 she came over from France to choose a spot in the graveyard of St Mary's Church at Limpsfield. She was not maintaining the early progress made following her operation and, possibly conscious of her own mortality, was anxious as ever to fulfil every last duty to Delius. Sunday 26 May 1935 was settled upon for the reburial and Jelka, though by then gravely ill, set out once more from France for England on the 22nd. Fenby travelled separately with Delius's coffin in a motor hearse from Grez-sur-Loing, arriving at Limpsfield at midnight in readiness for the next day's funeral.

A huge crowd, estimated by the police at 1,000, turned out for the service at

We are here to-day to bid farewell for ever to Frederick Delius, a great Englishman and a famous man. You have read that it was his wish to be buried in the soil of his native country.

I think it may be said that nowhere in the breadth of this land could a fairer spot be found than this to satisfy his wish, nor a more auspicious occasion than this beautiful day.

It may have struck some of you as requiring a little explanation as to why Frederick Delius, who left ~~this country~~ *these shores* as a very young man, a wanderer and almost an exile, has returned to ~~it~~ *them* finally only yesterday. You may like to know why it was he wished to lie here amid the countryside of the land which gave him birth. I think I am able to give you the explanation.

The England that we live ~~in to-day~~ is not by any means the England in which Delius was born, some 75 years ago. ~~Delius~~ *He* was born in those days which excited and provoked the rage of the sages of the time. Carlyle, Matthew Arnold, Ruskin raged and preached against the brutality, inhumanity, and insensibility of that age.

3.5 The first page of Beecham's funeral oration at Delius's reburial in 1935, with his own handwritten amendments (Archive of Shirley, Lady Beecham)

4 o'clock the following afternoon. Those who could not get into the church (which seated only 450) listened outside to a relay on loudspeakers. At the funeral, a section of the LPO played *Summer Night on the River*, the Serenade from *Hassan* and *On hearing the First Cuckoo in Spring* under Beecham's baton, and Paul Beard directed Anthony Pini in the *Elegy* that Delius had composed for Beatrice Harrison. Outside, after the committal, Beecham advanced to the head of the grave to deliver an oration (see Appendix 3). The whole service was recorded by the BBC, and parts of it were played from the records next day to Jelka Delius, who had, at the last, been too ill to attend and was lying in a nursing-home. 'Dear Tommy', she murmured as the oration ended. She died within hours, on 28 May and, a few days later, was laid to rest alongside her husband.

The day before she died, Jelka had signed a new will. It made provision for the establishment of a trust bearing Delius's name and directed that the income from her residuary estate should be applied:

> towards the advancement in England or elsewhere of the musical works of my late Husband Frederick Delius ... by means of (1) the recording upon the gramophone or any other instrument for the mechanical reproduction of music of those works of my late Husband, which in the opinion of my Trustees and their advisers are suitable for reproduction. (2) The publication and issue of a uniform edition of the whole body of the works of my late Husband or any part thereof or the publication and issue of any separate work hitherto unpublished under the editorship of Sir Thomas Beecham, Bart. (3) The financing in whole or in part of the performance in public of the works of my late Husband.

Jelka had sought Beecham's help in straightening out her affairs in the aftermath of Delius's death. With Norman O'Neill also now dead (the result of a street accident in London in February 1934) and Balfour Gardiner having withdrawn more and more from musical activity, she had few people to turn to and, as she wrote to the conductor, 'After all, you and I have Fred's interests more at heart and understand him better than anyone else.' When she came to London to hear both the BBC performance of *A Mass of Life* and the Royal Philharmonic Society's memorial concert, it was also so that Beecham's lawyers could assist her in finalising her intentions as to her own will: 'I must safeguard Fred's ultimate interests,' she wrote to Beecham before she set out. She was particularly concerned about a plan that Delius had discussed with Balfour Gardiner for a concert scheme that would benefit young composers whose works merited public performance. Gardiner was pressing for this to be carried through, but Jelka was adamant, arguing to Beecham: 'As to these programmes of young composers with only one Delius work – that is an absurd idea and there would be no public for such concerts. I feel we *must* change that'. In London she stayed at the home of Norman O'Neill's widow, Adine, where Beecham called upon her to discuss the plans that had been prepared for a Delius Trust. 'T.B. really came, as he had promised,' she told Eric Fenby on 14 November. 'Fred[eric] Austin was there and Mrs O'N[eill] and they greatly approved all his proposals ... He was splendid and I left with the happy feeling that I had accomplished all I had to do there.' So the Delius Trust came into being, with Beecham's solicitor, Philip Emanuel, and Barclays Bank as the first Trustees. Beecham became an Artistic Adviser, as did Frederic Austin, but it is easy to see where the power lay: indeed, the trustees were directed 'to obtain and faithfully observe the advice and opinion of Sir Thomas Beecham'. Beecham was to remain Artistic Adviser for the rest of his life. Balfour Gardiner felt sufficiently keenly about the abandonment of the concert scheme for young composers that he resigned as Delius's executor.

Another question that was settled before Jelka Delius died related to the biography of her husband that she wanted written: this was something that had also exercised her mind a great deal in the weeks since his death. Her first choice as its author was Eric Fenby, to whom she wrote on 25 September: 'Of course I most decidedly want you to do Fred's biography. I have a lot of old letters and we can make it most interesting.' But she also at some point approached the critic and writer Cecil Gray, who 'reluctantly acquiesced out of a sense of duty'.[7] He had no need to worry: on 14 December Jelka wrote to him:

> My dear Gray, Yesterday I had a letter from Beecham. He proposes to write the biography himself; in fact he says that most of it is already written in a number of essays on the Delius works, and he wants to do the remaining portions with the aid of a young writer under his leadership. This role you could, of course, never accept, and needs a willing collaborator under Beecham's orders. You will, I hope understand that I cannot do otherwise than accept Beecham's proposal. I never expected this, as he has already such multiple activities, but of course he holds all the threads of the Delius in his hands and it is natural for him to wish to be associated with him also in a literary way. Yours ever affectionately, Jelka Delius.

No doubt Jelka was embarrassed at this turn of events, although the matter was not quite as blunt as presented. The question of the biography had been dealt with a month earlier, at the meeting in London at which Beecham had presented his proposals for the Delius Trust to her. 'He also arranged about the biography etc.,' Jelka told Eric Fenby in her letter of 14 November. What was not known to anyone until then was that she had approached Beecham on 11 November to see whether he would undertake the biography, and that he had agreed. A complication then arose with the unexpected announcement that Delius's sister Clare was, with her brother-in-law, Ladbroke Black, planning a life of the composer to be published in the early spring of 1935. It transpired that a substantial portion of this was already complete, which caused sufficient alarm in the Delius camp for there to be moves made on behalf of Jelka and Beecham to suppress it; then they considered the idea of purchasing what had already been written, on the grounds that it would be valuable in providing ready-made information about Delius's childhood that would be difficult to obtain elsewhere. The Blacks, however, while at first seemingly not unwilling to accept a fee to cancel the contract with their publisher, rejected the notion that the work already done might be acquired by someone else; in the end, objection to their publishing was dropped.

The matter did, however, have the effect of forcing Beecham's hand, since during these negotiations it had to be revealed that he was going to write the authorised biography. At the beginning of 1935 he wrote to Eric Fenby in Grez-sur-Loing seeking a chronological list of Delius's compositions during the years 1884–89 and asking him to establish the exact dates of Delius's movements beginning at the Leipzig Conservatory and ending with his first visit to Grez-sur-Loing before he settled there. 'I think this is all – for the moment!' his letter ended. If this was evidence of Beecham's intention to begin work on a biography, indeed it was: nothing more was heard about it until the early 1950s. It was hardly surprising. In the course of 1935 he gave over 40 concerts, either with his own orchestra or as guest conductor of others such as the Berlin Philharmonic or the Hallé, undertook ten recording sessions and ran two international opera seasons at Covent Garden between April/July and September/November which involved him personally in conducting a total of 40 opera performances including a *Ring* cycle. Where Beecham ever imagined that he was going to find the time to write a biography of Delius as well remains a mystery. Perhaps, in his own mind, the project was one for the future, and any discussion about its early start was made out of tactful sympathy in the light of Jelka Delius's deteriorating health. Her death then effectively removed any urgency.

Instead of writing about Delius, Beecham threw himself into performing his music: in the first half of 1935, *Over the Hills and Far Away* was heard five times in various concert halls, including at his all-Delius concert in London (10 March), which also featured *Eventyr*, the Piano Concerto (Katharine Goodson) and the Double Concerto played by his LPO principals, Paul Beard and Anthony Pini;[8] elsewhere *Paris* appeared three times, and *Appalachia* once. All this was in addition to another major Delian project to which he now turned his attention. Despite his enthusiasm for the opera *Koanga*, which had manifested itself as early as 1910, Beecham had never conducted it: now he decided that he would open the Royal Opera's autumn season with it and then take it on tour to the provinces. As with *A Village Romeo and Juliet* 25 years earlier, the project was not without incident. An immediate obstacle was that the full score and all the orchestral material was missing, though the orchestral parts were soon located in a publisher's basement in London. While a search was undertaken for the score, Eric Fenby began to reconstruct one from the parts: he was about half way through this unrewarding task when the score was unearthed. Rehearsals began at Covent Garden, but when Act II opened in total darkness Beecham paused, before enquiring of his stage manager, 'Is anything going to happen, Mr Moor?' For once, the assurance that 'it would be all right on the night' apparently satisfied him, though it did not bode well. In the role of Palmyra, Oda Slobodskaya found Beecham difficult to follow because, she complained, he rarely gave a down-beat. 'But you don't need down-beats from Beecham,' retorted John Brownlee as her

3.6 *Koanga*: **programme of 1935 performance**

Koanga, 'you can *feel* where he is!' The costuming also seemed less than suitable.
Brownlee, in shorts, looked, in Fenby's words, 'like a goalkeeper', while the
unsuitably tall headdress Slobodskaya wore at first sight caused Beecham to laugh
so much that she threw a shoe at him. In the pit were two specially engaged banjo-
players, who turned out to be deadly enemies. At one rehearsal they were absent,
and when Beecham enquired where 'the exotic gentlemen' (as he liked to call
them) were, he had to be told that they were outside having a fight. None of this
improved his temper and for some time afterwards, when he was impatient with his
players, word went round that he was in a 'Koanga' mood.

Koanga received a very mixed press, most writers finding a series of beautiful
sounds little compensation for its lack of drama and what they considered to be
Delius's non-existent sense of theatre; few, consequently, were convinced of its
worth as an opera. As to the performances, criticisms ranged from 'highly
creditable' in *The Times* to 'inadequate' in the *Manchester Guardian*. Beecham and
the orchestra took most of the honours that were going, and the conductor provided
the popular dailies with some welcome material on the opening night by arriving
in the pit eight minutes late and – even more exciting – at a subsequent point
dramatically halting the opera, putting down his baton and leaving his desk.[9]
Matters did not improve greatly when the production went on tour. Despite rather
better notices and respectable audiences, Beecham was stung into criticism of local
music-lovers and music critics for not fully supporting him. He complained that
Liverpudlians were 'entirely uneducated when it came to opera', and that
Manchester 'used to be a real city: now it is only imitation'; and to Bradford, which
in not rallying to its local composer 'had insulted the memory of a great man', he
doubted he would ever return. The critics, meanwhile, 'never conveyed to the
public anything it might possibly want to know'; the musical press was 'only
concerned with its own peculiar views' – and so on. Battle was joined in Liverpool
when a young local writer, David Webster, wrote a long and reasoned response to
Beecham's tirades. But his description of Oda Slobodskaya as looking 'like a
corner cupboard with a vase on top' roused Beecham to a mock fury. 'I insist,' he
cried, 'that all copies of the offending newspaper be burned on St George's Steps,
and Mr Webster with them!'[10]

Fortunately, there were better things to come. In 1936 he first settled upon the
repertoire for the next Delius Society volume and then recorded it during April and
September/November. *Sea Drift* was the highlight, with John Brownlee, his
Koanga, as baritone soloist: a public performance on 22 March preceded the
recording on 3 April (though several sides were remade the following November).
The other works in Volume II were *In a Summer Garden*, *Over the Hills and Far
Away* and the Intermezzo from *Fennimore and Gerda*, and some of these were
given concert outings before being taken into the studio. This method of working
resulted in records that exhibited the qualities of the LPO to especially fine
advantage. Now in its fourth season, the orchestra was well established and
Beecham was obtaining practically unsurpassable results from it. A performance of

A Mass of Life at the Norfolk and Norwich Festival in September was described by Thomas Russell, then one of the LPO players but later to become its managing director, as 'one of the most living presentations of any music in my experience, even with Beecham. He conducted it from memory, which is a feat in itself, but did it to free himself entirely from the restraints of the score rather than as a feat. The performance became in effect a vast improvisation …'[11] Eric Fenby's opinion of the same performance remained unaffected by the passing of time: 'Passages such as the marvellous, evocative evening music in the third and fourth movements have never been given with such artistry since.'

Although there had been a few changes in the LPO's personnel (the most important being the replacement of Paul Beard as leader by David McCallum of the Scottish Orchestra), the woodwind principals of Geoffrey Gilbert, Léon Goossens, Reginald Kell and John Alexandra consistently imparted a lustre to its playing which no other London orchestra could match. This was particularly valuable in so evocative a score as *In a Summer Garden,* where Beecham could demand the utmost delicacy of nuance from his players and achieve it apparently effortlessly. Goossens's exquisite oboe-playing in this and the Intermezzo from *Fennimore and Gerda* goes a long way towards explaining why Beecham's Delius Society records created what amounted practically to a cult for the music in the 1930s. The *Fennimore and Gerda* item was unusual in that Beecham's record of it constituted the work's first performance. With Delius's approval Eric Fenby had linked together the preludes to Scenes 10 and 11 and added some bars from the end of the opera to make a short concert piece. It had never been performed, but it is likely that Fenby now drew it to Beecham's attention and possible that the conductor seized on it not only as a novelty for the Delius Society records but because it enabled him to include something from the one score that Delius had dedicated to him.

The year after the LPO's visit to Brussels in 1935, Beecham grasped a second opportunity to show off his orchestra to overseas audiences. He cared not a jot for criticism levelled at him at home on political grounds for accepting the German government's invitation to give eight concerts in Berlin and seven other towns and cities: the opportunity to demonstrate what England could achieve in the orchestral field was an ambition close to his heart and he was determined not to forgo it. In Brussels *Paris* had been played, but now Beecham chose the two miniatures, the *First Cuckoo* and *Summer Night on the River,* to represent Delius in his tour programmes, and they were heard together in Ludwigshafen, Frankfurt and Cologne. In Ludwigshafen, officials of the IG-Farben Company demonstrated to Beecham a means of recording on film; portions of the concert were recorded by this process and still survive, including part of the *First Cuckoo* in which, despite the primitive sound quality, Léon Goossens's oboe-playing can be clearly appreciated.

The Song of the High Hills now made a belated first appearance in a Beecham programme. Although he had evidently planned to introduce it as early as 1915, at

**3.7   Beecham on tour with the LPO in Germany 1936. Part of the concert
in Ludwigshafen included *On hearing the First Cuckoo in Spring*,
which was recorded by an early tape process**

the concert in question he had given the first performance of *North Country
Sketches* instead and it was a score he had not touched since; this is strange,
because it originated within that group of pieces composed in 1902–14 that he
promoted tirelessly all his life. The theory has been advanced that he was less
interested in it because its eventual first performance was conducted by somebody
else (Albert Coates, in February 1920): but Beecham had had every opportunity to
unveil it before 1920 had he wished to, and it is perhaps more likely that, while he
admired the music, he did not have as strong a feeling for it as for some of the other
pieces. Whatever the reason, he only ever performed it on four occasions. That
first, on 12 March 1936, was possibly a try-out for a Delius Society recording; if
so, nothing came of it. Other novelties also appeared, notably (in 1937) the *Florida*
suite. The student Delius had paid to have this, his first large-scale orchestral
composition, performed (informally in a Leipzig beer-cellar) while he was at the
Conservatory there in 1888, and it had not been played since; the orchestral
material had come to Beecham with the rest of Delius's manuscripts after the
composer's death. Although billed as the complete *Florida* suite, the work was
given with the second movement, *By the River*, replaced by the *Irmelin Prelude*.
All the same, as a 'first performance' it made a contribution that was both suitable
and significant to the Royal Philharmonic Society's all-English programme on
1 April to celebrate the forthcoming coronation of King George VI.

Aside from *Florida*, 1937 was a relatively quiet year for Delius performances, though there were two items of unusual interest. One was the return to Beecham's repertoire on 18 November of the Dance Rhapsody No. 1, which he had not conducted in England since the 1929 festival; the other involved the Hungarian pianist Edward Kilenyi, who had appeared as a soloist in Beecham's Sunday Concerts series in 1935 and 1937, playing concertos by Liszt and Chopin. It is possible that Beecham took the opportunity at one of these concerts to commend Delius's concerto to him, because Kilenyi played it at a second appearance in the same series on 28 November 1937, and thus became only the second international pianist (Benno Moiseiwitsch being the first) to essay it with him. Earlier that same month Beecham was in Berlin making recordings with the Berlin Philharmonic; at his only concert he included *Paris*, which had joined *Brigg Fair* as his Delian calling-card in foreign concert halls, while still figuring prominently at home. It had done so once again earlier in 1937 when, on 3 February, he paid another visit as guest conductor to the BBC Symphony Orchestra. The orchestra's principal viola, Bernard Shore, was compiling a book recording his impressions of some of the conductors who worked with the orchestra during its first decade, and describing their rehearsal methods this particular rehearsal (and concert) was the event he chose to study for the chapter on Beecham. To Shore's writings we owe one of the few extended observations of Beecham at work in rehearsal, and the only detailed description of him rehearsing a Delius score (see Appendix 2). It underlines the truism that Beecham's rehearsal methods were composed of a mixture of concentrated work leavened by fun and raillery. His charisma, of course, was such that he was able to obtain fine results from almost any band of players but, as Eric Fenby has pointed out, for his rehearsals to be completely fruitful precise requirements of phrasing and dynamics would already be present in the players' copies:

He would mark in blue pencil every bar of the score, exaggerating Delius's own nuances of expression to make the fullest impact in performance. Copyists would then transfer these markings to each of the orchestral parts of the work. The rehearsal existed in the main to familiarise the players, all of them experts, with the way he wanted the varying textures to sound in balance and attack. He would lean forward on the rostrum, shaping his phrases in exquisite flow, allowing the music to breathe and speak as Delius intended with pen and paper, but was unable precisely to convey: the stick often seemingly aimless, but poised to control some pivot chord on which the emotional tension hinged in his control of the melodic line. It was direction as if by mesmerism, his eyes anticipating every inflection. His verbal comments, often witty, reinforced the scrupulous observance of [his] editings, or exploded in humorous reprimand, or in mild rebuke of a player who had somehow missed his entry – 'Cor anglais! Will you kindly give me some indication of your presence!' Often he would draw attention to the operative note in a phrase, the pointing of which would make all the difference between telling at once or not at all. 'Clarinet!' he would say, 'a little more time before you get to the C' … or he would exasperate the first violins by making them repeat a long-drawn melody until he had flighted it to perfection. His chief concern with Delius was in tending the melodic strands that pass from voice to voice and give the piece its form, and, no less important, the balancing of timbres carrying the supporting harmonies.[12]

Volume III of the Delius Society discs appeared at the close of 1938. It contained *Appalachia*, which, in taking up five of the seven discs, left space only for some smaller works on the four remaining sides. While a final selection was being made Beecham actually recorded more music than there was room for, notably a purely orchestral passage from *A Mass of Life* (the opening of the third movement of Part 2) and several of the songs, sung by Dora Labbette, mostly in his own orchestrations. He also extracted Delius's first version of *La Calinda* from its original position in the first movement of the *Florida* suite and recorded that too, although he excised the dramatic passage that in the suite divides the two appearances of the famous oboe presentation of the dance melody. He had introduced this music, in this format, as the prelude to Act 2 in his performances of *Koanga* in 1935. For the records, however, he decided in favour of Eric Fenby's concert arrangement of *La Calinda*, which appeared in print that year, and none of the extra recordings made were used (though they achieved publication many years later). So the Closing Scene from *Hassan* and Fenby's version of *La Calinda*, together with the *Irmelin Prelude* completed the set. The *Irmelin Prelude* was another result of the Fenby period: he had helped Delius compose it in 1931, drawing on themes from the unstaged opera *Irmelin*. When Beecham had introduced it as an orchestral interlude during his 1935 production of *Koanga*, Fenby had been flattered by the 'smiles of approval and delightful comments' from the orchestral players as the work was rehearsed for the first time. It proved now to be an ideal encore piece and also good publicity for the new records; Beecham made a feature of it as an encore at nine concerts in the course of 1939. Reviewing the BBC Symphony Orchestra's February concert at Queen's Hall, which had included *In a Summer Garden*, Neville Cardus in the *Manchester Guardian* conjured up a vivid picture of Beecham in action:

> He swayed and pawed the air and caressed it. He dived and crouched, he cajoled, implored and commanded. Sometimes he looked like a conjuror using his wand to draw a symphony out of a hat ... For musical instinct pure and undefiled Sir Thomas Beecham has every other conductor of the present day easily beaten ...

Following the pattern established earlier, the appearance of another volume of records was followed by concert performances of the works on them to secure publicity. *Appalachia* was given in both London and Manchester, and *La Calinda* turned up in miscellaneous programmes. Nor was the repertoire from the two earlier Delius Society volumes neglected: *Paris*, *Eventyr*, *Over the Hills and Far Away* and *In a Summer Garden* were all programmed during 1939, and other shorter works such as *The Walk to the Paradise Garden* and *On hearing the First Cuckoo in Spring* were widely played (notably in the provinces) as part of the wider dissemination of the Delius message. In March 1939, the Piano Concerto was given another airing in Manchester, with R.J. Forbes as soloist.

So the most comprehensive decade so far in Beecham's crusade on behalf of Delius's music came to an end. Many people take the view that it was during the 1930s that its highest point was reached. In the course of it he consistently promoted the music in British concert halls, and played it in every European country he visited as well as in the USA. Few conductors anywhere in the world would have had the personal magnetism and authority to draw audiences consistently to all-Delius programmes or to hear largely unfamiliar works such as *Sea Drift*, *Appalachia* and *A Mass of Life* (particularly the last, which he conducted no fewer than five times). But it was through his recordings that he was able to demonstrate the range of Delius's achievement on a far wider scale: the three volumes of Delius Society records, published in the UK and the USA and exported to other countries, created a new audience for the music more effectively than if all his concert hall performances had been multiplied many times over.[13] In some ways, therefore, it is true that if Beecham had stopped conducting Delius's music in 1940 his self-imposed task would still have been well achieved; but much more was to come, all of it of the greatest interest, especially in the years following the Second World War.

Notes

*   Eric Fenby in *Beecham Remembered*.

1   The Dresden-born conductor Rudolf Kempe (1910–76) was appointed by Beecham to be his associate at the Royal Philharmonic Orchestra in 1959; when Beecham died, Kempe assumed the conductorship of the 1962 Delius Centenary Festival in Bradford.

2   After a month-long ballet season in London in April and May Beecham left for Munich to conduct opera and an orchestral concert (which included *Brigg Fair*): en route he visited the Deliuses. Dora Labbette was with him, and one evening they treated the household to a highly unorthodox encore of the performance they had just given for the BBC of *A Village Romeo and Juliet* by playing and singing most of Vreli's music, Beecham filling in the role of Sali. On another evening, 'he told us so many funny stories at dinner that I kept on laughing for three days afterwards', wrote a young German girl, Evelin Gerhardi, daughter of one of Jelka Delius's oldest friends, who was then helping out at Grez-sur-Loing.

3   In view of Beecham's immense workload at this time no doubt he could have provided a fascinating and quite unique contribution to a BBC broadcast series entitled *Seven Days Hard*, in which speakers were required to provide 'personal, informal and humorous commentaries' on the events of a specific week. It was, though, an inauspicious moment for the BBC to invite him, and they got what they deserved: his reply through his secretary, with its obvious sting-in-the-tail, was dismissive: 'Sir Thomas Beecham very much regrets that he is unable to accept as at present his musical activities forbid any sort of relaxation.'

4   Walter Legge (1906–79) became one of the most important and influential figures in British recording circles. Despite being self-taught he had a natural instinct where music

was concerned and, although not yet 30 when he first met Beecham early in 1934, even then he impressed the conductor sufficiently for Beecham to decide that he wanted him as his personal producer. At the time Legge was actually working for HMV, rival within EMI to Columbia for whom Beecham recorded, but special dispensation was obtained and for the next six years he took charge of all Beecham's recordings. Delius's *Paris* was the first music upon which they worked together.

5   'From all sides I hear what beautiful performances you gave throughout the Leeds Festival and especially those of the Delius works,' Jelka wrote to Beecham on 13 October 1934; 'Fenby was quite overcome with enthusiasm.' Although it had been decided not to publish the two Delius works recorded at Leeds (*Songs of Sunset* and *An Arabesque*), Beecham arranged privately for Jelka to have sets of both of them when she came to London the following month. To avoid any sort of misunderstanding such as that which had occurred over the *Paris* discs at the time of Delius's death, she decided against having them sent to Grez-sur-Loing and resourcefully transported them back herself: 'I told the customs about them and had nothing to pay,' she wrote to Fenby proudly. Following suit, in the new year he bore the newly published Volume I of the Delius Society records safely across the channel too, and they were soon, in her words, 'revelling in them'. To Beecham – her 'dear beloved and wonderful Thomas' – she described them as 'supremely beautiful … Eventyr is a revelation and it is so glorious to possess them all, and to be able to play and play them and get to know these great works better and better and appreciate at last every part of them and every inflection of your wonderful interpretation. Hassan and Koanga are most lovable too, and the Songs so beautifully sung and reproduced. Heddle Nash is splendid now …' And to Catherine Barjansky she wrote: 'My only joy throughout this whole time is the album of Delius's records. These records are wonderful, and I urge you to get them as soon as possible.'

6   Ralph Nicholson (1907–2001) described working with Beecham on *A Village Romeo and Juliet* as one of the six most thrilling events of his life. 'He always treated you like a gentleman,' he recalled. 'I remember he suddenly stopped and said to me, "Mr Nicholson, what do you consider the most efficacious bowing for this particular bar?" I took care not to lose my head and replied, "Well, Sir Thomas, as it's *piano*, up-bow at the point, I think, will get a smoother effect," or something like that. "Very well, that's adopted. Will you put it in the parts, ladies and gentlemen?" There was no real reason why he should have sought my advice on such a matter, but it was his way of showing the rest of the orchestra that he had established rapport with their leader. He somehow made you play better than you thought you could … he drew something out of you … he knew how to get the best, even out of a bad orchestra (not that ours was a bad one). Constant Lambert said that the secret of Beecham's Delius was that it was always moving; it never got stuck or slow; always marvellous rhythm and forward movement. That's why it was always so alive.' (Condensed from the *Delius Society Journal*, no. 63, April 1979.)

7   In Cecil Gray, *Musical Chairs* (Home & Van Thal, London, 1948).

8   The viola player Lionel Tertis (1876–1975), always intent on extending the viola repertoire, transcribed the Double Concerto (viola replacing cello) and performed this version at a BBC studio concert under Adrian Boult on 3 March 1935 with May Harrison. The result impressed Jelka Delius: 'Tertis was, of course, the soul of this performance,' she told Percy Grainger on 19 March, 'and imparted to it such a wealth of true Delius tenderness and feeling, carrying May with him quite beyond herself; Boult at his best where discreet following a master mind is required – Of course I know certain things could not help loosing their effect thro' the deep cello-tone not there. But as the

1   Beecham and the London Philharmonic Orchestra with which he recorded the first three Delius Society volumes in the 1930s

2 With the Hallé Orchestra in the (old) Free Trade Hall, Manchester in 1933: Beecham introduced most of Delius's works to Manchester, including his own first performance of the Dance Rhapsody No. 1 at his Hallé debut in 1911

3   Frederick and Jelka Delius in the composer's last years

4 Beecham delivering his funeral oration at Delius's reburial at Limpsfield Parish Church in Surrey on 26 May 1935

5   Beecham talking with Eric Fenby at Delius's reburial in 1935

6 Beecham rehearsing *Sea Drift* with Gordon Clinton (seated on his right) for his 70th birthday concert at the Royal Albert Hall London in 1949

7 Beecham conducting for television in 1952. *On hearing the First Cuckoo in Spring* featured in the programme

8   Nostalgic return: Beecham revisited Grez-sur-Loing in the 1950s at the time
    he was writing his biography of Delius

Cello part is almost all thro' in the high ranges it had not to be changed and sang out beautifully in Tertis's supreme playing.' In the 1920s Tertis had made a transcription for viola of Delius's second Violin Sonata and recorded it in 1929. Delius was delighted, writing to him: 'It is marvellously beautiful, and I am overjoyed. I cannot imagine it better played. You have got *so* inside the music, and I never thought the viola could sound so lovely ...' (1 December 1929). Encouraged by this reaction Tertis made a version of the third Violin Sonata as well and, on a visit to the composer in 1933, played both sonatas to him.

9   It would seem that Beecham became exasperated when the audience began to talk while he was conducting the *Irmelin Prelude*, which he had inserted as an entr'acte to cover a scene change. The curtain was down and he was heard to say sharply, 'Stop talking!' before bringing the music to a halt and leaving his desk. Afterwards he gave reporters a rather different account of the occurrence: 'What happened apparently was that there was some breakdown in the mechanism on the stage. I was conducting a very soft piece of music when there was such a row from the stage that I had to stop. I put down my baton and went on the stage to see what it was all about. I told them to stop – I won't say exactly what I said – and the noise ceased. Then I went back to my place in the orchestra and resumed the music ... what I wanted to achieve was ruined by the noise on the stage. I am not saying it was anyone's fault. Everyone was admirable, including the orchestra and singers ...' This account appeared in several newspapers, in the *Morning Post* headed by no fewer than four standfirsts: 'NOISE STOPS OPERA – Covent Garden Incident – STAGE DIN – Machinery out of control'.

10   David Webster, later Sir David (1903–71), became General Administrator of the Royal Opera House Covent Garden in 1945 and oversaw its post-war development. He and Beecham were hardly kindred spirits, although Webster was naturally keen to have him back in the opera house with which he had so long been associated, and Beecham did return to conduct *The Bohemian Girl* and *Die Meistersinger von Nürnberg* in the early 1950s. Some Beecham biographers state that Webster vetoed *A Village Romeo and Juliet* when Beecham thought to stage it at Covent Garden for the Festival of Britain in 1951.

11   In Thomas Russell, *Philharmonic Decade* (Hutchinson & Co., London, 1945). Beecham usually conducted *A Mass of Life* from memory. Of his altogether ten performances given between 1909 and 1951, all were sung in English except the last, although he had experimented with the original text as early as 1913 when the soloists on that occasion were to have sung in German. One of his five performances in the 1930s (24 October 1934, with BBC forces) was certainly planned as an all-German affair, but this intention was thwarted by the withdrawal of the baritone Hermann Nissen. At others, such as at the Leeds (1931) and Norwich (1936) festivals, it was not to be expected that the local choirs would be able to go to the lengths of specially mastering the German words. Beecham's desire evidently remained alive, however, because another performance in German was planned for 1938, with the distinguished German lieder and opera singer Herbert Janssen engaged for the baritone part; but this did not materialise. It was not until his last performance, in 1951, and his subsequent recording, that Beecham was finally able to give the work in German.

Interesting observations have been left by some of the soloists who sang in *A Mass of Life* with Beecham. The tenor Francis Russell was first engaged for the work at the Leeds Festival in 1931 (he sang it again in 1932 and 1946). At Leeds, he recalled, 'the usually very reliable Yorkshire choir fluffed their entry before the entry for the tenor, and Sir Thomas also tried to bring me in. It was far too early, but he said "Come on!"

I retorted between my teeth, "Shut up!" I had the score and he, as usual, was conducting from memory. When that movement was finished W.H. Reed, the leader of the orchestra, said to me as I sat down, "You were right, and T.B. was wrong." I said, "I know", and held up my vocal score. We continued until the interval, when T.B. said, "Thanks very much, my dear fellow." I heard the *Mass* done a few times by other conductors, but nobody understood the depth of this great work like Sir Thomas Beecham. In Delius he had an especial sensibility: I think that his early background undoubtedly contributed to this gift.'

Roy Henderson achieved fame overnight when he sang the baritone part in the work for the first time under Paul Klenau in 1925: this was its third performance in London following Beecham's two of 1909 and 1913. Then with Beecham he took part in six performances between 1929 and 1933. 'You may not notice any of my beats,' Beecham said to him, 'but the first beat of the bar you'll always know – the rest might do anything!' 'One had to be with Beecham absolutely. He treated the singer rather like a member of the orchestra. You weren't quite the individual you could perhaps be with, say, [Hamilton] Harty. Adrian Boult would ask, "Is this *tempo* all right for you?" Beecham would do nothing of the sort – but he was a great conductor of Delius.' Like Henderson, the contralto Astra Desmond first sang the work at Klenau's performance in 1925; but, while Henderson thought highly of the conductor, Desmond described him as 'a sadistic type [who] took a delight in reducing me to a highly nervous condition ... [and] I gave a bad performance'. Beecham was present ('It was terribly slow,' he told Roy Henderson) but when Desmond later recounted her experience with Klenau to him, he merely said, 'I wondered why you sang so badly', and engaged her to sing it with him at the 1929 festival (and again in 1934 and 1936). 'This time, with him conducting, all went well, and my morale, which had suffered a severe blow, was completely restored.' She remembered Beecham's 'great powers in drawing out a performer who gave him trust', though adding 'He could be merciless to the conceited or cocksure artist!'

12   Fenby continues: 'Why was Beecham so uniquely successful as an interpreter of Delius's music? It is sometimes said that the music would never have been heard but for [him]. This does not imply that there is only one way, Beecham's way, of playing Delius, but that no conductor has yet surpassed him in conjuring up to sheer perfection the hidden beauties of Delius's scripts. Beyond a word of warning that "it is imperative to maintain a tight control over the motion of the melodic line" there [can be] no attempt to "explain" his interpretations of Delius. The secret of giving flight to the line is his alone, and cannot be imparted. The clue, to my mind, lies in Beecham's temperament and the kind of music he pursued when left entirely to his own taste. Even his superb artistry was but the servant of this obsession, and this was the poetry of musical magic. Some composers have a richer vein of musical poetry than others in their invention. These always kindled an instant response in Beecham. There is a musical magic in Schubert wholly lacking in Beethoven. This was the quality that Beecham adored. He had found it in his incomparable Mozart, though rarefied and impalpable, but nowhere to such excess as in the musical imagery of Delius' (Stephen Lloyd (ed.), *Fenby on Delius*, Thames, 1996).

13   Figures from EMI's archives reveal sales of the three Delius Society volumes between 1936 and 1940 as follows: Volume I, published December 1934: 346 sets. (N.B. This figure should obviously be higher, perhaps nearer 1,000: no sales figures are shown in respect of 1935, the first full year of that volume's issue, though the documentation discloses that approximately 600 sets were ordered immediately it was issued.) Volume

II, published December 1936: 772 sets. Volume III, published December 1938: 540 sets. All three volumes were still obtainable throughout the 1940s and into the early 1950s. Of them the authoritative *Record Guide* (1950) said: 'the partisanship of Sir Thomas Beecham has achieved triumphs: the volumes of the Delius Society made under his direction … provide models for future conductors of the music'.

Chapter 4

1940–1949
'When there is no longer a Beecham to bring his burning sympathy to Delius's music …'*

The decade of the 1930s had been an especially taxing one for Beecham, both physically and mentally. For eight years he had carried virtually single-handed the combined weight and responsibility of running the LPO in tandem with the Royal Opera House; when not in London he was criss-crossing the country on tour with his orchestra or conducting at provincial festivals; in between he made regular guest visits to the Hallé, City of Birmingham and Liverpool Philharmonic orchestras, or darted overseas to conduct concerts or operas in New York, Berlin or Munich; he had made more than 200 gramophone records, including large-scale contributions to the Delius and Sibelius Societies, and in Berlin had recorded a complete *Die Zauberflöte*. By the end of the 1938–39 season the strain had become too much. In his customary speech at curtain-fall on the last night of the Covent Garden season (16 June) he announced that he hoped there would be a 1939–40 season, but he would not be conducting, 'partly on medical advice, partly for the sake of my sanity'. It transpired that a year's rest had been advised, and he was proposing to take it abroad before picking up the threads in a tour of Australia and Canada in the middle of 1940.

These plans were precisely made, but were thwarted by the declaration on 3 September of the outbreak of war. Within two weeks the company running the LPO went into liquidation though, with Beecham's approval and support, the players quickly reorganised themselves as a self-governing body and on 1 October confounded newspaper reports which were already announcing the LPO's disbandment by embarking on a five-concert tour beginning in Cardiff. This had originally been planned under Felix Weingartner's baton, but the new circumstances prevented him travelling from Germany, and so Beecham, with a characteristic utterance – 'I heard there was a national emergency: so I emerged' – resumed his former position as conductor-in-chief, throwing himself wholeheartedly behind the Orchestra's efforts. During the last three months of 1939 they appeared together at no fewer than 25 concerts; in between, an intensive round of gramophone sessions built up a bank of Beecham-LPO records to be released during his absence, though the three Delius volumes were not added to.

All these activities eventually delayed his departure until April 1940, but then he left for Australia, where his conducting tour was scheduled to begin on 22 June. Arriving in Melbourne, he duly rehearsed its orchestra for the first of five concerts spread over a period of three weeks, before moving on to other orchestras in Brisbane, Sydney, Adelaide and Perth. He had not conducted any Delius for many months, but *Summer Night on the River* found a place in his opening programme in Melbourne, to be joined later on the tour by its companion piece *On hearing the First Cuckoo in Spring*. All the Australian orchestras were new to him, but though he found them uneven on the technical side ('though remarkably musical', he told Walter Legge in a letter), he evidently felt confident enough of the reputation of the Sydney Symphony to programme both *Brigg Fair* and *Appalachia*. Both in Sydney and in Brisbane his soloist in concertos by Liszt and Schumann was a young Sydney pianist, Eunice Gardiner, but by the first of his two Adelaide concerts she had prepared the Delius Concerto for him. Neville Cardus, now writing for various Australian newspapers, thought her playing of the solo part among the best he had heard, 'free enough in style to match Sir Thomas's proud and virile treatment of the first and third sections, while she lent to the *Largo* a restrained eloquence of chording'. The performance of *Appalachia* in Sydney reunited Beecham with the baritone Harold Williams, who had sung in his *Messiah* and *Faust* recordings in London in the 1920s. Cardus commented that 'he lent the right note of Robesonian relish to his small solo part'. At the end of this concert Beecham declared that the Sydney Orchestra could be compared with the London Symphony Orchestra or the Hallé; he had been surprised to find the standard of playing as high as it was, he said.

After Australia came a tour of Canada and the USA, beginning in November 1940 and due to be completed the following April in New York when *Paris* was to figure in a Carnegie Hall programme. After that Beecham's sights were set on an early return to England, and for a particular reason. From San Francisco he wrote, on 7 January 1941, to Walter Legge in London:

> I expect to return to England about the beginning of April, and will remain there for something like six weeks, after which I shall go back to Canada. During my stay, I may give a few public performances, concerts of course, but what I should particularly like to do is a complete recording of A Village Romeo and Juliet. In this town, as in many others … there is a unanimous demand for this piece. Unlike A Mass of Life it is not difficult to execute as the chorus plays a very limited part in it, and can be of moderate size. The principal singers, there are really only three, should be easily procurable. The tenor is the only part about which there might be any difficulty, but there must be someone, somewhere capable of singing it in the right way. Perhaps Lisa [*Dora Labbette*] might have some ideas about this; at any rate it would be worthwhile to talk it over with her.

This was an exciting prospect, though one which was going to be especially difficult to realise in wartime. An important factor of which Beecham was doubtless unaware was that orchestral recording in London had virtually ceased because of the danger from aerial bombing. Legge was only able to keep EMI's HMV and Columbia catalogues stocked with fresh material by moving outside the capital to use the Hallé, City of Birmingham and Liverpool Philharmonic orchestras, as well as the BBC Symphony Orchestra which had relocated to Bristol. Beecham would certainly have wanted the LPO for a Delius opera recording, and it is difficult to imagine that any of the provincial orchestras would have been an acceptable substitute. Nevertheless, Legge did not hesitate to explore the venture with his superiors, but they turned him down flat, pointing to the heavy restrictions on the public's purchasing power in wartime and citing the future uncertainty, all of which made recovery of the expenditure involved unlikely. They also doubted 'if there are suitable singers who are available today'. Legge fought back, not hesitating to use Beecham's name as a powerful weapon. Beginning his letter ominously, 'Before I communicate to Sir Thomas Beecham your decision not to record *A Village Romeo and Juliet*', he went on to contradict the idea that suitable singers were not available: 'It is quite easy to get the best cast in the world for this work. Sir Thomas will insist on Lisa Perli and either David Lloyd or Webster Booth for the principal parts and rely on the singers who took part in the famous broadcast of the work for the other parts'. He advanced cost projections of his own which suggested that the sale of 500 albums – 'a conservative estimate' he was convinced – would show a profit on the project, and he sought permission to approach former subscribers to the Delius Society to obtain their assurances that they would support the new venture as they had done in the 1930s. This he was given, and he made the most of it in the columns of the May 1941 issue of the *Musical Review*:

> We have the opportunity of recording A Village Romeo and Juliet under Sir Thomas Beecham's direction. This is a project with which every member of the Delius Society will be in sympathy. It is a duty to music and to the memory of Delius which should be fulfilled as soon as possible. The work will fill fourteen or fifteen double-sided records and we propose to publish them in two volumes – the first in the Autumn, the second in the spring of 1942. The quality of the performance and recording is vouchsafed by Sir Thomas Beecham's direction and Columbia's recording, but this plan can be realised only if every member of the Delius Society guarantees beforehand to subscribe for both volumes. Written guarantees should be forwarded to the Secretary of the Delius Society.

But Legge was handicapped by not being able to announce who the singers were likely to be nor what the records would cost, and the hoped-for support was not forthcoming. No more was heard of the idea, and Beecham stayed on in the USA where he was by this time contracted to conduct the 1941–42 season of the Seattle Symphony Orchestra. Having been approached by that Orchestra's officials almost as soon as he set foot in Canada in June 1940, he had agreed to direct their subscription series beginning on 20 October 1941. Since Seattle's orchestra was a completely unknown quantity to him Delius's music was not planned to loom large in his programmes, though *The Walk to the Paradise Garden* was down for the opening concert and the Piano Concerto a few weeks later. The idea for the Concerto seemingly came from the Seattle Orchestra's board, which was keen to promote a young locally-born pianist, Randolph Hokanson, whose credentials as a one-time pupil of Myra Hess doubtless helped to make him acceptable to Beecham.

Another pianist now came back into his life, though this time with far-reaching consequences. He had met Betty Humby in 1937 when she was involved in organising a series of Sunday Night Mozart concerts at London's Cambridge Theatre. He had lent his name to the venture and even conducted one of its concerts, though not one of those in which she featured as soloist. Their paths then diverged, but now she and her young son Jeremy arrived in the USA as evacuees. Needing to support them both, she made her American debut in February 1941, and then her name came up on a list of suggested soloists for concerts which Beecham was planning to fill the gap between New York in June and the opening of the Seattle season in October. 'But I know Betty Humby!' he exclaimed, agreeing readily to her inclusion on his approved list. No time was lost: together they broadcast the Delius Concerto for CBS from its New York studios on 22 June. It was to be the first of many such collaborations, as Betty Humby quickly became not only his day-to-day companion but also the pianist who appeared with him most during the rest of the war years. Other concertos – two by Mozart, Saint-Saëns's in G minor and a work based on Handel's music which Beecham concocted for her in 1944 – were given occasional airings by them, but from that moment (with the one pre-arranged Seattle exception mentioned earlier) he never again conducted Delius's Concerto for anybody else.

With his plan to return to Britain in the autumn of 1941 aborted, Beecham had time on his hands before taking up the reins in Seattle on 20 October. The gap was filled by concerts in various parts of the USA, most notably with the Chicago Symphony Orchestra, which he directed in a total of eight concerts at Ravinia Park, and three in Canada with the Montreal Symphony Orchestra at the Montreal Festival. There was little Delius at these concerts, although *The Walk to the Paradise Garden* was heard at Ravinia Park (presumably Beecham considered it the most likely of all the Delius works to make an impact in that vast open-air setting), but on 21 September, back in New York, he broadcast *Sea Drift* with soloist Moser Nicholson, the Collegiate Chorale and the Columbia Broadcasting Orchestra. Then, after a few concerts in Detroit and Vancouver, he headed for Seattle.

The time he spent as conductor of the Seattle Symphony Orchestra – ultimately one complete and two half-seasons – was typically colourful. Seattle had never seen anything like Beecham, and the newspapers were soon devoting more column inches to his doings and sayings than to his music. Quite by accident, Delius's music caused upsets at both his first rehearsal and his first concert. Upon meeting the players for the first time and electing to begin the rehearsal with *The Walk to the Paradise Garden*, he stopped them within a few bars. 'What's this?' he cried, seizing the music from the nearest music-stand. 'I thought as much. An old and very bad arrangement, which cannot be played in any civilised part of the globe!'[1] He also called it something else highly uncomplimentary (the puritan Seattle press avoided printing the actual word he used) and shook himself as though to rid his being of something unpleasant. His own edition was hurriedly sent for. At the subsequent concert Delius's gentle rapture had proceeded for less than a minute when Beecham's ear registered the click of a camera. Rapping for silence, he whirled round and ordered the hapless photographer – seated in the front row with, as he thought, permission to snap the conductor in action – to leave the Hall, calling after him that he was 'an insult to the audience'.

Such imperiousness left his listeners breathless; and things went on in much the same colourful way. The American press had always painted Beecham a larger-than-life character, and he was well aware that they expected him to behave like one; so, even if Seattle was not New York, he duly obliged. All the same, he could overdo it: his well-known utterance in which he seemed to label Seattle 'an aesthetic dustbin' was not easily ignored or forgotten, and would later be used against him.[2] For the moment, however, having announced his presence in no uncertain manner in the course of five pre-Christmas concerts, which drew full houses and were acclaimed by both press and public, he left to fulfil engagements with the Detroit Symphony and Philadelphia Orchestras. Two pairs of concerts in each city included Delius's Piano Concerto with Betty Humby. On his return to Seattle in February, his re-engagement for the next season (1942–43) was announced, and it was given out that one of his concerts would include *Appalachia*. He primed his audience for this work through a lecture, when he told how Delius's desire to become a musician, a composer, 'filled the souls of his father and mother with rage'; how these misguided parents sent their son to Florida 'in an effort to stifle all inspiration, all yearnings and all heart-burnings, but where he listened to the Negroes and wrote real Negro music'. Warming to his subject, he went on:

> He wrote not the Negro music you hear today, which is doctored up by college professors, has its hair curled and face washed and is all prettied up and palmed off on you as 'spirituals' ... No! He wrote the Negro music of the 70s and 80s in Florida. The works of Delius are a perfect compound of European music and music of the Southern states of the United States. Delius's mighty contribution to music is his inborn, inherent, unforced, unmanufactured, original scheme of harmony, with the imperceptible shifting of chords giving at once a complexity and simplicity to the composition.

The subsequent performance of *Appalachia* on 16 November 1942 was an undoubted success. In a speech at its end Beecham praised the contribution to it of the 100-strong group of singers from the University of Washington, and told the audience which had thronged Seattle's Music Hall and filled it to capacity: 'This is the audience I have been looking for all my life.' Whether this was meant completely sincerely or was merely intended to keep Seattle's enthusiasm alive while he conducted elsewhere for the next six months is not clear. Certainly he was

4.1   The pianist Betty Humby, whom Beecham married in 1943

anxious to leave Seattle without delay, for he and Betty Humby boarded a train for Chicago within a few hours of the conclusion of the concert. At the station, where they arrived arm-in-arm, Beecham dodged questions from a Press that clearly scented romance in the air following reports which were circulating that he was seeking a divorce from his first wife. The reports were right. In January 1943 it was learned that he had indeed obtained a divorce from the first Lady Beecham, and the next month he married Betty Humby in New York.

He may also have sensed by this time that the battle he had been waging with the music critics in Seattle was lost. The rapturous tone of the first season had turned sour and, despite a series of thrilling concerts and unprecedented full houses, to which satisfied patrons pointed in letters' columns, the music writers now seemed hell-bent on sniping at Beecham in a manner which did not exclude the personal. Even on the day following his triumphant *Appalachia* the *Seattle Post-Intelligencer*, while acknowledging his 'conductorial magic', referred to him as 'the pompous little Britisher'. When he returned for the start of the 1943–44 season the knives were really out: a concerted critical attack was waged upon him from all sides, mostly on the grounds that Seattle's music could never be properly served by a music director who was absent so much. They were also peeved that their orchestra did not already figure among the top 16 ensembles in the USA after two seasons playing under Beecham, and they revived the 'aesthetic dustbin' jibe. Some of his responses, as he mounted a typically spirited rearguard action, were crushing. 'What is so perfectly obvious,' he observed disdainfully in an address to the Orchestra's patrons, 'is that there is no one in this town writing in the press who has the slightest knowledge of music at all.'

At the height of the row, in an unprecedented move, he convened a public session at which he first played recordings made at some of his concerts and invited his listeners to judge for themselves whether what had been written about them in the newspapers reflected accurately what they were now hearing. He had with him a sheaf of criticisms, from which he quoted while the music was playing 'Weak horns?' he queried incredulously at one point when the sound of the horns was filling the hall. Then he compared some of the Seattle recordings with commercial discs made by himself and other conductors, all unidentified, and invited the audience to declare a preference by a show of hands. Seattle won handsomely. The demonstration was complete enough. He labelled the critics 'ignorant and malicious', at one point going so far as to call them 'damned liars'; he gave a warning that if they did not desist he would pack up and leave. Far from desisting, they kept up the pressure; so, after taking charge of three more concerts while the controversy continued to rage, he was as good as his word.

Aside from single appearances of *On hearing the First Cuckoo in Spring* and *Summer Night on the River*, and a studio broadcast for CBS of, unusually, *Songs of Sunset* (with Mona Paulee, Robert Nicholson, the Collegiate Chorale and the Columbia Broadcasting Orchestra), Beecham played no Delius at all in the early part of 1944, most of which found him in the pit of the Metropolitan Opera in New York. He was by this time planning to return to England in the autumn to take up again with the LPO, and an extensive tour had been arranged beginning on 18 September in Birmingham. But suddenly a highly interesting Delian project arose in New York in the shape of a ballet entitled *Romeo and Juliet* utilising Delius's music. This was the brainchild of Anthony Tudor (1907–87), who had considered Prokofiev's score before rejecting it in favour of Delius's music. The Ballet Theater had actually staged the piece for the first time in April 1943 at the Metropolitan

Opera House while Beecham was conducting opera there, but if he was aware of it he took no direct interest until the following year's revival, when the producer Sol Hurok suggested that he conduct some of the performances. Although there would appear to be no link between Tudor's choice of subject or music and the presence in the USA at that time of Beecham, Tudor knew the conductor through working in London in the 1930s: before settling in New York in 1940 he had been a dancer and choreographer with the Ballet Rambert, and in 1935 he had arranged the dancing for Beecham's production of *Koanga*.

One immediate problem had been that the printed orchestral material was not easy to obtain under wartime conditions, so the company's musical director, Antal Dorati, in arranging the music for a small pit orchestra, constructed at least parts of his score by listening to the music on records. The date set for the première was 6 April 1943 and, even though the ballet was not quite complete, the performance went ahead under Dorati's baton; four days later the finished piece played to general acclaim from both audience and critics. Lasting 55 minutes, the music drew on *Over the Hills and Far Away*, *The Walk to the Paradise Garden*, *Eventyr*, *Brigg Fair* and the *Irmelin Prelude*, all of which were played complete except for some cuts in *Eventyr* and *Brigg Fair*. When Beecham came to examine Dorati's handiwork he declared it, 'Astounding! Perfectly astonishing! It is precisely as written by my late friend.' He readily agreed to conduct some of the performances scheduled for April and May 1944 and, in the event, conducted nine out of the eleven given, Dorati taking the remaining two. *Romeo and Juliet* shared the bill with other ballets, notably Stravinsky's *Petrouchka* and de Falla's *El Amor Brujo*, under other batons, and the run broke all box-office records. Every performance was sold out, and 'standees' were three-deep each night.

Beecham's arrival on the scene at first had a disconcerting effect on the dancers, because in his hands the music sounded quite different. 'Sir Thomas's *legato* obliterated the landmarks they were used to,' wrote Edwin Denby in *Looking at the Dance* (4 June 1944):

> He made the Delius selections of which the score consists shimmer and glow, swell out and sink to a whisper. Ballet Theater's orchestra, unusually good this season, never played so well; the rather ponderous music never sounded more sumptuous. The great Sir Thomas ... also proved how immensely valuable a conductor can be to the dancers ... As a performer, he has to yield the spotlight to the ballerina ... as a musician he can't let the music take the spotlight. He has to adjust the score to the rhetoric of the drama on stage – and when a ballet has been composed for another purpose, the points of emphasis are often quite different ones ... Dancers and conductor didn't have an easy time getting together in *Romeo and Juliet* ... in this ballet there isn't any groove for them to get into. The Delius selections ... don't by nature follow the logic of the action, nor is their beat clearly distinguishable in the web of luxurious sonorities.

Gradually, however, the dancers seem to have identified a new set of landmarks to the ones they had previously listened out for, and began to adjust. The ballet grew in sureness and towards the end achieved supremacy. Of the final performance, in which the principal dancers were Alicia Markova and Hugh Laing, Denby wrote:

> The audience saw throughout the most brilliant and the most exact performance the ballet has ever had. This time the orchestra was astonishingly transparent. One heard distinctly the variety of impetus the interwoven musical phrases have; their devious and delicate qualities of motion as they rise to the surface and shift and overlap and get lost again in a sort of harmonic undertow. The dancers not only recognised their cues, they could find in the musical phrases they were cued to the exact impetus which suited their momentary phase of dancing. Tudor had counted on these correspondences of impetus from the first. But only Sir Thomas understood completely on the stage and in the orchestra what aspect of the score it was that Tudor had counted on, and he made this aspect musically plausible and expressive. The result was a unique performance by the entire company; in fact the delighted dancers, especially Miss Markova and Mr Laing, probably inspired Sir Thomas as much as he did them.

Beecham's dalliance with *Romeo and Juliet*, and a further delay as a result of his lawyers' recommendation that he should go through a second marriage ceremony with the new Lady Beecham 'to ensure compliance with the technicalities of English law', delayed Beecham's departure from the USA, and he did not arrive in England until 30 September, two weeks after the LPO tour should have started. Immediately, however, he plunged into rehearsals for the rescheduled first concert, on 2 October. Delius's *First Cuckoo* and *Summer Night on the River* were supposed to figure in it, but the orchestral material following him from the USA had not arrived. *Brigg Fair*, however, made it into the next night's concert at Leeds. For the following two months, travelling the country and conducting the LPO everywhere from Bristol to Sheffield kept Beecham busy. The LPO would have been pleased to keep him exclusively to itself, but he found time for visits to an old conducting haunt, Liverpool, where *Eventyr* featured in one of his programmes with the Liverpool Philharmonic. He had been a welcome guest there for thirty years and, as though the five-year gap since he had opened the City's new Philharmonic Hall on his last appearance in 1939 was as nothing, his disarming greeting to the players was, 'What would you like to play?'

He also found time to resume work with Walter Legge in London in the recording studio. Doubtless, they were taking stock of the orchestral situation in England, because Beecham was unimpressed by what he saw and heard. In particular he was dissatisfied with the quality of his old Orchestra, while its self-governing basis, which had been unavoidable in 1939, was now anathema to him. It is clear that he was soon contemplating the formation of another orchestra of his own, and that he envisaged Legge helping him to run it. He returned to the USA at the end of January 1945 for a five-month conducting stint: in Rochester, Cleveland, Buffalo and San Francisco he conducted the Piano Concerto with Lady Beecham, and between 5 and 28 April undertook several more performances of the *Romeo and Juliet* ballet at the Metropolitan Opera in New York. From there he wrote to Legge in strict secrecy to tell him of his plans. The new orchestra was to be launched with a flourish, under conditions similar to those of the LPO in 1932. Its name, he said, would be the Beecham Symphony Orchestra, and he was prepared to contribute £10,000 on his own account towards its upkeep from 1 January 1947. It would also play at concerts sponsored by the Delius Trust and, if asked, for the Royal Philharmonic Society, but only if it became the Society's resident orchestra as the LPO had been.

This presented Legge with a dilemma. For some time he had had his own ambitions to form a new British orchestra, initially (at least) as a 'house' orchestra for EMI's recording purposes. He now had EMI's backing, and Beecham's letter must have made him realise that he and the conductor were on a collision course. It is clear that they had discussed Legge's project because Beecham wrote that the title 'Philharmonia', which Legge favoured, was 'preposterous'; similarly rejected was the suggestion of a collaboration beginning in a more modest way than Beecham envisaged with a reduced combination giving some Mozart programmes. Despite this, and possibly hoping that even then some sort of accommodation might still be reached, Legge went ahead with his plans and, when Beecham returned to England in the May, invited him to conduct the Philharmonia's debut concert, planned for 27 October. Beecham accepted. In the weeks leading up to it he and Legge made some last recordings with the LPO, including four Delius titles (although none was published). These were his first-ever attempts at recording the Piano Concerto with Lady Beecham, as well as *A Song before Sunrise*, Dance Rhapsody No. 2 and two of the *North Country Sketches* ('Autumn' and 'Winter').[3] Concerts during this period took in the Piano Concerto in London and Glasgow, *Appalachia* in Liverpool (twice) and *Over the Hills and Far Away* with both the BBC Symphony and BBC Northern orchestras. In addition, he conducted *In a Summer Garden* in Liverpool and with the Scottish Orchestra in Glasgow, and also with the Paris Conservatoire Orchestra in a 'Victory' concert marking the end of the war, for which the French Orchestra came to London in an exchange with the LPO.

Beecham now turned his attention to the debut of Legge's new orchestra. No doubt he reasoned that, if it turned out satisfactorily, it would save him the trouble of forming his own ensemble, and he would retain Legge's services as well. The debut programme, despite his earlier rejection of the idea, was after all an all-Mozart one, though that may have been dictated by the fact that the total strength of the ensemble was only 52 players. But the instrumentalists Legge had gathered were among the very best, and Beecham saw immediately that they would serve admirably as a basis for his own requirements. He had changed his mind about the title Beecham Symphony Orchestra, and intended to call the new orchestra the Royal Philharmonic, because of the link he had by this time re-established with the Royal Philharmonic Society. A few days after the concert he and Legge met, and it was at this point that Legge dug in his heels, insisting that the Philharmonia Orchestra was to remain under his control. The inevitable parting was stormy. Beecham was not a man who enjoyed having his ambitions thwarted and, besides, he knew he needed some of Legge's players, such as the brilliant young horn-player Dennis Brain, to fully realise his ambitions for the new orchestra.

It was now clear that he was going to have to go it alone, although he made no announcement before leaving for another visit to the USA, which occupied him from February to May 1946. During these months, he and Lady Beecham shuttled between New York, Montreal and a dozen towns and cities in between: it was now the turn of St Louis, Miami and Havana to hear the Piano Concerto. In St Louis the close partnership between husband and wife impressed itself on a Delius-loving local, John W. Titzler, who observed in the Beecham Society's journal that:

> All during the performance, Sir Thomas and the soloist worked in close communication, even when he would take hold of the piano lid with his left hand, lean backwards and appear to be lost in reverie. At its close, the audience applauded long and gratefully, perhaps hoping for an encore. Finally, after many recalls, Lady Beecham raised her hands and said, 'Thank you very much, but I am a bit winded after that.' With that the enthusiasm rose again, but soloist and conductor had retired.

While in New York Beecham gave the *Idyll* in a broadcast concert from the CBS Studios (3 April), for which he had unusually distinguished soloists in the American artists Eileen Farrell and Mack Harrell. As he had not conducted the work for fourteen years (it was the second of only two performances he ever gave of it) it is possible that he was already formulating in his mind programmes for another large-scale Delius event and took the opportunity that CBS's rehearsal time afforded him of reassessing a work that he had not conducted since 1933.

In between rehearsals and concerts, and while travelling, Beecham doubtless mulled over his future plans. When he returned to England in June he had a mere handful of engagements to fulfil, all with BBC orchestras; this may have been intentional, allowing him to identify some players he wanted to engage for his new orchestra, though he later denied any poaching. Naturally, it quickly became known that he was forming another orchestra, at which the cry 'He'll never get the players!' went up just as it had done in 1932. Beecham was unmoved: 'I always get the players,' he retorted. 'Among other considerations, they are so good they refuse to play under anybody but me …'[4] Recruiting Victor Olof as his orchestral manager, he began to enrol his personnel, first going after those instrumentalists he knew and who had worked for him before, especially in the key positions. The clarinettist Reginald Kell and flautist Gerald Jackson, together with timpanist James Bradshaw and double-bass Jack Silvester, all founder members of the LPO in 1932, were persuaded to rejoin him, and the oboist Peter Newbury came in from the current LPO. The woodwind line-up was completed by the veteran bassoonist Archie Camden who, after many happy years in the Hallé Orchestra and 13 thoroughly demoralising ones in the BBC Symphony Orchestra, thought he had finished with orchestral playing for good; but such an invitation was not to be turned down, especially when Beecham, who understood players' psychology perfectly, tracked him down at a Cornish holiday resort in order to speak to him personally. Camden had been swimming and only came in reluctantly to answer the summons of some unknown person on the telephone: he was amazed to find Beecham at the other end of the line. The conversation ended on a typically Beechamesque note: 'Now, go back to the ocean, my dear fellow, but for God's sake, and mine, pray do not drown.'

From the BBC came Raymond Clarke as principal cellist, and the oboist Terence Macdonagh was to follow. Among the younger generation, Beecham somehow secured Dennis Brain as his first horn, despite the fact that Brain was already occupying the same chair in the Philharmonia. As if registering a claim to Brain's services, at the launch of the RPO Beecham declared: 'The horn quartet will be the finest in Europe. First horn, Dennis Brain, is a prodigy.' Brain's position naturally soon became impossible, because neither Beecham nor Legge was willing to share their first horn and each demanded him for their own concerts. Somehow he contrived to carry both jobs between 1946 and 1954, except for 1949 when Beecham tried to force the issue and lost him for a whole year. One prominent position that was not wholly satisfactorily filled immediately was the all-important one of leader. Since Beecham knew all Britain's concert-masters at first hand it may be assumed that he decided not to try to entice any of them away, as he had done in Paul Beard's case in 1932. His choice ultimately fell on John Pennington, who had been first violin of the London String Quartet from 1926 to 1934, subsequently pursuing a career in the USA that included the leadership of the San Francisco and Los Angeles orchestras and an 11-year stint in Hollywood's film studios. The association was, however, short-lived: within a few months Oscar Lampe, a man who eschewed most social graces but played the violin divinely, was in the leader's chair, while the tried-and-tested David McCallum from the LPO of the 1930s hovered in the background (he rejoined Beecham eventually in 1949 and stayed until 1954). Among new and untried material among the first violins was 18-year-old Martin Milner, later to lead the Hallé Orchestra for 29 years.

On 11 September 1946 Beecham met with his new orchestra for the first rehearsal. Drawing up the list of 80 or so players had taken less than a month, but now the first concert was only four days away. Cannily, this was not given in London but at the Davis Theatre in Croydon, so that the new orchestra did not appear in the capital for another six weeks. Beecham 'played in' his latest orchestral venture in a series of out-of-town engagements in seaside towns such as Folkestone and Eastbourne, varied only by inland forays to Oxford and Cambridge. Only once did the RPO venture into London, and that was for its first-ever recording session for EMI at the Abbey Road Studios (3 October): although Beecham had already identified a long list of works he proposed to record with his new orchestra, for this first occasion he selected a piece which the Orchestra had not yet played in public: Delius's Dance Rhapsody No. 2.

This soon came to be seen as part of a deliberate plan. Delius's music featured in the RPO's debut concert in the shape of *Over the Hills and Far Away*, *In a Summer Garden* was heard in Folkestone and Margate, and Lady Beecham played

4.2 Rehearsing the Royal Philharmonic Orchestra for its first concert in 1946. The Delius Festival that year marked the orchestra's first appearance in London (Courtesy of EMI)

the Piano Concerto in the two university towns; and in the midst of these southern perambulations Beecham found time to dash north for a pair of concerts with the Liverpool Philharmonic, one of which included *Paris*. All this was soon seen as preparation for a series of events that had evidently been in the planning for some time – a seven-concert Delius Festival spread throughout several venues in London. Beecham's publicity indicated straightaway that he had made his plans adroitly: the Festival was to be given 'by the Royal Philharmonic Society in conjunction with The Delius Trust under the direction of Sir Thomas Beecham Bart'; the RPO would play throughout after making its London debut at the first concert, and that concert would also open the RPS's 1946–47 season; the BBC, it transpired, had agreed to broadcast some of the concerts and sponsor the last, at which *A Mass of Life* would be performed by the BBC Choral Society and the BBC Symphony Orchestra. Meanwhile, Beecham had arranged with the Delius Trust to support the recording of the greater part of the music to be heard at the festival.

Beecham decided to share the conducting with Richard Austin, conductor of the Bournemouth Municipal Orchestra between 1934 and 1940 (and son of the baritone Frederic Austin, whose association with Beecham went back to his earliest performances of *Sea Drift* almost 40 years before and who was now involved with him in the Delius Trust). Characteristically, Beecham never said why he invited the younger Austin to be his assistant conductor, although one of the first things Austin had done upon taking over the Bournemouth Orchestra from its founder, Sir Dan Godfrey, was to invite Beecham to be a guest conductor: Delius's Piano Concerto, played by Katharine Goodson, and *Over the Hills and Far Away* had featured in the programme (25 March 1935). Richard Austin later ruefully described being Beecham's assistant as 'a fraught but flattering position!': his own conclusion was that Beecham's interest in him had come about because he had been conducting some Delius on his own account around the time, and Beecham must have got to know of it.[5] Nor was there any discussion as to which works were to be allocated to him although these included excerpts from *Koanga* and *A Village Romeo and Juliet*, *An Arabesque* and a selection of the songs, all of which Beecham might have been expected to want to conduct; less surprising was the handing over of the Concerto for violin and cello and the *Idyll*, both of which Beecham had conducted only twice before. Austin was particularly gratified, in view of Beecham's long association with it, to be given the scenes from *A Village Romeo and Juliet* to conduct.

From the complete list of the Festival's programmes that follows it will be seen that, aside from former associates such as the tenor Heddle Nash and violinist Jean Pougnet (who had led the LPO during the two years of Beecham's return to it) he called mainly upon the newer generation of solo performers, especially for his singers. Some of these emerged from auditions he held in London after instructing all the concert agents to send along their most promising material. A typical case was that of the baritone Gordon Clinton, who was eking out a living in a concert party at Worthing. 'Can you sing a top F, boy?' came the unseen Beecham's voice after he'd sung. Throwing caution to the wind, Clinton responded, 'Yes, Sir Thomas' – though he knew he couldn't – and was amazed to find himself down to sing *An Arabesque* at the Royal Albert Hall. It was an especially nerve-racking prospect as it would be the first time he had ever sung with an orchestra. Another baritone, the Welshman Redvers Llewellyn, was listed for *Sea Drift* and *Songs of Sunset*, seemingly on the strength of having sung a single performance as Valentine in Gounod's *Faust* under Beecham's baton in Bradford some 13 years before. But only after he had sung these works was he engaged to take part in the Festival's climax, the performance of *A Mass of Life*. According to the singer's widow, Beecham coached her husband, as the music was quite unknown to him and he was nervous about its size and importance. 'Yes, I know it seems to go on and on about nothing at all,' Beecham remarked casually to him, 'but with the band it sounds grand.'

THE DELIUS FESTIVAL
October–November 1946
given by
The Royal Philharmonic Society in conjunction with the Delius Trust
under the direction of Sir Thomas Beecham Bart.

THE

ROYAL
PHILHARMONIC
SOCIETY

In conjunction with the Delius Trust and the
British Broadcasting Corporation

has pleasure in announcing a

DELIUS FESTIVAL

under the direction of

SIR THOMAS BEECHAM
BART.

ROYAL PHILHARMONIC ORCHESTRA

Conductors :

SIR THOMAS BEECHAM, Bart.
RICHARD AUSTIN

1946
Programmes

4.3 A page from the 1946 Delius Festival programme

Programmes

26 October 3 pm   Royal Philharmonic Society Concert
Over the Hills and Far Away
The Song of the High Hills – Freda Hart, Leslie Jones, Luton Choral Society
Suite, Hassan – Intermezzo & Serenade; Chorus for Unaccompanied Female
  Voices; Intermezzo with Female voices; Procession of Protracted Death; Final
  Scene
Appalachia – Bruce Clark, Luton Choral Society

4 November 7.30 pm
Paris
Piano Concerto – Betty Humby Beecham
Sea Drift – Redvers Llewellyn, BBC Choral Society
On hearing the First Cuckoo in Spring
Dance Rhapsody No. 1

8 November 7.30 pm
Symphonic Poem, Paa Vidderne
In a Summer Garden
Violin Concerto – Jean Pougnet
Koanga – Act 3 and Epilogue (conducted by Richard Austin) – Victoria Sladen,
  Roderick Jones, Leslie Jones, Bruce Clark, Trevor Anthony, Croydon
  Philharmonic Society, Stock Exchange Male Voice Choir (Chorus Master Alan
  J. Kirby)

15 November 7.30 pm
Eventyr
Brigg Fair
Songs of Sunset – Nancy Evans, Redvers Llewellyn, BBC Choral Society
A Village Romeo and Juliet – Scenes 5 and 6 (conducted by Richard Austin) –
  Freda Hart, Estelle Applin, Ethel Lyon, Eileen Pilcher, Heddle Nash, Leslie
  Jones, George Pragnell, Bruce Clark, Redvers Llewellyn

18 November 7.30 pm
Dance Rhapsody No. 2
Idyll – (conducted by Richard Austin) – Elsie Suddaby, Roderick Jones
Songs of Farewell (last movement omitted) – Croydon Philharmonic Society
Three Symphonic Poems (first performance: conducted by Richard Austin)
  Summer Evening; Winter Night (Sleigh Ride); Spring Morning
Songs with Orchestra, sung by Elsie Suddaby
  The Violet; Twilight Fancies; Whither; Il pleure dans mon coeur; The Bird's
  Story

Summer Night on the River
A Song before Sunrise
Cynara – Roderick Jones
Double Concerto (conducted by Richard Austin) – Paul Beard, Anthony Pini

21 November 7.30 pm
North Country Sketches
Three Unaccompanied Choruses (conducted by Arthur Davies) – Luton Choral
  Society
  The Splendour Falls; On Craig Ddu; Midsummer Song
An Arabesque (conducted by Richard Austin) – Gordon Clinton, Luton Choral
  Society
Songs with Orchestra sung by Marjorie Thomas (conducted by Richard Austin)
  In the Seraglio Garden; Black Roses; I-Brasîl; Le ciel est, par-dessus le toit;
  Homeward Journey
Irmelin Prelude
Marche Caprice
Songs with Orchestra sung by John Kentish
  A Late Lark; The Nightingale has a Lyre of Gold; Irmelin rose; La lune blanche;
  Daffodils
La Calinda
Prelude, Act 3, *Folkeraadet*

11 December 7pm
A Mass of Life – Lilian Stiles-Allen, Muriel Brunskill, Francis Russell, Redvers
  Llewellyn, BBC Choral Society, BBC Symphony Orchestra

The first four and the last of the seven concerts took place in the Royal
Albert Hall, the other two at the Central Hall, Westminster; the first, fourth and
last were broadcast by the BBC. Attendances, as was only to be expected in the
austere immediate post-war period, did not replicate the full houses of the 1929
festival, but Beecham's prestige, the first appearances in London of his new
Orchestra, and the chance to hear such a wide cross-section of Delius's music
(notably the major works, very few of which had been played in Beecham's
absence during the previous five years) combined to produce houses that were
at least respectable. Novelties included *Paa Vidderne*, incomprehensibly identified
in the festival's pre-publicity as 'Under the Pines', a translation defying all
logic: in the subsequent concert programme its full title, 'On the Mountains,
Symphonic Poem after Henrik Ibsen's Paa Vidderne', was abbreviated to
'Symphonic Poem, Paa Vidderne', but then the work was erroneously described
as receiving its first performance. (In 1891 it had been the first orchestral work
of Delius's to be performed publicly, and a second performance had followed
at Monte Carlo in 1894.) Other novelties were the three short symphonic

poems *Summer Evening*, *Winter Night (Sleigh Ride)* and *Spring Morning*, which
were handed over to Richard Austin to conduct, and the little miniature *Marche
Caprice*, discovered in an early orchestral suite, which Beecham directed himself.
Several larger works, notably *An Arabesque*, *The Song of the High Hills*, *Songs
of Sunset*, *Cynara* and the excerpts from the operas had not been heard for at
least a decade, while very few of the songs had ever been heard with orchestra:
several were orchestrated specially for the festival. The Choral Songs, too, were
rarities.

Beecham made his own selection of movements from the incidental music to
Hassan, beginning with the Intermezzo and Serenade, which he had published in
his own edition in 1940, and ending with the celebrated Closing Scene, 'We take
the Golden Road to Samarkand'; in between were some short choral passages for
female voices, together with the purely orchestral 'Procession of Protracted Death'.
He also elected to conduct for the first time (for him) one of the works that Delius
had completed during his last years with the aid of Eric Fenby, *Songs of Farewell*.
In the event, however, he performed only four of its five movements, omitting the
last which he considered not to be 'authentic' Delius. This intention worried Felix
Aprahamian, to whom Beecham had entrusted the job that Philip Heseltine had
done in 1929 of writing the programme notes. His association with Beecham had
begun two years earlier when he was working at the LPO; one day he answered the
telephone to an unmistakable voice which said: 'Is there anyone there who can tell
me the lowest note a bassoon can play?' His prompt reply, 'B flat, Sir Thomas', led
to him joining a line of people whom Beecham at various times identified as useful
to him, and the association continued sporadically for the rest of Beecham's life.
At this time, however, Aprahamian felt their relationship was not sufficiently
established to entitle him – as he later told Eric Fenby – 'to argue with the greatest
Delius conductor' over *Songs of Farewell*, and so the work was performed, for
Beecham's one and only time, incomplete. The programme simply stated 'The
fifth song will be omitted at this performance', without further explanation. All the
other works in the festival in which Fenby had a hand – *A Late Lark*, *Cynara*, the
Irmelin Prelude and Fenby's version of *La Calinda* – Beecham had conducted
before. The song orchestrations were mostly his (*Twilight Fancies*, *The Violet*,
Whither, *The Bird's Story*, *To Daffodils*) while Norman Del Mar, then a
horn-player in the RPO, did the others, apart from *Homeward Journey* (Robert
Sondheimer), and the three Verlaine settings for which Philip Heseltine's
orchestrations of 1915 were called up; these three French songs were distributed so
that each was sung by a different singer. Elsewhere, Oda Slobodskaya was
announced as Palmyra for the excerpts from *Koanga* but was replaced by Victoria
Sladen, and in *A Mass of Life* Francis Russell was the tenor soloist instead of Frank
Titterton. The programme fell back on Philip Heseltine's synopsis of the *Mass*
which had been used at the 1929 festival and did not offer the complete text.
Musical Opinion, in a succinct overview, was in no doubt as to the Festival's
success:

Sir Thomas Beecham's Delius Festival, consisting of seven generous programmes, began on October 26th at the Albert Hall ... The undertaking brings back to mind Sir Thomas's similar festival of 1929, and although the conditions of 1946 are less propitious it should be said at once that the conductor's feeling for the music seemed to be more passionate and deeper than ever, and its expression of surpassing fineness. The Royal Philharmonic Orchestra gave in the course of this series the best performances by far of the autumn's multifarious music-making, and the festival stands out as the distinguished feature of the season ... Some of the music brought forward was secondary, and if hardly any of it was without some magical gleam one was aware that this depended on the conductor's personality and passionate exertion to a degree that does not promise well for the future of secondary Delius ... It is clear that if Delius's music is to survive Beecham the publication of a Beecham edition is necessary.

When there is no longer a Beecham to bring his burning sympathy to this music the vocal works are likely to be the first to fall into the background ... *Songs of Sunset* were beautifully sung by Nancy Evans and Redvers Llewellyn, but the composer's complaisance towards the feeble moans of his poet, Dowson, excited impatience. And yet it was one of the vocal works, *Sea Drift*, which stood out as a pure masterpiece ... We have heard many routine performances of *Paris* that made it sound at least twice too long, but on this occasion, thanks to Sir Thomas's unflagging energy and unrivalled command of dynamics, the playing of the Royal Philharmonic Orchestra invested the music with a sense of urgency and direction that compelled attention throughout its considerable length.

The Festival came to a triumphant conclusion at the Albert Hall on December 11th when the BBCSO and BBC Choral Society ... gave the great *Mass of Life* ... the BBC Choral society sang splendidly and made light of the work's formidable problems ... as for the orchestral playing, only Sir Thomas could have evoked the spell-binding sound of, *inter alia*, the preludes to the sixth and seventh movements, or shown so firm a grasp of the massive stucture. The Festival has served the valuable purpose of demonstrating the remarkable variety and richness of Delius's output ... and in our view has also fully vindicated Sir Thomas's estimate of Delius as the greatest composer since Wagner.

In an advertisement in each of the festival programmes, EMI, proudly displaying their boast that 'Sir Thomas Beecham records exclusively for "His Master's Voice"', announced that 'Arrangements have been concluded for recording selected works in collaboration with The Delius Trust'. In fact, he had already begun his recordings in parallel with the concerts and, ultimately, between 3 October and 21 December, the following works were captured in the studio with the same artists as at the festival:

Dance Rhapsody No. 1*
Dance Rhapsody No. 2*
Piano Concerto
Violin Concerto
Songs of Sunset*
The Song of the High Hills
Brigg Fair
On the Mountains*

On hearing the First Cuckoo in Spring*
A Song before Sunrise*
Irmelin Prelude
Marche Caprice

None of the above works marked with an asterisk was issued at the time, though in the case of *On hearing the First Cuckoo in Spring* completion and issue followed two years later after the second side was re-made. Of the other titles, *On the Mountains*, Dance Rhapsody No. 2 and *Songs of Sunset* were eventually published during Beecham's centenary year (1979) despite the fact that the second number in *Songs of Sunset* was missing (it had not been recorded).

Once the Delius Festival and most of the recordings arising from it were completed it was time to move on to other major events Beecham had in his sights. In 1947 these included an important contribution to a festival of the music of Richard Strauss, commercial recordings of Handel's *Messiah* and Gounod's *Faust* and several large-scale projects in BBC studios for its new arts channel, the Third Programme, which had taken to the air on 27 September 1946. In October Beecham had broadcast Wagner's *Tristan und Isolde* followed in December by *Die Walküre*, even though they were in uncomfortably close proximity to the Delius Festival concerts. But now the BBC, anxious to display really convincingly what the new medium could offer in terms of the highest standards, contracted him for a series of high-profile events including both parts of Berlioz's *The Trojans* as well as his *Requiem*, Cherubini's *The Water Carriers* and Strauss's *Elektra*. In falling in readily enough with these schemes, what must have crossed Beecham's mind quite early was that, since there was virtually no prospect in the foreseeable future of putting any of Delius's operas on the stages of either of London's opera-houses, such a thing might very well be possible in a BBC studio. If that could be achieved, then *A Village Romeo and Juliet* would be the opera most suited to broadcasting, and it might even bring about the opportunity for him to revive the idea (first mooted five years earlier) of a recording. Almost as if to put down a marker, he included *Appalachia* in a studio broadcast from London and conducted an entire Delius programme that included *Appalachia* and the Violin Concerto with the BBC Northern Orchestra in Manchester.[6]

Meanwhile Beecham set about establishing his new orchestra on all his old provincial conducting routes. Apart from visits to Switzerland and Holland, where he conducted *The Walk to the Paradise Garden* in Winterthur and three performances of *Paris* with the Concertgebouw Orchestra in Amsterdam and The Hague, he journeyed extensively around England and Scotland, whenever practical including a Delius work in order to publicise the records which were beginning to appear in the wake of the Festival. Jean Pougnet was heard in the Violin Concerto, though plans for the Piano Concerto with Lady Beecham during the London Music Festival at Harringay Arena in June fell through because she was recovering from an operation. *Eventyr* was heard in both Leeds and Liverpool, though it was

4.4   Jean Pougnet, soloist in Beecham's recording of the Violin Concerto

presumably Sir Thomas's quixotic nature that persuaded him to include *Summer Night on the River* in December in Nottingham during what is remembered as one of the most severe English winters of the 20th century.

1948 began quietly enough on the Delius front, almost as if Beecham was preserving his energies for *A Village Romeo and Juliet*, which the BBC had now agreed to broadcast on two evenings in April. It was, however, the calm before the storm. The BBC was privately smarting over the fact that, in the wake of his pair of studio performances of *Elektra* for them, he had recorded the opera's final scene commercially. Though this was perfectly legitimate, there was a suspicion that two extra rehearsals he had demanded were for his own commercial ends. The Corporation was in a quandary. The two *Elektra* broadcasts had been attended by a delighted Strauss and acclaimed by the critics – 'Never can such vast shining *nouveau riche* mansions of sound have been transported across the air' was one of the happier descriptions – and the last thing anybody wanted to do was to upset Beecham. All the same, because of the extra rehearsals provided, *Elektra* had far exceeded its budget, and with an operatic project looming which was even closer to Beecham's heart something had to be done to ensure that a similar situation did not arise again over Delius's opera. Eventually, he was taxed about *Elektra*, when a BBC delegation sought a meeting with him on 15 January. Its spokesman, Kenneth Wright, subsequently reported back to his superiors:

In the course of a very friendly conversation I seized the opportunity to say how concerned we had been at the very persistent rumour – I put it at that – that more rehearsals for Elektra had been asked for when the commercial recordings of this opera were fixed for the week following our broadcast. Sir Thomas was obviously nettled at the suggestion and emphatically denied it. But we pushed the point home saying that we would not admit any difference in standard aimed at for a broadcast or for commercial discs. If 'x' number of rehearsals were necessary at the outset for a good performance of an opera, then we should stick to 'x' whether recording afterwards came into the picture or not ... He conceded this point and I feel that should there be any question of him recording A Village Romeo and Juliet after a BBC performance he will come out in the open from the very beginning.

Beecham's seemingly conciliatory reaction at the interview undoubtedly caused the visiting BBC men to return with the feeling that they had settled the matter amicably and rather to their advantage. The very next day, however, a letter arrived demanding the withdrawal of what Beecham described as 'a scandalous and unwarrantable libel upon my honesty' and, moreover, 'before I have any other dealings of any kind with the British Broadcasting Corporation ... To my certain knowledge, never before in the history of this difficult and complicated piece by Richard Strauss has any conductor been known to undertake its adequate representation with such a limited programme of preparation ...' An apology was swiftly forthcoming, but when the matter reached the BBC's top echelons, Controller George Barnes asked for an estimate of the cost of broadcasting *A Village Romeo and Juliet*. The figure of £2,455 alarmed him to the extent that he spoke of cancelling all future Beecham broadcasts.

Stanford Robinson, the BBC's Music Productions Director, now came on the scene. He had prepared choruses for Beecham on several occasions (including the 1932 broadcast of *A Village Romeo and Juliet*) and when he made his conducting debut at Covent Garden in 1937 in *Die Fledermaus* it must have been at Beecham's invitation or at least with his approval. Early in 1935, however, Beecham had taken exception to a broadcast performance he had conducted of Humperdinck's *Hansel and Gretel*, denouncing it in a letter to a newspaper as a 'travesty' and a 'massacre'. Now Beecham's increasing activity in BBC studios brought them together again and, whatever attitude Robinson adopted towards Beecham in their face-to-face dealings, within the private and confidential world of the BBC memo he lost no opportunity for bitter complaint. A reference in Beecham's letter concerning the *Elektra* debacle to 'certain of your people who may reasonably be presumed to have some running acquaintance with this particular composition' he doubtless took as a slight upon himself, and it caused him to boil over:

No further invitation should be extended to Sir Thomas to conduct studio opera. I don't agree with Sir Thomas's fans that he is our best opera conductor nor does, I think, any experienced continental or international opera singer, producer or conductor. His lack of sympathy with singers and producers has, in my experience, prevented any of his performances being anything better than an orchestral tour de force. In the matter of studio opera his contempt for the BBC and his absolute inability to collaborate has made his rehearsals a nightmare for all my department. We have no pride in the transmissions which are ill-balanced and from a professional radio point of view – amateurish. I implore you, therefore, not to make any attempt whatever to persuade Sir Thomas to conduct any more studio opera.

Despite this remarkable attack, of which no notice was seemingly taken within the BBC, *A Village Romeo and Juliet* went ahead on 23 and 25 April – and a week later, Beecham began recording it for HMV under the auspices of The Delius Fellowship.[7] One cannot help wondering how affected Robinson was by the ironical outcome of the whole affair when the soprano Vera Terry, who sang the role of Vreli in the broadcasts, was replaced for the recording by Lorely Dyer, who was Mrs Stanford Robinson. Unfortunately, Miss Dyer's part in the proceedings was generally found wanting. When the records were issued, most of the praise went to Beecham's conducting and the orchestral playing, while the *Music Review* (February 1949) seemed to sum up what most commentators felt about the singing: 'Gordon Clinton as The Dark Fiddler is evenly satisfying (sometimes a little dry). René Soames is intense and perceptive as the full-grown Sali. As Vreli, Lorely Dyer fails to be moving: her style is too much that of the "light soprano" of musical comedy.'

While these operatic controversies were raging in private, another arose in the public arena of the kind Beecham was inclined to enjoy rather more. On 13 May at Oxford he conducted the RPO in a formidable all-English programme consisting of Delius's *Paris*, Bantock's *Fifine at the Fair*, Bax's *The Garden of Fand* and Elgar's *Falstaff*, planning to repeat it in London's Royal Albert Hall on 21 May. But when, as the London date approached, only a hundred or so tickets had been sold, he cancelled the concert with a fine display of outrage and invective, inveighing against those who 'wanted only bread-and-butter routine concerts which his orchestra was obliged to give to satisfy the present public demand for an embarrassingly limited number of well-known compositions'. Seizing the moment, the Bournemouth Corporation wrote to say that if he would give the same programme with their Municipal Orchestra they would guarantee him a full house in their Winter Gardens there. Beecham accepted and Bournemouth officialdom was as good as its word: it sold every seat (within two hours), enlarged the orchestra to 76 players to meet the challenge of such large-scale works, and in a pleasant tribute the orchestra's regular conductor Rudolf Schwarz took over the celesta parts so that he could play under Beecham's baton.[8] The concert was a huge success, and Bournemouth must have felt that its display of enterprise had been well rewarded.

By late summer Lady Beecham was sufficiently well to be able to join her husband for a tour of South Africa that occupied them during August and September. With orchestras in Cape Town, Johannesburg and Durban, each augmented by players from the South African Broadcasting Corporation Orchestra, they embarked once more on a series of performances of Delius's Piano Concerto.

Lorely Dyer (Vreli)

René Soames (Sali)

Gordon Clinton (The Dark Fiddler)

Beecham

4.5   Beecham and his principal singers for the recording of *A Village Romeo and Juliet* in 1948 (Courtesy of EMI)

And, once back in England, there were four more, in Bradford, Manchester, Hanley and Wolverhampton. More unusual were two Delius events involving Beecham alone. In November he undertook for the BBC the last two of the only four performances he ever conducted of *The Song of the High Hills,* engaging as soloists for it the Sali and Vreli from his recording of *A Village Romeo and Juliet,* Lorely Dyer and René Soames, together with the Luton Choral Society which had sung the work both at the 1946 festival and on his recording. Then, on the very last day of the year, in a BBC studio for the General Overseas Service, he conducted the RPO in *North Country Sketches*: once again he outsmarted the BBC, because he was preparing it for a commercial recording six weeks later.

When the records appeared they offered a curiosity in that the order of the second and third of the four movements as printed in the score was reversed, so that the *Dance* preceded *Winter Landscape*. It was thought that Beecham had perhaps done this to allow the breaks between the 78rpm sides to fall more gratefully, but it is doubtful whether he would ever have compromised musical integrity merely to accommodate a technical requirement; in any case, later public performances show that he was not averse to a revised order. More Delius was recorded a few days later, including his first attempt since 1935 to capture the elusive *Summer Night on the River;* which was now needed as companion to the *First Cuckoo,* already completed. *A Song before Sunrise* was also taken down at this time and, together with *Summer Evening* and *Summer Night on the River,* the three works were fitted onto four 78rpm sides. One of the sides that gave trouble was repeated successfully on 6 April, when Beecham also made his first-ever recording of *Heimkehr* ('Homeward *Journey'*, the third of the *Seven Norwegian Songs* of 1889) in the orchestration by Robert Sondheimer that had been used at the festival. The singer was again Marjorie Thomas, but the recording was not published at the time (and indeed remained unpublished until 1979 when it was unearthed with others during Beecham's centenary year celebrations). Although *Summer Evening* had received its première at the festival, the BBC seemed unaware of this, because they announced the official première under Beecham in an evening broadcast on 2 January 1949: the error was understandable, since it was the first time that he had conducted the piece himself. He included in the same programme his own edition of *Marche Caprice,* which brought the tally of Delius works for that particular day to three: in the afternoon, he and the Orchestra had given a concert in the Trocadero Cinema in the East End of London at which Lady Beecham had played the Piano Concerto.

The official celebration of Beecham's 70th birthday occurred on 2 May, when the *Daily Telegraph* sponsored a concert in the Royal Albert Hall. (Their photograph of the occasion, taken from the side of the Hall looking towards the platform, reduced Beecham to so tiny a figure that an identifying arrow had to be superimposed to show where he was.) The centrepiece of the programme was Delius's *Sea Drift* with Gordon Clinton, now established as a Beecham regular, as soloist, and the RPO augmented to 130 players. Writing in the *Daily Telegraph* next day, Richard Capell described the performance of *Sea Drift* as the concert's supreme achievement:

> It is a work – a masterpiece – of peculiar technical problems, and the presentation of its difficult texture with an effect of clarity and pure beauty is rare indeed. Delius's nostalgia and pathos are so far from obvious or common! It spoke for Beecham's art that on this festive night he should have transported all, performers and audience alike, into a faraway world of tragic longings and passionate regrets. The beauty of the performance was poignant beyond all one's experience of *Sea Drift*.

The BBC did not broadcast the concert, but to mark the conductor's birthday invited him to give an all-Delius programme from the studio (24 June): besides *Sea Drift* and the Piano Concerto with Lady Beecham, *North Country Sketches*, *A Song before Sunrise* and the Dance Rhapsody No. 1 were all played. There was trouble over Gordon Clinton's participation because he had not passed a BBC audition. 'Then pass him!' was Beecham's uncompromising rejoinder when he heard about it; and passed Clinton was.

In August he and the RPO travelled to the Edinburgh Festival for three concerts, though his only Delius offering was the movement from the *Folkeraadet* incidental music that he had revived at the Delius Festival after a gap of 30 years. Upon returning to London he conducted the *Two Songs from the Danish* ('The Violet' and 'Whither') for Elsie Suddaby, who had sung them at the 1946 festival, but once again the disc was not issued at the time. The remainder of 1949 was spent mostly guest-conducting in the USA with different orchestras in Washington, Dallas, Baltimore and Houston: each of his programmes offered *The Walk to the Paradise Garden*, though he gave a single performance of *Brigg Fair* with the San Antonio Symphony Orchestra. The very end of the year found him making recordings in New York for American Columbia and burying the hatchet after falling out with them (in 1942) over some discs of his that he said had been issued against his wishes. Now a new contract with Columbia was drawn up which, in the 1950s, was to be the means through which he would realise some of the most important of all his Delius projects.

Notes

* From the review of the 1946 Delius Festival in *Musical Opinion*.
1 This can only have been the arrangement made by Keith Douglas, published in 1934. While it differed in minor matters of scoring from Beecham's own arrangement (which was not published until 1940), more important from the conductor's point of view at that moment was the fact that it did not contain his detailed editing and phrasing.
2 Beecham actually said (as reported verbatim in the *Seattle Post-Intelligencer*): 'If I were a member of this community, really I should get weary of being looked on as a sort of aesthetic dustbin.' He was urging Seattle to become a model in the arts, not waiting as at that time for artists to come there as a kind of afterthought after performing in the big cities. Unfortunately, it was the 'aesthetic dustbin' phrase that stuck.

3 A *Song before Sunrise*, Dance Rhapsody No. 2 and two of the *North Country Sketches* from these sessions were issued on compact disc in 2000.

4 The author remembers how quickly Sir Adrian Boult's irritation surfaced during an interview as late as 1980 as he recalled how the two new orchestras, the Philharmonia and the Royal Philharmonic, made inroads into the personnel of the orchestra of which he was principal conductor, the BBC Symphony, which lost 40 out of 96 players. He was particularly scathing about the role of 'Master Beecham', possibly remembering that, when asked whether the BBC players he wanted to engage for the RPO would come, Beecham was reported to have said: 'Yes, and for one very good reason. They are bored to death where they are.'

5 This was a modest self-assessment. Richard Austin (1903–89) had himself conducted some major works by Delius during his six Bournemouth years, including *Paris*, and the Violin Concerto with May Harrison. A recording of the latter performance taken from the broadcast (13 May 1937), though missing 38 bars, was published in 1989 (Symposium CD1075).

6 The concert was on 26 June 1947. Beecham enjoyed particularly harmonious relations with the players of the BBC Northern Orchestra in Manchester, and between 1945 and 1950 frequently conducted them in broadcasts and public concerts. On one occasion he brought out their conductor, Charles Groves, and deflected the applause to him, 'to whom all the credit is due'. All the same, this rather daunting all-Delius programme may have been the occasion when, with the players at rehearsal responding rather cautiously to his beat, he murmured to the concerto soloist, 'Don't look now, Mr Pougnet, but I believe we may be being followed.' Jean Pougnet's recording of the Concerto with Beecham, made in the wake of the 1946 Festival, appeared during 1947, and he played the work at the Proms each year between 1947–51, variously conducted by Basil Cameron, Sir Malcolm Sargent and Sir Adrian Boult.

7 The Delius Fellowship resumed in 1948 where the Delius Society had left off in 1938, the chief difference being that whereas the Society discs had to be subscribed to in advance the Fellowship records did not and could be purchased outright from dealers. Although the Delius Fellowship publicity hinted at further issues, *A Village Romeo and Juliet* was the only publication under its auspices. The opera was issued in two albums of seven and five 78rpm discs respectively, and had to be acquired in that format as the individual records were not available separately. They appeared on EMI's HMV label, whereas the Society discs had been issued by Columbia, and came with an accompanying booklet containing an essay and synopsis by Eric Fenby.

8 The concert was on 30 May 1948. Beecham had first appeared with the Bournemouth Municipal Orchestra on 1 December 1928 and paid further visits in 1935 and 1936, including works by Delius on all three occasions. He had always retained an interest in its fortunes, along with those of Britain's other provincial orchestras, and was no doubt interested to see how it stood following its reforming in 1947 under Rudolf Schwarz. At the first rehearsal he startled the players by announcing 'We'll take the easiest piece first', before plunging with an encouraging shout into Elgar's *Falstaff* (!). Schwarz told the author that he was extremely apprehensive as to how his orchestra, then only six months old, would acquit itself in such a taxing programme, not to mention under Beecham whom personally he had never seen before. But afterwards Beecham made a speech in which he congratulated Bournemouth on having 'an orchestra of these dimensions and quality and the ability to lick itself into shape under the direction of its able conductor. After six or seven months' experience the orchestra has played four of the most difficult modern works in the world. It not only played well, but as an

established, solid, secure, reliable body of instrumentalists it has enabled me to interpret these works for you. I will have to go a long way before I can get better performances than I have had tonight.' The Bournemouth Corporation was quick to secure a return visit from Beecham, and this took place on 19 February 1950 when he included *In a Summer Garden* in a more manageable programme of Mendelssohn, Mozart and Sibelius. In 1954, when the orchestra changed its name to Bournemouth Symphony, he shared the inaugural concert with its then conductor, Charles Groves, including *Scenes from Irmelin* in his portion of the programme.

Chapter 5

1950–1961
'You know, the old b—— really loves that music!'*

Although EMI had been recording on tape since October 1948 it was another four years before they began to issue their own long-playing records; even then the old process of recording in 78rpm segments continued up as late as 1954, and some extended works were still being issued in both formats up to that time. Three major Beecham-Delius projects – *North Country Sketches,* recorded in 1949, *Eventyr* in January and April 1951, and the Dance Rhapsody No. 1 in October 1952 – were affected: while all three were issued as 78s none of them achieved release in microgroove format in the UK until many years later. American collectors were luckier: *Eventyr* was quickly paired with *North Country Sketches* on an American Columbia LP, while the Dance Rhapsody was included in a Delius compilation issued by RCA along with other miniatures which had also achieved issue in the UK only as 78s (the *First Cuckoo, Summer Night on the River, Summer Evening,* and the Intermezzo and Serenade from *Hassan*). Especially irritating from the English point of view was that the RCA disc also offered an item completely new to the Delius-Beecham discography in the shape of the song *Twilight Fancies,* sung by Elsie Suddaby to Beecham's orchestration and recorded in London in April 1951. The Dance Rhapsody and some but not all the miniatures made their eventual debut on LP in 1962 to mark the centenary of Delius's birth; Suddaby's song, however, was denied to the UK until Beecham's centenary celebrations in 1979.

Sea Drift and the Closing Scene from *Koanga* were also recorded at this time (January 1951), and the *Koanga* excerpt was issued as a single 78rpm disc. *Sea Drift* was not issued at all, despite being an apparently successful piece of recording and Beecham assuring his baritone soloist, Gordon Clinton, 'My boy, those records will enhance your reputation immeasurably.' After that, Clinton recalled, he never heard another word about them. (Eventually, in 1992, the tape was exhumed and published, when it was found to be the swiftest of Beecham's four recordings of the music.) But the disc that really inaugurated Beecham's 1950s series of Delius recordings on LP was *Over the Hills and Far Away,* coupled with *In a Summer Garden.* The first was recorded in February 1950, and some public performances around that time pointed to a session for the latter piece; but

5.1   Beecham with Lawrance Collingwood, EMI's producer of his Delius recordings from 1946 onwards (Courtesy of EMI)

Beecham became ill as he brought *In a Summer Garden* to a close at one of these, and he was out of action for six weeks. Such was the complexity of his workload that it was 18 months before the work could be scheduled again.

All was now geared to an extended tour of North America, which was to occupy him and the RPO throughout the last three months of 1950. Before it they took the Dance Rhapsody No. 1 to the Leeds Festival. It was one of the Delius works chosen to figure prominently on the American tour with seven performances, exceeded only by *On hearing the First Cuckoo in Spring* with nine, though that ultimate total included two occasions when it was played as an encore. *Brigg Fair*, *Over the Hills and Far Away* and *Summer Night on the River* were also played, together with the Piano and Violin Concertos. David McCallum received unanimously good notices for his four playings of the Violin Concerto, but Lady Beecham was not so fortunate and these proved to be her last performances of the Piano Concerto. As it was, her scheduled five tour appearances were reduced through illness to three and one of those, in Chicago, drew some harsh critical words. Beecham would have been incensed (if he saw them) by reports such as that of the city's *Journal of Commerce* – 'It [the Concerto] isn't much of a piece. Lady Beecham isn't much of a pianist, and between them they didn't add up to anything inspiring' – while on another level the curious wording of a Boston review which spoke of 'the pleasant *First Cuckoo* being done to a turn' would surely have put him in mind of his Seattle days. Nevertheless, the tour, which involved 56 concerts in 52 days, was in general terms a huge success, with virtually every house full and rave notices for Beecham and his orchestra.

Back home, 1951 was the year of the Festival of Britain, and Beecham took full advantage of the surfeit of British music being played everywhere to programme Delius from Bath to Birmingham and London to Liverpool. *Paris, In a Summer Garden* and several of the miniatures were heard countrywide – *In a Summer Garden* was in the opening concert of the Royal Philharmonic Society's season on 17 October, which also was the occasion of Beecham's first appearance at London's Royal Festival Hall – and the Violin Concerto was brought out no fewer than five times by the ever-reliable McCallum. There was talk of putting *A Village Romeo and Juliet* on at Covent Garden, but that came to nothing and the high point of the year for Beecham was probably his performance of *A Mass of Life* on 7 June at the Royal Albert Hall: it was 42 years to the day since he had given the work its first complete performance anywhere. But now there was a difference: whilst all his performances since had been sung in English – even those at the 1929 and 1946 festivals – now he was finally able to give it in the original German. (William Wallace's English translation, which he had specially commissioned for his first performance on 7 June 1909, was published alongside it in the programme book.) The previous night he gave a broadcast talk on the work. His ingrained reluctance to conform to the BBC's strict code of conduct by not preparing a detailed script, together with his declared intention to illustrate the music by playing some of it on the piano, must have filled the BBC's men with misgivings, no doubt heightened when he remarked casually to the listening audience as he moved to the studio piano, 'The music is essentially orchestral, and I am possibly one of the world's worst pianists.' The soloists next night were Sylvia Fisher, Monica Sinclair, David Lloyd and Dietrich Fischer-Dieskau. The last was making his concert debut in England, and it was a typically good stroke on Beecham's part to engage him for the work's major role. Fischer-Dieskau was quite unknown in England, a factor reflected in the phonetic spelling of his name in the programme as 'Fischer-Dieskow', with no hint of a Christian name. He was then only 23, but already experienced enough to appreciate what he termed Beecham's 'sense for the German language in which the piece is written'. He also recalled 'an incomparable moment' at rehearsal when Beecham, 'during an enormous crescendo of all the masses', suddenly stopped and turned to him with the casual observation: 'Pretty piece, isn't it?'

Fischer-Dieskau scored a considerable success in the *Mass* – 'he threw immense conviction into his enunciation of the German text, so as to touch poetry in Zarathustra's soliloquy at Midnight,' ran one critical evaluation. Beecham wanted him for his planned recording of the *Mass*, scheduled for the Autumn of 1952; but this did not work out and Bruce Boyce sang instead. With the tenor Charles Craig taking David Lloyd's place, only Monica Sinclair survived from the previous year's public performance, though Sylvia Fisher sang in the early stages of the recording before the Australian Rosina Raisbeck took over the soprano part. Quite why Sylvia Fisher dropped out seems not to be clear, but Miss Raisbeck has never forgotten receiving the score on a Friday and being told that Beecham wanted to hear her sing it on the following Monday. Ultimately the sessions spread themselves from November 1952 to May 1953 before Beecham was satisfied that justice had been done to Delius's score. 'On the whole it is a really good job,' he told Eric Fenby, 'not to be bettered, possibly, in our time.'[1] Beecham was a realist and doubtless was acknowledging tacitly that these were likely to be his last thoughts on the *Mass*, certainly so far as recording was concerned, and also possibly on *Appalachia* which was captured on tape following performances during August at the Edinburgh Festival and in the studio for the General Overseas Service of the BBC. Beecham had wanted to record *Appalachia* in Edinburgh immediately after the Festival performance while it was fully prepared and so that he could use the same chorus, but it proved too difficult for the recording equipment to travel to what he liked to call 'The Modern Athens', and eventually the recording was done in London.

A *Mass of Life* and *Appalachia* were the last of his Delius recordings to appear in England on EMI's Columbia label. They were also the last Delius records to appear for two years because, even while they were being made, a crisis was blowing up in Beecham's recording affairs. He had effectively left EMI in 1949 when he signed a new contract, initially for three years, with the American company Columbia Records International (CRI). This contract included provision for recordings of Delius's music sponsored by the Delius Trust to be released both in the UK and the USA. All Beecham's records would still be made in London under EMI's auspices, however, and in the UK would simply be produced and marketed on EMI's Columbia label. So far as he was concerned, the difference was barely noticeable, but by the time the contract ran out at the end of 1952 CRI had engaged another company, Philips Electrical of Holland, to make all its European recordings. This was a different matter altogether: not only were EMI's familiar facilities and staff at their Abbey Road Studios now no longer available to him, but Philips brought in its own recording team, secured a recording venue new to him (Walthamstow Town Hall), and marketed its records under its own name. He went along with the new arrangements for a while: after all, they gave him virtual *carte blanche* to record whatever he liked, which would not have been the case at EMI with its roster of conductors all needing a share of whatever repertoire was to be recorded; nor was he dissatisfied with the technical quality of his records, which he found 'excellent', and he described Philips's chief producer, Us van der Meulen, as 'a most intelligent man, who had two competent assistants'. But there were now long gaps between recording sessions, followed by lengthy delays before he got to hear the test-pressings of his recordings to approve their release, and this slowed down the whole recording programme. It affected his Delius output as much as any other composer's, especially when nothing happened in the period between the completion of *A Mass of Life* in May 1953 and December 1954 when he recorded *Sea Drift*; at one point it began to look as though through lack of activity on the Delius front CRI/Philips might be in breach of its contract with the Delius Trust. Unsurprisingly, Beecham was soon agitating to return to the EMI fold.[2]

Meanwhile, the endless round of concerts continued. Early in 1952 he left for a two-month tour of the USA as guest conductor. In Boston, Washington, San Francisco and Los Angeles, Delius miniatures were in the programmes. Beecham had long recognised that the huge USA market was of far greater importance in terms of record sales than any other, and on this tour he seized the opportunity to promote the RCA long-playing disc newly issued in America by including works on it such as the *First Cuckoo* and *Summer Night on the River* in his concerts. While in Boston he gave a radio interview to Station WGBH in which he affirmed once more his belief in Delius as an international composer. Invited to name the three outstanding British composers of the 20th century, he replied unhesitatingly:

Oh, that is very simple. Delius, Elgar and Vaughan Williams. Those are by far and away the outstanding – and the *only* outstanding – composers.
Questioner: And probably, of the three of them, Vaughan Williams has had the most recognition?
Beecham: I don't think so.
Questioner: Well, who would you say?
Beecham: Undoubtedly Frederick Delius.
Questioner: But did Delius have the recognition during his lifetime?
Beecham: Oh, most certainly. He was played everywhere. As far back as 1929 I gave a festival – a whole week, six concerts – the greatest musical event known in England in the last fifty years. He was brought over, crippled, paralysed and blind, and the whole town rose to greet him and thronged the concert halls. What more could you want? It was like the return of Voltaire to Paris in 1778 ... A year or two ago I recorded for Victor an album of Frederick Delius, three works ... in the same year I produced albums of Mozart – symphonies and concertos, which Mr Heifetz played – Richard Strauss and others. The sale of the Delius album was more than twice as large as any classical composer.
Questioner: Is that right?
Beecham: That seems to signify recognition on the part of somebody ...

Later in the year, back in England, he embraced the opportunity to conduct for a television audience through a BBC programme called *The Conductor Speaks*: all the pieces in it were short, but *On hearing the First Cuckoo in Spring* was found a place among them. In December there was another performance of the Violin Concerto with David McCallum, and *A Song before Sunrise* made a rare concert appearance, again obviously to publicise the recording recently released in England.

The year 1952 was notable in another respect because it saw the beginnings of serious work on his projected life of Delius. Little had been heard of this since the 1930s, although when Beecham went to conduct in Australia, the USA and Canada in 1940 he had left his secretary in London, Dr Bertha Geissmar, the task of listing the various letters and other material that had come into his possession and translating some of it. (While in Sydney in 1940 Neville Cardus remembered him 'dictating for hours' to Dora Labbette, who was travelling with him, though that will have been for his autobiography *A Mingled Chime* which appeared in 1944.) By the early 1950s, however, according to Beecham's biographer Charles Reid, 'masses of material had been collected [including] hundreds of letters to and from Delius dating back to the [1880s], which had been made over to him by Delius's widow'. Many of the letters had been translated by Dr Geissmar. In the spring of 1952 he and Lady Beecham domiciled themselves on Round Island near Poole Harbour where, during the summer months, working in a room set aside in what was the only house on the island, the Delius material was sifted and considered. Beecham had only a handful of concerts and recording sessions at this time, because the RPO was engaged at the Glyndebourne Opera, where each summer it became the Glyndebourne Festival Orchestra for the season (which that year ran from the beginning of May to the end of July). The same pattern applied to the next and subsequent years, and he made the most of these quiet periods, at one point in 1954 inviting Eric Fenby to spend some time with him: 'I shall be collating all the material I have been acquiring for many years past for my life of Frederick, and should welcome your assistance,' he wrote, thus reviving the idea he had expressed to Jelka Delius in 1934 of using a young writer to help him complete the work. (There is no evidence that Fenby did so.) In the same letter Beecham touched on a subject that must have raised acute misgivings in Fenby. He wanted his advice

upon whether or no I am to cause the publication and performance of some of those earlier works remaining in manuscript. I have for some time past been forming the view that it is next to impossible for either this generation or any succeeding one to appraise the value of this man's work from his mature accomplishment only. For instance, one of his very finest songs, admired particularly by Grieg and sundry French musicians, has been neither heard nor seen these fifty years. Fred never laid an absolute embargo upon either the performance or publication of any of these earlier compositions: he only requested me first to do all I could to make known those of his middle and later periods, before touching or handling the pre-twentieth century pieces. If we could peruse these together carefully, we might decide that some of them at least should see the light.

Fenby had very definite views in this direction because he remembered only too well a series of sessions with Delius at Grez-sur-Loing when he played all his early works to him, and how the composer had rejected them one by one and charged him to see that they were not unearthed. 'He made it perfectly clear that he didn't want any of the works we'd looked at either published or performed, and in one of our last conversations he made me promise that they would not be,' Fenby stated in a newspaper interview in 1986.[3] In actual fact, Beecham had already selected two such early scores, *Summer Evening* and *Marche Caprice*, and these had been heard as novelties at the 1946 Festival and were already in print. As it happened, there was only one further Delius-Beecham arrangement to come, and that arose because his thoughts had begun to turn to the possibility of staging one of the operas he had not previously performed.

In April 1952, he had commissioned Eric Fenby to construct a piano score of *The Magic Fountain*. 'Personally I think the work of great interest and in many ways highly different from anything else of Frederick,' he declared. 'In other words I think it worthy of publication, which Boosey and Hawkes will undertake.' The job took Fenby just over a year, at the end of which the fee he suggested for his work Beecham considered 'unduly modest': at his most grandly seigneurial, he informed Fenby that he had already suggested 100 guineas to the Delius Trust, 'who will forward you a cheque for this sum when their next ship laden with fat royalties arrives in harbour'. But if it was *The Magic Fountain* he was thinking of putting on the stage, by the beginning of 1953 he had changed his mind in favour of *Irmelin*, and the Sadler's Wells producer Dennis Arundell, who had worked with him before on operatic projects, was preparing a vocal score of that opera. Things moved quickly: as early as March Beecham wrote a newspaper article describing the opera and its plot in detail, although he stopped short of making a firm commitment to a performance (see Appendix 2). The article's final paragraph nevertheless contained a broad hint: 'Lastly, *Irmelin* is the only one of Delius's six operas which has a satisfactorily happy ending, thus making it suitable for performance at a moment when all of us hope to be taking part in joyful celebrations'. This was a reference to the forthcoming coronation of HM Queen Elizabeth II, due in June that year.

Irmelin reached the stage of the New Theatre, Oxford on 4 May 1953, with Edna Graham as Irmelin and Thomas Round as Nils. The staging was fairly primitive (it was rumoured that some of the scenery was from the previous season's pantomime, *Cinderella*), but that hardly mattered. The orchestra was the RPO, which was widely complimented on the quality of its playing: 'The orchestral music ... provided Sir Thomas Beecham with the opportunity of pouring forth a constant stream of ravishing sound, produced with rare beauty of tone by the RPO,' recorded *London Musical Events*. Beecham was assisted by the conductor Bryan Balkwill, Dennis Arundell was the producer, and Oxford's Professor Jack Westrup prepared a chorus consisting of College undergraduates, Glyndebourne understudies and a contingent from Sadler's Wells. Thomas Round had been singing minor roles at the Wells: he was amazed to be summoned to audition for Beecham, and even more to be offered the role of Nils. At rehearsals he discovered that the only way of pitching his entries accurately among 'the mass of orchestral sound flooding the stage' was a tuning whistle: finding that he still needed to rely on it at the performances he carried it about in Nils's pouch, 'part of a sack-cloth costume that didn't lend itself to a lot of dignity', as he later recalled. One of his entrances he found especially difficult to time: a few bars of horns off-stage were its cue, but after several failed attempts, he summoned up the courage to approach Beecham and ask for a personal cue. There was an ominous silence while Beecham

NEW THEATRE – OXFORD

Chairman and Managing Director: Stanley C. Dorrill, M.B.E.
Proprietors: Oxford Theatre Co. Ltd.   Manager: Ben Travers

On Monday, 4th May, 1953, at 7.0

First Performance on any Stage of

IRMELIN

An Opera in Three Acts by

FREDERICK DELIUS

Four subsequent performances will be given on
Tues., 5th May; Wed., 6th May, and Sat., 9th May, at 7 p.m.

Special Matinee of "Irmelin" will be given on Thursday, 7th May, at 2.15

The Royal Philharmonic Orchestra

(Leader: David McCallum)

Conductor:

SIR THOMAS BEECHAM

BART.

Cast includes

**EDNA GRAHAM   CLAIRE DUCHESNEAU,   JOY PIERCE
THOMAS ROUND,   GEORGE HANCOCK,   ARTHUR COPLEY
ROBERT EDY,   NIVEN MILLER,   DAVID ODDIE**

Producer: DENNIS ARUNDELL

Scenery and Properties by Mary Owen   Costumes by Beatrice Dawson
Choreography by Pauline Grant

Associated with Sir Thomas Beecham, Bart., in this enterprise are:
The Arts Council of Great Britain and The Delius Trust

OPERA PRICES OF ADMISSION (including Tax):
STALLS 21/-, 17/6, 15/-, 10/6; CIRCLE 21/-, 17/6, 12/6, 8/6; BALCONY 6/-;
UNRESERVED 3/6

Box Office open daily from 10 a.m. to 7 p.m. at the New Theatre, and at Keith Prowse,
159 New Bond Street, W.1 (REGent 6000), and usual Agents

Special facilities will be offered to Patrons returning to London after each
performance by the provision of a train service scheduled to leave Oxford at
10.30 p.m. each evening (except Thursday) arriving London at 1.15 a.m.

5.2   Handbill for Beecham's performances of *Irmelin* in 1953

considered this, stroking his beard, but then he said, 'Very well, Mr Round. Off you go, and we'll try again.' This time Nils had taken about three paces onstage when there was a roar from the pit: 'There's your damned cue, Mr Round!' and Beecham's baton landed at his feet. The tension was broken, and the entry gave no further trouble.

Five performances of *Irmelin* were given, one conducted by Dennis Arundell, but, despite Beecham's prestige – and his clarion-call to the audience at an orchestral concert sandwiched in on 8 May before the final performance next day – 'Come to the opera! – Don't worry about music you already know! – Come to "Irmelin"!' – it was not well supported at the box office. The noble sentiments and encouraging words of *The Times* that '[Beecham] knows as no one else where Delius kept his magic; we have come to expect this, but what is astonishing is that he can, merely by taking a train to Oxford, shake out of his suitcase an unknown and exquisite opera all of a piece and without apparent effort', may have been of some consolation. In the *Sunday Times* Ernest Newman described *Irmelin* as 'true Delius, immature but prophetic', but put his finger on its principal weakness: 'Delius at that time lacked the most rudimentary sense of stage technique ... there is practically no action.' This had already struck the orchestral players who, having spent six wearying hours in rehearsal reading through the orchestral material simply to establish its accuracy, expected that the arrival of the singers would inject a bit of life into the proceedings. But it did not: 'In the love scene,' recalled Harry Legge, one of the viola players, 'the man started at one side of the stage, the girl started at the other, and it took them half-an-hour to meet in the middle!' When the cost was counted, the project had lost £9,259, which took a little time to pay off. But, as Beecham's accountant, Thomas Hazlem, averred many years later, 'while the financial loss represented a lot of money in those days, to Sir Thomas money never mattered: it was the performance'.

The following year, introducing excerpts from *Irmelin* on BBC television in another programme in the series *The Conductor Speaks*, Beecham had some fun at the expense of English methods of opera-giving, citing the fact that *Irmelin* had only just reached the stage after 60 years: 'There are excellent reasons why these pieces are so belatedly heard,' he informed the viewing audience, 'the principal one ... is that they are of extraordinary charm and beauty. Those qualities, of course, are fatal in the eyes of most of the British public, the British Press, and those responsible for the production of opera ...' He then launched into a vivid account of the plot of *Irmelin*, lightening it with humorous asides about the hero Nils 'who doesn't think very much: like most operatic heroes he thinks very little'. At the end he referred to the Oxford production of the previous year, which he described as 'unlucky'. 'I may say unlucky,' he told viewers, 'because from the commercial point of view it was the most complete and fatal flop' – adding ruefully (to the barely suppressed amusement of the players and technicians in the studio), 'like every other operatic project with which I have been associated in this country'.

He did have the consolation of *Irmelin* reaching a wider audience through a BBC studio broadcast of it six months after the Oxford stagings. (This took place on 22 November 1953 and was preceded by a radio talk by Beecham on 'Delius's Operas'.) As in the TV presentation, the role of Princess Irmelin was taken by Joan Stuart. Then, between the Oxford performances and the broadcast, perhaps fearing that without his continuing attention the music would disappear altogether, he arranged some passages from Act 2 into a continuous 16-minute concert suite for orchestra entitled *Scenes from Irmelin*. This was unveiled at the Swansea Festival on 14 October, and afterwards taken determinedly around the country during the 1953–54 season – including to Oxford, exquisitely timed to coincide with the first anniversary of the 'unlucky' New Theatre staging. Later on, he introduced it to the USA and Canada in concerts with orchestras in Houston and Toronto. The programme note covering the work is worth recalling since it was obviously of Beecham's own composing: after giving the dates of composition and referring to 'the World Première in Oxford by Sir Thomas Beecham as part of his contribution to the Coronation Festival', it continues:

> The story tells of the lovely Princess Irmelin whose hand is sought by suitors far and wide, but voices in the air persuade her that her true love has yet to appear. Nils – a youth who has been following a silver stream which will lead him to his love – had been lured away from the stream and had been detained by Rolf, a robber, at his castle, as a swineherd. One day he finds again his silver stream which brings him to Irmelin on the day she is, against her will, about to be betrothed to a powerful neighbouring prince. The betrothal party departs on a hunting expedition leaving Irmelin, who flees to the woods with Nils, to joy and happiness.
>
> Tonight's excerpts from Act II provide fifteen minutes of delightful music. The whole of the tranquil prelude, with its melodic groundswell, is first heard. Then we move to a more sinister scene, with suggestions of cloud and thunder. Thereafter there are pages from the episode in which Nils is tempted by women summoned by the robber chief to detain him. But the character of the music suddenly changes as he spurns their seductions and seeks the silver stream. Then follows the music of the rippling water. The women (now wood-nymphs) again try to hold him back. But Nils rises quickly and vigorously follows the stream, to the ecstatic music of the end of the Act.

Within a few days of the broadcast of the complete *Irmelin* he conducted the BBC Symphony Orchestra in *Over the Hills and Far Away* at a London concert (25 November, and repeated it next night in a studio broadcast), while *Cynara*, which he had not given since the 1946 festival, was revived the following month in two studio performances with his own orchestra for the BBC. His own principal concert contribution to the Coronation celebrations had occurred earlier at the Royal Festival Hall (24 May) when *Appalachia* figured in one of the Royal Philharmonic Society's Coronation Concerts; two weeks later, in the same hall, he and David McCallum collaborated for the final time over the Violin Concerto. McCallum was shortly to retire as leader of the RPO and Beecham seemingly did not find another violinist to replace him in the Delius concerto; he never conducted it again.[4]

Highlights of 1954 included the long-awaited recording in December of *Sea Drift*, sung by Bruce Boyce, who had taken over the Delius baritone repertoire from Gordon Clinton, and the BBC Chorus. Then, at a packed Henry Wood Promenade Concert in September, more people heard the orchestral *Scenes from Irmelin* than had attended all five of the Oxford stagings of the opera, quite apart from the huge audience listening to the broadcast from the Royal Albert Hall. The work was also played in five more towns and cities. In October, the orchestral material, coming on from a performance in Bournemouth a few days earlier, had not arrived in Birmingham by the time Beecham did. Harold Gray, the city orchestra's deputy conductor, who was looking after the conductor during his visit, squared up to the unwelcome task of imparting this news. But all Beecham said for the moment was: 'Well, that *simplifies* matters, Mr Gray, don't you think?' All the same, everyone heaved a sigh of relief when the parts turned up in time to be rehearsed for the concert. In November, evidently with an eye to the future survival of the music that he so loved and believed in, he included the *Irmelin Prelude* as well as *La Calinda* at one of the long series of youth concerts organised in London by his old friend Sir Robert Mayer. At Christmas, when the BBC invited him to record a concert for transmission on Christmas night, he included the Dance Rhapsody No. 1 in the hour-long programme.

Beecham's life now settled into a pattern that, during his last decade, created opportunities for spreading the Delian gospel on the kind of international scale that his previously all-consuming commitments in England had denied. Each year he spent some time touring the USA as a guest conductor of various orchestras before returning to England for concerts and recordings with his own players. In March 1954 he introduced *Summer Evening* to American audiences in support of his recording; during March and April 1955 he toured with the Houston Symphony Orchestra in and around the city's environs – *The Walk to the Paradise Garden* was heard at three of the ten concerts, *Scenes from Irmelin* at one. Among his concerto soloists in Houston was Benno Moiseiwitsch, with whom he had not worked since their collaboration over three performances of Delius's Piano Concerto in London 40 years before. In June, he visited Norway, where the *First Cuckoo* and *Summer Night on the River* featured in programmes with local orchestras in Oslo and Bergen. Back in England during August, the Philips recording team took down *Paris* and, during October and November, *An Arabesque* and most of the incidental music from *Hassan*. *An Arabesque* was sung in the original Danish by the baritone Einar Nørby, while the BBC Chorus coped nobly with its choral demands. In the concert hall, Beecham gave what turned out to be his last two performances of *Eventyr*, in Sheffield and London.

The 1956 tour of America and Canada was an altogether longer affair, lasting from January to April. As the guest of major orchestras, Beecham was able to programme substantial works such as *Brigg Fair* (Cleveland), *Paris* (Philadelphia and Dallas) and *Scenes from Irmelin* (Toronto). Returning to the UK he made records throughout the whole of May for EMI, to which he had now returned after

5.3 Beecham conducting the City of Birmingham Symphony Orchestra in 1954 at a concert that included *Scenes from Irmelin*

breaking with Columbia and Philips. The arrival of the recording industry's newest development, stereophonic sound, raised the prospect of an enormous recording programme for him but, so far as Delius was concerned, he decided to embrace the medium to deliver new accounts of mainly those pieces he had recorded before at various times on 78rpm and 33rpm discs. He did, however, set his sights on two large-scale works of which no previous recordings existed at all, *Songs of Sunset* and the *Florida* suite. With the exception of *Summer Night on the River* (not recorded until March 1957), *Brigg Fair* and all the shorter pieces – *On hearing the First Cuckoo in Spring*, *A Song before Sunrise*, the Intermezzo from *Fennimore and Gerda*, *Irmelin Prelude*, *Summer Evening*, *Sleigh Ride* and *Marche Caprice* – were successfully completed during October and November 1956; work also started on *Florida*, but it was to take four more sessions before the suite was recorded to his satisfaction. *Songs of Sunset* lay some way ahead. At the end of the year there was another BBC transmission on Christmas Day, the third in the series that had begun in 1954. On previous occasions Beecham had included some Delius, and this time he put *Paris* down for the programme. It was the first Delius work he had ever conducted back in 1907, in the exciting days of exploration of this 'new and strange-sounding music' which had knocked him sideways, and this proved now to be the last of the 48 performances he had given since.

A significant omission from his recording programme at this time was *In a Summer Garden*. Its inclusion at concerts in London and Leeds in the midst of the other Delius recording sessions suggested that he was polishing it for EMI's microphones, but in the event it was not done. The fact was that ownership of all the material he had recorded for Columbia Recordings International since 1949 had passed to Philips, who were busily reissuing it on their own labels. Besides *A Mass of Life*, *Appalachia*, *Eventyr*, *North Country Sketches* and *Over the Hills and Far Away*, their list included *In a Summer Garden*. Beecham's 1951 monaural recording, therefore, stands as the best representation of this Delius orchestral masterpiece of which he thought so highly and which he conducted so supremely well. His performance of it at the 1956 Edinburgh Festival (24 August) had caused a small sensation. Long after the music ceased, nobody moved: the music, in the words of his old friend Lord Boothby, 'reduced the audience to a stricken silence'. At the previous night's concert the packed Usher Hall audience had gone to the opposite extreme, quite unable to resist bursting into spontaneous applause in the middle of a suite of Grétry pieces he was conducting. The concert was broadcast, and listeners in several countries were startled to hear Beecham's voice break in as the ovation died: 'Ladies and Gentlemen, I deeply regret to say that we haven't come to the end of this piece yet' – followed by more delighted uproar. Beecham was in particularly good form that year at Edinburgh: asked if he was willing to share a concert with The Master of the Queen's Musick (Sir Arthur Bliss), he enquired mischievously: 'Will he appear *in uniform?*'

Beecham's book on Delius was now reaching its final stages. What might have been a valuable contribution to it was suggested to him by Felix Aprahamian. It arose out of the paucity of authentic information available about the composer in the period before he and Beecham first met in 1907: virtually all Delius's English friendships dated from around the same time and little was known about his activities during the years before he finally settled down in Grez-sur-Loing in 1897. Aprahamian offered to try to trace someone who had known Delius in his Paris days in the 1890s:

> I found such a person for Sir Thomas: the composer Florent Schmitt, who, born in 1870, and only eight years younger than Delius, was one of his few French musician-friends. Schmitt, who prepared the vocal scores of Delius's first two operas, lived to a very lucid 87, and was probably the last to remember 'Le grand Anglais' of the Latin Quarter, as he told me Delius was known ... I whisked him away in a cab to the Abbey Road Studios where Sir Thomas was recording; Delius, as it happened – the *Songs of Sunset*. But all was not well, and Beecham was in one of his moods. The session had not gone as he had hoped, and there were domestic as well as musical pressures weighing on him. And although I had taken Florent Schmitt there at his express wish, all a testy Sir Thomas did was to greet him with a 'How do you do?', shake him by the hand, and pass down the corridor. The interview was at an end. But it was the kind of behaviour that Schmitt, himself once a stormy petrel of Paris musical life, understood well enough. Passing it off with 'Il était toujours un homme curieux,' he smiled, and we returned to his hotel ... Two years later he died, and with him the last of those who remembered Delius in his formative period.[5]

The 1957 tour of the USA in January and February involved Beecham in a total of 16 concerts in New York, Chicago and elsewhere, but the only Delius work played was *On hearing the First Cuckoo in Spring*, and that only once. He played it again, this time coupling it with its companion piece *Summer Night on the River*, at the Salle Pleyel in Paris when he took his own orchestra on a European tour in the autumn, but the remaining eight places visited on the tour (including Vienna, Zurich and Geneva) heard *The Walk to the Paradise Garden;* so did Madrid, when Beecham went on there to guest-conduct the National Orchestra of Spain. In between touring he spent much time at the Abbey Road studios in London and the Salle Wagram in Paris making records, and these sessions took in the last of his recordings of Delius's music. There were three: *Summer Night on the River*, a new version of *Over the Hills and Far Away* to make a coupling for the *Florida* suite, and his third and final attempt to capture *Songs of Sunset* for the microphone. Two previous attempts at the choral work, in 1934 and 1946, had been unsuccessful for one reason or another, and once again complete success was to elude him. The earlier attempts had at least had the advantage of taking place around concert performances: this time there was no previous performance of any kind, so it is not surprising that Beecham had reservations about what was achieved; he never personally approved the recording's release. Denis Vaughan, his chorus-master, volunteered that he felt he was to blame for mistaking Sir Thomas's intentions and training the Beecham Choral Society to sing Ernest Dowson's words in the *mezza voce* which he thought was what Beecham required. The disc was, however, eventually released after Beecham's death, when it provided a much-needed document of his conducting of a work which he launched in 1911 and with which he had a greater association than any other conductor.[6]

In 1958 there was no American tour: instead, with huge demands being made upon him by the gramophone men, Beecham used much of the year for recordings. These were done mostly in Paris and, during April, in London. A handful of guest-conducting engagements in Monte Carlo and parts of Switzerland (the latter with L'Orchestre de la Suisse Romande) culminated in Basel on 1 April where his programme took in *On hearing the First Cuckoo in Spring* and *La Calinda*. Then between July and the end of September he had a season at the Teatro Colón in Buenos Aires. During three months there he conducted only two orchestral concerts, though one of them, with the Buenos Aires Philharmonic Orchestra on 26 September 1958, was of special significance: in the programme he included *The Walk to the Paradise Garden*, possibly as a personal farewell to Lady Beecham, who had died three weeks earlier on 2 September. Another, more lasting, tribute to her was now arranged to appear on the flyleaf of his forthcoming Delius biography: 'To the memory of a beloved companion, brave and beautiful, gracious and gay, to whom the music of Delius was ever a joy and a mystery.'

The reappearance in British concert halls in the Autumn of 1958 after an absence of 18 months of England's greatest conductor was naturally the occasion for considerable rejoicing and packed houses. For Beecham, though, there was an early disappointment that must have irked him considerably. Confident of his own drawing-power and in the continuing appeal of the music, he announced an all-Delius concert in London for 4 November. The programme was to be Dance Rhapsody No. 1, *Appalachia*, *Eventyr* and the *Florida* suite, the last intended partly to publicise his new recording. For once, however, the public was not attracted, and *Eventyr* and the *Florida* suite had to be jettisoned in favour of a Sibelius symphony. So Beecham never conducted the *Florida* suite in its entirety in the concert hall, and publicity for the new record had to be served instead by a few isolated performances of its second movement, *On the River*. The Dance Rhapsody he repeated in a Christmas Day broadcast for the BBC.

1959 saw the American tour reinstated during January and February but, though the orchestras he guest-conducted were again major ones – those of Philadelphia, Chicago and Houston – Beecham contented himself with *The Walk to the Paradise Garden* and, from his new record, *Sleigh Ride*. The latter fitted especially well in the programmes of short works he had devised – 'lollipops' programmes, as they were known – which were becoming very popular in America. The same Delius works featured in a tour of West Germany with the Royal Philharmonic in October, before he returned to England to attend to an event that marked the culmination of his work for Delius, the launch of the biography he had written of the composer whose acquaintance he had made just over a half-century before.

On 4 November, Beecham conducted a studio concert with the RPO for the BBC. This included *North Country Sketches*, notable for the transposition of the

**5.4   Beecham rehearsing the Royal Philharmonic Orchestra for a last
broadcast in 1959 that included *North Country Sketches***

two middle movements (as in his 1949 recording's original format). Photographs
taken during the preparation for the broadcast suggest an atmosphere of intensive
rehearsal: when conducting, Beecham can be seen completely rapt in the music
and, when not, holding the score up to study it intently while the players wait
expectantly for a fresh instruction. At the end of the session, the cellist Cedric
Sharpe, who had played for Beecham on-and-off for 30 years in various orchestras,
was heard to remark admiringly: 'You know, the old b—— *really loves* that music.'

One of the most interesting of the events surrounding the launch of his book
Frederick Delius – aside from an hilarious speech at a Foyle's Literary Luncheon
– was the extended interview he gave to the critic Edmund Tracey for the BBC
television programme *Monitor*. The 15-minute session was shown on 22
November, and the soundtrack was also broadcast later on the BBC's Third
Programme; portions were subsequently issued as a commercial recording, but not
the whole of it. One of the passages not published caught Beecham's reaction of
pained surprise when it was suggested to him that perhaps the public's lack of

interest in the Delius operas was because they were not dramatic. While on one level it made amusing listening, on another it restated the essence of his case for Delius's operas, and for *A Village Romeo and Juliet* in particular:

> Well, I don't know what is dramatic ... I understand that there is a view rather prevalent in England that an opera cannot be dramatic unless half-a-dozen people are slaughtered on the stage under conditions of horror, or very unpleasing circumstances – or, as in *Tosca*, where you have the lively scene in the second Act of a gentleman chasing a lady around the table in spite of the comparative unoriginality of the motive ... That thrills the public, they think that's dramatic. But a charming idyll, a story of young people, which is not lacking in interest, and certainly not in musical beauty, and which ends in a tragic way that is, in my view, quite remarkable – without horror – lots of pity – but no terror ... No, that isn't dramatic ...

The final year of his conducting career began once again in the USA and Canada, where concerts in Pittsburgh, San Francisco, Chicago, Washington, Vancouver and Toronto occupied him between January and April. He even returned to, and was fulsomely welcomed in, Seattle. There, as elsewhere, it was Delius to the last: room was found in his programmes of 'lollipops' for *On the River*, which he alternated with the Intermezzo and Serenade from *Hassan*. On 24 April he reappeared in London with the RPO at the Royal Festival Hall and on 7 May at the Guildhall in Portsmouth. Both concerts featured *On the River*, and at both *Sleigh Ride* was given as an encore. The performance at Portsmouth proved to be the last music Sir Thomas Beecham conducted: the next month he was struck down by a coronary thrombosis and, although he seemed to be making a steady recovery, a second attack on 8 March 1961 proved fatal.

Every obituary without exception paid tribute to the singular work he had done for Frederick Delius, and many openly raised the question of what the music's position would be had there been no Thomas Beecham. When Edmund Tracey had asked him precisely this question in his *Monitor* interview, Beecham had replied:

> I can't tell you. I can't even begin to imagine what would have happened. But I do know one thing: that the vast majority of the performances of the works would have been totally unrepresentative of Frederick Delius. And that, possibly, would have meant his disappearance from the scene twenty or thirty years ago. That I do know. What I have done, really, is to uphold the banner of his integrity, as a great originator, pathfinder, and a man of genius in respect of the ability to transmit into music human emotions of all kinds; an extraordinary kinship with nature – not equalled but very closely approached by Berlioz – but nobody else has done it; and also an extraordinary sense of beauty of sound, which has not been surpassed by any composer, dead or alive, in the world.

Among the pieces played by the Royal Philharmonic Orchestra, conducted by Sir Malcolm Sargent, at the Memorial Service for Beecham held in Westminster Abbey, London on 29 May 1961, *The Walk to the Paradise Garden* was chosen to represent the composer whose music he had loved, cherished and fought for all over the world for more than half a century. Afterwards, one of the players observed to a newspaperman: 'He [Sargent] won't mind if I say that we were playing for HIM today ... and we were ... especially in the Delius.'

Notes

*   Comment by RPO cellist Cedric Sharpe at rehearsal in 1959.

1   Eric Fenby had now come back into the picture. In the years after the deaths of Delius and his wife, he worked briefly as Beecham's musical secretary. Then for a period leading up to the 1939–45 war he advised the publishers Boosey & Hawkes on building up a catalogue of works by emerging as well as established English composers, and also wrote scores for films such as *Jamaica Inn* (1939). After the war he returned to his native Yorkshire to teach, but in 1948 he contributed the synopsis of the opera and other supporting documentation to Beecham's recording of *A Village Romeo and Juliet*. Now a letter from Beecham (21 April 1952) revived their former acquaintanceship. As it began 'Dear Mr Fenby', one deduces that they had perhaps not been in touch since the mid-1930s: however, the mode of address soon progressed from the formal through 'My dear Fenby' to 'Dear Eric'. Columbia Records now asked Fenby to provide the supporting documentation for Beecham's recording of *A Mass of Life*. He naturally needed to know the layout of the music on the discs and whether the movements followed the score or appeared in the varied order Beecham usually adopted in his concert performances. Beecham reassured him (25 August 1953): 'The Mass has been recorded according to the printed edition. There will almost certainly be two L.Ps – i.e. – four sides. I cannot tell you exactly what will be played on each side: A man – by name Boyle [Nicholas Boyle, the assistant producer who had worked on the recording] – can give you this information. He is to be found any day at the Studio in Abbey Road ... I will ask Boyle to give you all particulars of the recording. I should like to see your writings on the subject before going finally to press – All the best. Yours, T.B.'

2   Beecham's dealings with RCA, Columbia, Philips and his return to EMI at this period have been fully explored as part of a study of Beecham's contractual negotiations with his various record companies between 1941 and 1959 by Dr David Patmore of Sheffield University ('Sir Thomas Beecham: the contract negotiations with RCA Victor, Columbia Records Incorporated, and EMI, 1941–1959: artistic aspiration vs. commercial reality', unpublished paper, 2002). They are intricate and fascinating but, for the purposes of this study, I refer to them only insofar as Beecham's Delius recordings are concerned.

3   Interview with the present author published in *The Independent*, 10 December 1986. It arose because the Royal Philharmonic Society had accepted a suggestion to programme at one of its concerts Delius's early orchestral rhapsody *Appalachia*, composed in 1896 and previously unperformed. As well as topical references to *Yankee Doodle* and *Dixie*, it contained one fine theme which Delius extracted six years later and used as the basis of his 'Variations on a Negro slave song'; to this work, which in scale and concept eclipsed the earlier one, he also gave the title *Appalachia*. 'I have no quarrel with the Royal Philharmonic Society,' Eric Fenby told me, 'but my primary allegiance is to Delius. He would have been absolutely livid if he had known what was happening all these years later.' He also provided a glimpse of how he and Delius had systematically examined each of the early works: 'I would begin to play at the piano, calling out the

orchestration to refresh his memory. But we wouldn't get far – ten pages of full score at the most – before he'd start fidgeting in his chair. "That's enough," he'd say, shaking his head in mock reproval. "Did I really write that? Well, *really*" ... You see, they were 'prentice works containing early ideas, and he was quite ruthless in dismissing them.' I pointed out that Beecham had already revived some of those early pieces. 'Yes, I know, but Beecham was Beecham. He'd known Delius long before my time, and he had *carte blanche* to do whatever he liked. Mind you, even with Beecham Delius used to warn me, "Whatever you do, don't let him tamper with the notes!"'

4   When I was preparing Yehudi Menuhin's 80th birthday tribute for BBC Radio 3 in 1999 I took the opportunity to ask him whether he was the violinist who had said of Delius's Violin Concerto to Beecham, 'It is hardly a concerto, but it is a lovely poem' (Beecham, *Frederick Delius*, 1959). He confirmed that it was, and he thought the occasion was a concert at the Bath Festival in May 1955 when he played a Viotti concerto under Beecham's baton. It would seem possible that Beecham, looking for another violinist for Delius's Concerto after David McCallum retired, felt that to have it played by an international figure was just what it needed. But the work was not then in Menuhin's repertoire, though he did take it up later and recorded it in 1976.

5   This incident is recounted in Felix Aprahamian's Introduction to the 1975 reprint of Beecham's *Frederick Delius*, published by Severn House Publishing.

6   The soloists in Beecham's last recording of *Songs of Sunset* were Maureen Forrester (b. 1930) and John Cameron (1920–2002). In her book entitled *Out of Character* (published in Canada in 1984 in French and English), Miss Forrester recorded her memories of her dealings with Beecham, beginning with auditioning successfully for him for a planned recording of 'four songs by Delius' (unspecified). Then, she said, he changed his mind, and she was called to record *Songs of Sunset* instead. 'When I flew to London for the recording session', she recalled, 'Sir Thomas was in a playful mood. The piece called for orchestra, chorus and two soloists, and the huge BBC Symphony and choir were all in place. But he decided to begin by rehearsing only the harpsichord and strings. We all had to stand around and wait for hours. This was to be a one-day session, but it was dragging out interminably. Suddenly, with half the piece still left to record, Sir Thomas put down his baton, bowed to the orchestra and the rest of us, and said, "Ladies and gentlemen, thank you very much. I'll see you in eighteen months," and walked out ... We never did get to finish that session and not long afterwards, Sir Thomas died. But eventually a recording of him conducting *Songs of Sunset*, listing me as a soloist, appeared on the market. The critics raved that it was stupendous, but when I listened to it, I was sure that was not Sir Thomas playing, and one thing I had absolutely no doubt about: that was not my voice I was hearing. I can only assume that the record company wanted to recoup its investment and re-did the work with a new cast. Although I could have caused a scandal protesting, it was such a delicate matter that I didn't want to raise a fuss. But the voice which is supposed to be Maureen Forrester's on that record is, I believe, actually that of a young mezzo-soprano who was then just starting out on her career. I only hope she got paid, because if it's who I think it is, she ought to have gotten her name on the credits as well: Janet Baker.'

It is difficult to attach any credence whatever to this version of the circumstances under which *Songs of Sunset* was recorded by Beecham (see Chapter 5 and Appendix 1). There is, for example, no harpsichord in the work, the orchestra was not the BBC Symphony and, far from the work being left incomplete, the whole recording was finished in one day. There is also no question other than that the voice in the recording is Miss Forrester's: her participation at the recording session has been confirmed by, among others, Denis Vaughan who, as chorus-master of the Beecham Choral Society, was present throughout. It is also inconceivable that EMI would knowingly issue a recording in which one of the soloists was incorrectly identified. (The recording in which Janet Baker sang, conducted by Sir Charles Groves, was not made until 1968.)

Appendix 1

A Critical Discography

> I have been very much helped by the invention of the gramophone, through listening to records ... frequently records of other musicians. It has been of great use to me ... knowing what to avoid.
>
> Thomas Beecham

Although Sir Thomas Beecham made commercial records over a 50-year period (1910–60) his systematic recording of Delius's music did not begin until the acoustic process was superseded by the electrical system in 1925; then, between 1927 and 1958 he placed on disc over 30 titles, several more than once. Major milestones during the era of the 78rpm disc were the three albums for the Delius Society, issued on 21 discs in the 1930s, and the opera *A Village Romeo and Juliet*, recorded for the Delius Fellowship in 1948; after that, with the advent of the long-playing disc at the end of the 1940s, came *A Mass of Life* (1952) while the second half of the 1950s produced his final tapings for the stereophonic medium.

Virtually every one of these recordings issued originally on 78s or LPs has achieved reissue on compact disc where, just as in the LP era, they have been regularly coupled and recoupled by the various record companies involved. To reproduce the catalogue details of all these recordings issued in the UK, the USA and other countries would result in a plethora of disc numbers that would be of academic or specialist interest only. It is in any case an acknowledged fact that any discography is overtaken and becomes out of date as soon as it appears, and Beecham recordings continue to be recoupled as this book goes to press. It is proposed, therefore, to show only the details of the first issue in the UK (as the country of origin) of each of the recordings listed. In a few cases, reference may be made in the accompanying text to a particular reissue on either LP or CD, but the purpose of this Discography is to survey and discuss Beecham's legacy of recorded Delius based on the formats in which the performances originally appeared.

The Discography falls into three parts:

I: A chronological list of all Beecham's Delius recordings
II: The recorded works in alphabetical order
III: The songs.

I: A Chronological List of Sir Thomas Beecham's Delius Recordings

1927   The Walk to the Paradise Garden
        On hearing the First Cuckoo in Spring

1928   Brigg Fair†
        Summer Night on the River
        Sea Drift

1929   Songs: Irmelin
               Cradle Song
               Twilight Fancies
               Le ciel est, par-dessus le toit
               The Violet

1934   Paris*
        Eventyr*
        Hassan (excerpts)*
        Koanga (excerpt)*
        Songs of Sunset
        An Arabesque
        Songs: To Daffodils†
               So sweet is she†

1935   Summer Night on the River
        Appalachia (public performance)

1936   Sea Drift**
        In a Summer Garden**
        Over the Hills and Far Away*
        Intermezzo from Fennimore and Gerda**

1938   Appalachia***
        Irmelin Prelude***
        Hassan (excerpt)***
        La Calinda (arr. Fenby)***
        La Calinda from Florida suite
        A Mass of Life (excerpt)
        Songs: Autumn
               The Violet
               I-Brasîl
               Klein Venevil
               Twilight Fancies†

1945   Dance Rhapsody No. 2
       A Song before Sunrise
       Piano Concerto†
       North Country Sketches ('Autumn' and 'Winter Landscape' *only*)

1946   Violin Concerto
       Piano Concerto
       Dance Rhapsody No. 1†
       Dance Rhapsody No. 2
       On hearing the First Cuckoo in Spring
       The Song of the High Hills
       Brigg Fair
       On the Mountains
       Songs of Sunset
       Marche Caprice
       A Song before Sunrise†

1948   A Village Romeo and Juliet
       Dance Rhapsody No. 1†
       A Mass of Life (excerpt)

1949   North Country Sketches
       Summer Night on the River
       A Song before Sunrise
       Summer Evening
       Songs: Heimkehr
               Autumn
               The Violet

1950   Over the Hills and Far Away

1951   Sea Drift
       In a Summer Garden
       Eventyr
       Koanga (excerpt)
       Song: Twilight Fancies

1952   A Mass of Life
       Appalachia
       Dance Rhapsody No. 1
       Hassan (excerpts)

1954   Sea Drift
       Scenes from Irmelin (public performance)

1955   Paris
        Hassan (excerpts)
        An Arabesque

1956   Florida suite
        Brigg Fair (and broadcast performance)
        On hearing the First Cuckoo in Spring
        Dance Rhapsody No. 2
        A Song before Sunrise
        Irmelin Prelude
        Summer Evening
        Intermezzo from Fennimore and Gerda
        Sleigh Ride
        Marche Caprice

1957   Songs of Sunset
        Summer Night on the River
        Over the Hills and Far Away
        The Walk to the Paradise Garden (public performance)

1959   North Country Sketches (broadcast performance)

* ** ***   Recordings so marked were included in the Delius Society Volumes I, II and III
            respectively.

†   The recordings marked † have never been issued. The details are appended here
     for the sake of completeness:

Brigg Fair. London Symphony Orchestra. 12 July 1928

Songs: To Daffodils; So sweet is she. Dora Labbette *soprano*, Sir Thomas
    Beecham *piano*. 4 December 1934

Song: Twilight Fancies. Dora Labbette *soprano*, LPO. 11 February 1938

Piano Concerto. Betty Humby Beecham *piano*, LPO. 3 October 1945

A Song before Sunrise. RPO. 19 December 1946

Dance Rhapsody No. 1. RPO. 6 November 1946; 4 May 1948 and 18 February
    1949

II: The Recorded Works in Alphabetical Order

In the following entries the participating artists are shown first, followed by the recording date(s), recording venue (where appropriate) and catalogue number(s) of the first issue in the UK. Except in a very small number of cases, all Beecham's Delius recordings were undertaken in Studio 1 at the EMI Studios opened in 1931 in Abbey Road, St John's Wood, London. It has not been thought necessary to repeat this information each time, though naturally all other recording locations are shown.

Orchestra titles and symbols
Apart from the earliest discs, made in the 1920s with either unnamed symphony orchestras, the Royal Philharmonic Society Orchestra or the London Symphony Orchestra, all Beecham's Delius recordings were made with the London Philharmonic Orchestra or the Royal Philharmonic Orchestra. The following abbreviations are used throughout:

LPO = London Philharmonic Orchestra
RPO = Royal Philharmonic Orchestra

Titles of other orchestras are given in full.

Disc and catalogue numbers
The Columbia record prefix SDX was allotted to each of the 21 (78rpm) discs of the three Delius Society volumes published in the 1930s. The prefixes SHB32 and SHB54 are the catalogue numbers of two LP compilations (of five and six discs respectively) issued by EMI on its World Records label during the 1970s. The first of these (SHB32) transferred to LP the complete contents of the Delius Society albums published in the 1930s, and was valuably supplemented by some titles recorded at that time but not then issued. The second (SHB54) comprised all the published and a few unpublished recordings made at the time of the 1946 Delius Festival, together with a few others made between 1946 and the end of the 78rpm era in 1952.

Public and broadcast performances
Five of Beecham's Delius performances emanating from public concerts or radio broadcasts that have been published on compact disc have been included. The most important of these is *Scenes from Irmelin* in Beecham's only known recorded performance. Other recordings from various sources which have circulated from time to time, but which have never been generally available, have not been included.

Appalachia, Variations on an old slave song *chorus and orchestra*
LPO, Royal Opera Amateur Chorus. 10 November 1935. Queen's Hall, London.
   EMI 5 75938 2 (CD)
LPO, BBC Chorus. 6–7 and 31 January 1938. Columbia SDX15-19 (78rpm)

RPO, unnamed chorus. 29 October, 6–7 November, 13–18 December 1952.
  Columbia 33CX1112 (LP)

Beecham's 1938 version of *Appalachia*, which appeared in Volume III of the
Delius Society discs, was considered an outstanding achievement in its day,
while the manner in which it had been caught on record was thought to be little less
than miraculous. Even given his 30-year association with the score, the ease with
which he welded all the variations into a cohesive whole and gave full value to
incidental passing beauties (such as the unaccompanied choral passage, 'After
night has gone comes the day') while sustaining the overall shape of a piece which
can easily become diffuse, compelled admiration. The 1952 remake was
remarkably similar, though naturally its total effect was enhanced by the
recording's greater depth, range and clarity. And without the restrictions imposed
by the 4-minute 78rpm sides Beecham's reading could expand a little, although in
fact the only significant difference is in the Introduction where a marginally slower
tempo contrives to make it even more atmospheric than before. The 1935 live
performance from Queen's Hall that was published in 2003 is highly interesting to
hear, affording as it does a unique glimpse of Beecham in this piece at a concert.
Possibly because of those circumstances it is perhaps the best performance of all,
as it is so very full of spontaneity and an excitement that neither of the studio
versions can quite match. Beecham gives some of the quicker variations their
heads, and unsurprisingly shaves 2 minutes off the 36 taken up by the two
later recordings; at many points it is thrilling to hear him caught up in this music
he so obviously loved. The sound, for such an historic document, is surprisingly
good.

An Arabesque *baritone, chorus and orchestra*
Roy Henderson *baritone*, Leeds Festival Chorus, LPO. 3 October 1934. Leeds
  Town Hall. Somm-Beecham 8 (CD)
Einar Nørby *baritone*, BBC Chorus, RPO. October–November 1955.
  Walthamstow Town Hall, London. Fontana CFL1009 (LP)

Though he only twice performed it in public – at the 1929 Delius festival and the
1934 Leeds Festival – Delius's *Arabesque* was a work for which Beecham had a
high regard; he thought it was 'not only in its composer's ripest style but in point
of sheer opulence of sound unsurpassed by anything else he ever wrote'. Part of the
explanation for the paucity of performances lay with the words. Delius had
composed *An Arabesque* to his wife's translation into German of the original
Danish words (of Jens Peter Jacobsen), and Philip Heseltine had then made an
English version from the German. Although Beecham had himself amended
Heseltine's text (and employed the result in both his concert performances), he
later came to the conclusion that Danish was the only possible language for the

work to be sung in. The earlier of his two recordings is actually of one of the two public performances mentioned above, recorded during rehearsals for the 1934 Leeds Festival, and is sung in English. It offers a fine piece of singing by Roy Henderson, notable for that artist's customary pin-point accuracy of intonation, and the words are surprisingly clear. The music moves here rather more swiftly than in the later version and, though the orchestral part is indifferently caught, the work's outline is well defined. In the second recording, which is sung in Danish, much more of Delius's fascinating orchestration can be heard and the music responds equally well to Beecham's slightly more expansive view of it. The Danish baritone's vocal quality is not perhaps ideally focused, but the BBC Chorus meets its linguistic challenge with complete professionalism.

Brigg Fair, An English Rhapsody *orchestra*
Unnamed symphony orchestra, 11 December 1928 and 10 July 1929. Portman
    Rooms, London. Columbia L2294/5 (78rpm)
RPO. 26 November 1946. HMV DB6452/3 (78rpm)
RPO. 22 October 1956. BBC Studio 1, Maida Vale, London. BBC Legends
    BBCL4113-2 (CD)
RPO. 31 October 1956 and 2 April 1957. HMV ALP1586 *mono* ASD357 *stereo*
    (LP)

Judged purely as performances of the music, none of the others listed above comes within striking distance of the first, which remains one of Beecham's greatest gramophone achievements. It gave him a deal of trouble (no fewer than 11 attempts at the first side, for instance), but if ever there was a case of the end justifying the means, the way in which those first few minutes are ushered in, and then how the music surges joyously along after the announcement of the theme by Léon Goossens's oboe, is the proof. Nor, in any of the other versions, does Beecham succeed in making the whole Rhapsody as much of-a-piece as here; each section flows effortlessly into the next with the greatest naturalness, while the quiet interlude in which violins soar over a murmuring clarinet background before giving way to cor anglais and french horn, is pure magic. Sonically, of course, what we have here is a mere relic (made worse in one compact disc transfer which reproduces it above pitch) making the pity greater that none of Beecham's other recorded performances are its equal. In 1946, a considerably broader conception was achieved in the customary two 'takes' of each of the four sides, but it is a less engaging performance and nothing like so well constructed. The BBC studio account was taken down shortly before the commercial recording for EMI was begun, and is akin to a rehearsal for it; neither it nor the EMI performance hang together too well, though the stereo LP naturally has much of beauty to offer. But, somehow, here we never quite enter the same world of subtlety and eloquence as … once upon a time.

Concerto for Piano and Orchestra
Betty Humby Beecham *piano*, RPO. 4 and 16 December 1946. HMV DB6428/30
 (78rpm)

Few commentators have found much to say in favour of Delius's early and
completely untypical Piano Concerto – the Composer himself grew to dislike it and
in his last years tried to avoid hearing it – and when Beecham used to claim that
'the public likes to listen to it', what he was really saying was the public liked to
listen to it when he was conducting. As the main text records, after 1941 he
conducted the work for nobody else but Lady Beecham, and one guesses that many
of the 30 or so public performances they gave together are likely to have projected
the music in a more favourable light than their one commercial recording. What the
Concerto needs is a commanding player with a strong sense of structure who can
make the episodes hang together and sweep through the music in virtuoso style. On
this showing Lady Beecham was none of these things: instead she pulls the time
about (so that her husband sometimes has a job to synchronise the orchestra's
participation, for all his art at 'papering over the joins'), fails to maintain the
essential basic *tempi* and, in the quieter passages, tries to invest the material with
a grandeur it will not bear.

Concerto for Violin and Orchestra
Jean Pougnet *violin*, RPO. 31 October and 1 November 1946. HMV DB6369/71
 (78rpm)

When this recording was first issued there was already competition in the field; no
mean competition, either, since Albert Sammons was the Concerto's dedicatee, had
given its first performance and played it with Beecham at the 1929 Delius Festival.
Beecham always admired Sammons's playing and it is a great pity that an
opportunity was not seized to unite them on disc for what surely would have been
a definitive account; in the 1930s, for instance,when Sammons was at the height of
his powers, it would have made the high point of a fourth volume of Delius Society
discs. In 1944, however, when English Columbia decided to embark on their
recording with Sammons, Beecham was still in the USA and the 1946 Delius
Festival was not even on the horizon. Sammons's version has, as might be
expected, special qualities (*The Record Guide* in 1951 described it as having the
'dumbfounding splendour of a sunset') and there is no doubt that its nobility and
unaffectedness give it special authority. But the orchestral background is grey in
tone, rhythms are flabby and quite a lot of important orchestral detail fails to
register. Against Sammons, Pougnet is clearly a lesser executant, but his sweet-
toned playing is of undeniable beauty, his technique is equal to the score's
demands, and his version has the advantage in nearly every bar of the presence of
Beecham's guiding hand. This is evident right from the forthright opening, and

indeed throughout the whole of the opening section with its attractive rhythmic zest; the *tempo* here is swifter than Sammons's, but this gives Pougnet no qualms. In the slow central section the orchestral contribution is incomparable, and in the last Beecham points the rhythm of the dance with perfect poise.

Dance Rhapsody No. 1 *orchestra*
RPO. 29 October 1952. HMV DB9785/6 (78rpm)

The single listing above hardly tells the full story of Beecham's attempts to capture on disc this tricky piece (incidentally entitled 'A Dance Rhapsody' when its score was first published in 1910: six years later Delius embarked on a second piece of a similar caste, which had of necessity to become 'A Dance Rhapsody No. 2'). It was a work which Beecham conducted quite frequently in concert halls both at home and overseas, yet getting it down on disc seemed fraught with difficulty: dissatisfied with two earlier efforts, in 1946 and 1948, success was only finally achieved in 1952. At the first of the earlier sessions, attempted in the wake of his 1946 Delius Festival performance, it was evident that the bass oboe player was having problems with his cruelly exposed opening solo. After a few attempts, Beecham enquired mildly: 'Is anything the matter, Mr —— ?' 'I'm suffering, Sir Thomas', came the reply. '*You're* suffering!', expostulated Beecham, 'My dear fellow, we're *all* suffering!' In 1952, however, all was well and the piece was captured in one session without the necessity for later retakes. Beecham makes the tune upon which the variations are based sound truly 'bewitching' (Arthur Hutchings) and then dives headlong into the vigorous passage that temporarily interrupts them. Once the variations resume he manages, by means of tonal variety and adroit adjustments of *tempo* and emphasis, to avoid the music sounding repetitious (which it so easily can); even he, though, feels the necessity to excise one of the louder variations (by making a cut of 11 bars from 2 bars before cue 17 to cue 18). The music's culmination, in that most glorious quiet rhapsody for solo violin (David McCallum) against a wash of muted harmonies is, despite the relatively restricted monaural recording, quite breathtakingly beautiful.

Dance Rhapsody No. 2 *orchestra*
LPO. 16 October 1945. Somm-Beecham 10 (CD)
RPO. 3 October 1946. World Records SHB54 (LP)
RPO. 7 November 1956. HMV ALP1697 *mono* ASD329 *stereo* (LP)

The second of the above discs has the distinction of being the first recording that Beecham made with his new Royal Philharmonic Orchestra: even so – and despite its being given a catalogue number – it was not issued in the UK at the time, and only surfaced in 1979 for Beecham's centenary. It is a spirited performance, much more so than the stereo LP of ten years later, though the most spirited of the three is actually the earliest: this is the one that bears out Beecham's own view that 'the music halts nowhere, all the sections being knit together with a firm and unwavering hand'. That might describe his performance, too, but unfortunately an almost ideal conception is spoiled by orchestral playing which is not up to the mark: it is occasionally sketchy, and in the opening bars the mazurka theme on the flute is obscured by the strings. It is not difficult to see why this version was rejected at the time, though it is highly interesting to have this glimpse of the music in preparation in the conductor's workshop, as it were. The two RPO versions are not dissimilar in length, though the mood of the first is more fanciful than the second; the variations of *tempo* are more marked, it is generally livelier and the music dances more. The stereo version has greater subtlety in its phrasing of individual passages, but it seems almost stately by comparison, partly (at least) because those sudden outbursts on the brass which Delius marks 'quicker' are played at much the same *tempo* as the rest.

Eventyr (Once upon a time) *orchestra*
LPO. 14 November 1934. Columbia SDX4/5 (78rpm)
RPO. 12 January and 3 April 1951. Columbia LX8931/2 (78rpm)

Delius's 'Ballad for Orchestra' of 1917 is scored for a large contingent of players and successfully combines his characteristic harmonic methods in a sizeable but concise structure that recalls the tone poems of Richard Strauss. Beecham revelled in its strong rhythms and wild effects (it includes two shouts for men's voices) and often conducted it outside England, doubtless to show another side of a composer too often thought of as a pastoral dreamer. His two recordings are very little different from each other; both are sterling performances, though the second (recorded on tape) is naturally able to accommodate the often heavy scoring more easily as well as pointing up the brighter colours with enhanced clarity.

Fennimore and Gerda: Intermezzo *orchestra*
LPO. 28 September 1936. Columbia SDX11 (78rpm)
RPO. 5 November 1956. HMV ALP1586 *mono* ASD357 *stereo* (LP)

The first of Beecham's two recordings of this piece comes into that somewhat unusual category where a recording also constitutes a first performance. The main text discusses the possibility that Eric Fenby, who had with the composer's approval linked two of the opera's preludes to make a short concert piece, brought his score to Beecham's attention while he was working for him as a musical secretary in the mid-1930s. The 1936 record that resulted contains a slight variation from the later printed score in that the final chord beneath the sustained clarinet note is a continuous *diminuendo* in the accompanying strings, rather than two chords with a break between them. Beyond that, this is not so much Beecham's record as that of his oboe-player Léon Goossens, whose highly individual and idiosyncratic playing contrives to give the second half of the piece a completely spontaneous air; with Beecham exercising the lightest of hands on the accompanying strings, the effect as Goossens's slender sound hovers in the air is almost of music being improvised. In the 1956 remake, the RPO's Terence MacDonagh does not attempt anything of the sort, though he plays quite beautifully and Beecham is just as considerate. But the earlier disc is a miracle of fragile beauty for all time.

Florida, suite for orchestra
LPO. 7 January 1938. World Record Club SHB32 (LP)*
RPO. 10, 19, 21–22 November and 14 December 1956. HMV ALP1697 *mono*
    ASD329 *stereo* (LP)

The time and care that Beecham expended in the creation of his completely captivating account of Delius's first major orchestral work is reflected in the number of recording sessions it took. *Florida* has been described as best-quality light music (though it is doubtful if the composer took that view of it) and in the sense that it is brimful of the kind of delightful melody that sticks in one's brain after a single hearing then perhaps it is. Beecham takes each of the suite's four orchestral impressions at face value and lavishes all his art on them, phrasing the tunes with an instinct that invariably seems right, and revelling in the rich orchestral colour. High points are the opening with its oboe solo over shimmering strings proclaiming dawn, the imaginative tone-colour he draws from his first violins at the beginning of part two of the third movement, and the mood of reflection and even regret that pervades the final picture, *At Night*. The whole of the second movement, *By the River*, which he sometimes extracted to play on its own at concerts where the programme was made up of shorter pieces, is a perfect little tone-poem in its own right.

*The isolated 78rpm side contains music from the second section of the first movement, *Daybreak*, in the truncated form in which Beecham used it as a prelude to Act II of his 1935 production of *Koanga*.

Hassan: incidental music to the drama by James Elroy Flecker *soloists, chorus and orchestra*
Interlude between scenes I and II – Serenade *solo violin* – Short interlude – Chorus behind the scenes – Ballet: Dance of the Beggars – Chorus of Women – Prelude to Act III – Chorus of Soldiers – Procession of protracted death – Serenade *solo viola* – Closing Scene

Leslie Fry *tenor*,* Stanley Riley *bass-baritone*, BBC Chorus, RPO. 23 and 29
   October 1955, Walthamstow Town Hall, London; 29 May and 12 October 1956,
   Studio 1, Abbey Road, London. Fontana CFL1020 (LP)

Closing Scene
Jan van der Gucht *tenor*, Royal Opera Chorus, LPO. 28 June 1938. Columbia
   SDX20 (78rpm)

Intermezzo and Serenade *edited and arranged Beecham*
LPO. 11 December 1934. Columbia SDX7 (78rpm)
RPO. 29 October 1952. HMV DB9785/6 (78rpm)

The Fontana LP contains nearly 30 minutes of music from the score that Delius
composed for *Hassan*, first staged in Germany and London in 1923. Some
ambiguities between the above titling and the published score might be cleared up:
the first recorded excerpt is the music that later became familiar in Beecham's own
published arrangement as the Intermezzo; the 'Short interlude' consists of part (six
bars only) of the instrumental music that precedes the unaccompanied 'Chorus
behind the scenes'; in the Chorus of Women there is a cut of seven bars in the
opening orchestral passage and, since the music ends in mid-air, Beecham
obligingly provides a concluding chord; the Prelude to Act III runs on to include
the music accompanying the rise of the curtain; and in Act III Beecham disdains
Delius's second, more fully scored, version of the Serenade in favour of the
original strings-only version, merely replacing the solo violin by a solo viola. That
said, Beecham everywhere enjoys himself up to the hilt, sweeping soloists, chorus
and orchestra through these ten picturesque numbers with considerable élan.
Although he always stuck to the original orchestration, the small theatre orchestra
that Delius wrote for can hardly have sounded like the RPO here, at something like
full strength in a large resonant Hall; but the idiom is right even if the effect is
occasionally outsize. The Closing Scene, in which the departing pilgrims repeat the
refrain 'We take the Golden Road to Samarkand' (so often, observed one
commentator, that we begin to doubt their resolution) was recorded in Studio 1 at
Abbey Road and benefits from its tighter acoustic. The solo violin and solo viola
in the well-known Serenade are Arthur Leavins and Frederick Riddle respectively.
   The earlier (1938) recording of the Closing Scene was an inclusion in Volume
III of the Delius Society discs: it gives us a snapshot of the tenor Jan van der Gucht,
who sang Sali to Dora Labbette's Vreli in Beecham's 1932 broadcast performance
of *A Village Romeo and Juliet*. In 1934, Beecham recorded the unaccompanied
wordless 'Chorus behind the scenes' with the London Select Choir: it went
unpublished at the time but was included in SHB32. His own arrangement of two
of the movements under the title 'Intermezzo and Serenade' was first recorded in
1934 for Volume I of the Delius Society, and he repeated them in 1952 to make a
fourth-side 'filler' for his recording of Dance Rhapsody No. 1.

*Delius's score calls for tenor and baritone soloists. In all the issues of these ten Beecham excerpts over 40 years the tenor Leslie Fry has been listed incorrectly as a baritone. It is a pleasure now to record that it is Leslie Fry who sings the tenor solo at the beginning of the Closing Scene. He and the (correctly listed) bass-baritone Stanley Riley were members of the BBC Chorus.

In a Summer Garden *orchestra*
LPO. 2 October 1936. Columbia SDX13/14 (78rpm)
RPO. 27 October 1951. Columbia 33C1017 (LP)

The earlier of Beecham's two recordings of this Delius masterwork was highly regarded in its day, though here and there the strings use a degree of unfashionable *portamento* that the modern ear will find hard to accept. The second is a different matter altogether, a performance that might be described in the same words – 'well nigh flawless' – that Beecham chose when discussing the work itself. Delius employs a sizeable orchestra to conjure his vivid evocation of the garden and river at Grez-sur-Loing, but in Beecham's hands the soft-grained quality of the strings and the eloquence of the woodwind playing, together with his unique sensitivity to the balancing and blending of the music's timbres, at times suggest chamber music. The recording reproduces this masterly piece of orchestral interpretation with great fidelity.

Irmelin Prelude *orchestra*
LPO. 18 July 1938. Columbia SDX21 (78rpm)
RPO. 21 December 1946. HMV DB6371 (78rpm)
RPO. 31 October and 7 November 1956. HMV ALP1586 *mono* ASD518 *stereo* (LP)

The material of this short orchestral work originates in four themes found in Acts I and III of the opera *Irmelin*. Beecham first used it as an interlude in his 1935 production of *Koanga*, and substituted it for the second movement of the *Florida* suite when he first gave that in 1937. There is very little difference between his three recordings. The first, which has the advantage of Léon Goossens's oboe-playing, is the swiftest, the 1956 version the more leisurely by half a minute; the 1946 disc has Dennis Brain as first horn, and its timing lies between the other two. All three recordings are exquisite in their way, though the last, because the phrases are able to expand effortlessly in its more opulent sound, may be thought to be nearest to the kind of performance that Beecham gave in the concert hall.

Irmelin: Concert Suite from Act II, 'Scenes from Irmelin' (edited and arranged Beecham) *orchestra*

RPO. 16 September 1954. BBC Promenade Concert. Royal Albert Hall, London.
  BBC Legends BBCL 4068-2 (CD)

Of the small number of Beecham broadcasts of Delius's music to have come down
to us, that containing the concert suite that he fashioned from the music of Delius's
second opera and entitled *Scenes from Irmelin* is perhaps the most important: he
never recorded it commercially, and though he conducted it a dozen times at
concerts (and once on television) this seems to be the only transcript of any of
those performances to have been made. It was fortunate that somebody in the BBC
of the day, having decided to record selected works from the only two concerts that
Beecham gave at the Proms – not counting one almost 40 years before in 1915 –
most fortuitously decided to include the Delius, thereby earning the gratitude of
posterity (not to mention Delius lovers). All the material in this continuous 16-
minute orchestral work is drawn from Act II of the opera: its overriding impression
on the listener is likely to be one of beauty and charm, though not even Beecham's
persuasive baton can altogether disguise the music's occasional conventionalities.
These are generally most obvious in the quicker passages; elsewhere the ebb and
flow of the exquisite phrases are realised in playing of such quality that one is sure
one is listening to a miniature masterpiece. The monaural sound is good enough to
allow this unique recording to be enjoyed to the full.

Koanga, opera in three Acts

Closing Scene
London Select Choir, LPO. 4 and 11 December 1934. Columbia SDX6 (78rpm).
[Unnamed] soloists and Chorus, RPO. 26 January 1951. Columbia LX1502
  (78rpm)

This brief glimpse of Beecham conducting something from one of Delius's operas
is immensely valuable, even if it is mainly an orchestral excerpt (beginning 3 bars
after cue 40 in Act III and running to the end of the opera). The mood of tragedy
and regret that he establishes immediately is immensely striking, and the quiet
string interlude at mid-point is quite heartrending (in both versions). The uncut
1951 recording contains 29 bars more than the 1934 one, so we hear the voices of
the slave-girls briefly reflecting upon the sad tale that Uncle Joe has been telling
them in the course of the opera.

La Calinda (edited and arranged Fenby) *orchestra*
LPO. 11 February 1938. Columbia SDX21 (78rpm)

Eric Fenby's familiar arrangement for concert orchestra of music from Act II under
the title *La Calinda* finds its place here on account of its relationship to the opera.

There have been many recordings of the piece over the years, but Beecham's, with its main theme inimitably phrased by Léon Goossens, has never quite been equalled.

Marche Caprice *orchestra*
RPO. 19 December 1946. HMV DB6430 (78rpm)
RPO. 31 October 1956. HMV ALP1586 *mono* ASD357 *stereo* (LP)

Marche Caprice was originally the third of three *Morçeaux Caracteristiques* dated 1889–90. It became one of two early Delius pieces upon which Beecham alighted: he introduced it at the 1946 festival and published his own 'edited and arranged' score in 1951. It is a sprightly little march, full of attractively light-hearted ideas in Delius's formative style, and it may be thought that the first of these two versions, which has more of the flavour of a *jeu d'esprit* than the later one, is to be preferred. On the LP, however, the playing is distinctly superior and the woodwind solos taken with more confidence.

A Mass of Life *soloists, chorus and orchestra*
Rosina Raisbeck *soprano*, Monica Sinclair *mezzo soprano*, Charles Craig *tenor*,
  Bruce Boyce *baritone*, London Philharmonic Choir, RPO. 8 and 11 November,
  12–13 December 1952, 1 and 20 January, 10 April and 14 May 1953. Columbia
  33CX1078/9 (LP)

After the original Columbia LPs were reissued in equivalent form by Fontana in the 1960s and CBS in the 1970s, there was an excessive wait before this celebrated recording finally made it onto compact disc in 2001; this was a fine way to treat a unique document whose place among the pantheon of truly great recordings of the 20th century was absolutely secure. Only Beecham really had the true measure of this music, and the ability to convey its ecstatic pantheism white-hot to the listener. Aided by a more than adequate chorus and truly superb orchestral playing, Delius's genius is revealed to us by a conductor who seems to be re-creating the music, not merely interpreting it. Time and again, in orchestral interjections, postludes and longer passages such as the 'On the Mountains' section and the prelude to the second 'Dance Song', the ear is caught by phrasing of exquisite sensitivity, while the famous 'drenched' string tone that Beecham was able to command so effortlessly highlights those moments when the performance seems to dispense with bar-lines and takes on the nature of an improvisation. The soloists are good, too: Bruce Boyce, who has the largest share, grows in stature as the work proceeds, while the others all make the most of their briefer passages. (Apparently, Beecham began the recording with Sylvia Fisher as his soprano soloist, and it seems that her voice can still be heard in some early passages.) Monica Sinclair manages her long and touching solo (beginning 'O Zarathustra') at the end of the first 'Dance Song' with fine, steady tone so that it makes its full effect.

The *Mass* is sung in German but, incomprehensibly, the accompanying booklet to the first issue of this recording on compact disc (Sony SMK2K89432) reproduces the original, hopelessly unidiomatic, Bernhoff English translation of the text with its laughable nonsenses (for a full account see Chapter 1 above). It is doubly ironic that this should appear now in conjunction with this particular recording, since it was Beecham himself who rejected the Bernhoff text at the time of his 1909 première and commissioned his own from William Wallace. Wallace's version, which has done valiant service ever since, naturally graced the booklet of the original Columbia LP issue, together with an admirably sensitive note on the work which Beecham arranged to be commissioned from Eric Fenby: that, too, has gone, and colloquialisms such as 'Zarathustra snoozes' are not an improvement. But nothing can really detract from the impressiveness of Beecham's achievement. Past performers of the *Mass* under his baton who recalled the experience in phrases such as 'a vast improvisation' and 'the most living presentation of any music in my experience' were surely not exaggerating, while for the present day listener it is of the greatest significance to have this direct link back to the work's first performer.

Note:
On 11 February 1938 Beecham recorded the prelude to the third movement of Part II with the LPO; and on 8 May 1948 the prelude to Part II with the RPO. These were issued in SHB32.

North Country Sketches *orchestra*
LPO. 16 October 1945. [Autumn; Winter Landscape *only.*] Somm-Beecham 10 (CD)
RPO. 14 February 1949. Columbia LX1399/1401 (78rpm)
RPO. 4 November 1959. BBC Studio 1, Maida Vale, London. Music & Arts CD-281 (CD)

Only one of the above recordings is a really credible proposition. The first comes from that period in the autumn of 1945 when Beecham took up again with the orchestra that he founded; several Delius works were recorded at the time, but none was approved for release and, of them, *North Country Sketches* was, in any case, incomplete. Several years later he made a fresh start on the music with his new RPO, and this was successfully captured on 78s. With its prodigious range of sound, alternation of the fullest scoring with the lightest and its wealth of instrumental detail, the music must have been difficult for the gramophone men to deal with but, fortunately for the engineers, Beecham's blue pencil had been at work to good purpose, ensuring that what should be heard *was* heard. This was not so apparent at first on the 78s (though they were a good specimen), but the recording quality seems to have improved with each subsequent transfer (the work has been reissued at least four times on either LP or CD) and now one's only regret can be that it pre-dated the stereo era for which such a score cries out. As to Beecham's performance, it is surely definitive: only a virtuoso conductor possessing a kaleidoscopic beat could manage so effortlessly the many *tempo* changes in the Dance movement and 'The March of Spring' so that the essential flow is preserved, and so that each movement sounds complete in itself; as well, the imagery conjured up in both 'Autumn' and 'Winter Landscape' is startlingly visual. On the 78s the movements appeared in the order 1–3–2–4, possibly for the convenience of the side breaks, though the recording's first issue on LP and subsequent reissues followed the order of the printed score. In his broadcast of 4 November 1959, however, Beecham opted for the irregular order: this reading took a much swifter overall view of the music (at 21'55" it is almost 3 minutes quicker than the commercial version) and, while it is interesting to hear, it does not, on the whole, promote the music nearly so comprehensively as the 1949 version.

On hearing the First Cuckoo in Spring *orchestra*
Royal Philharmonic Society Orchestra. 19 December 1927. Fyvie Hall, London.
    Columbia L2096 (78rpm)
RPO. 19 December 1946 and 8 May 1948. HMV DB6923 (78rpm)
RPO. 31 October 1956. HMV ALP1586 *mono* ASD357 *stereo* (LP)

Only a few seconds separate the two recordings made during the 78rpm era. The first opens magically into Léon Goossens's matchless phrasing (a reminder that it was a chance radio hearing of this very record that so arrested Eric Fenby's attention in 1928, leading to his unique partnership with Delius). Like *The Walk to the Paradise Garden* from the same session, Beecham's record achieved legendary status, and even now, heard under good conditions, it can still exert its own very special brand of nostalgia. The second, a good but not outstanding performance, is remembered more as an example of Beecham's occasionally haphazard recording methods. Having recorded both parts of it on 30 October 1946 he remade the second side on 19 December, before deciding that he also wanted to repeat the first. But for one reason or another the new attempt on the first side was not made until 18 months later, by which time several key players in the RPO had changed and the orchestral balance in the studio was different. The result is that after the break between the sides (at 3'43") the sound quality changes, and in particular the cuckoo, impersonated in Part 1 by Jack Brymer, sounds much further away when heard from Reginald Kell in Part 2. In Beecham's last recording the phrases expand and breathe with infinite tenderness at a marginally slower *tempo*: the balance between the string sections is perfect, as it is between the string body and Delius's handful of woodwinds and horns, so that their all-important contributions are perfectly judged. The result is a great Beecham-Delius creation, outstanding even by his standards.

On the Mountains: Symphonic Poem after Henrik Ibsen's *Paa vidderne* *orchestra*
RPO. 26 November 1946. World Records SHB54 (LP)

In 1888, Delius composed a melodrama in which Ibsen's poem *Paa vidderne* was recited against an orchestral background. Two years later, the same Ibsen poem inspired an orchestral work which, when first heard in Oslo in October 1891, was described as a Concert Overture; after revision, a second performance followed at Monte Carlo in 1894, by which time it was being called a Symphonic Poem; after that, it was forgotten until Beecham unearthed it for his 1946 Delius Festival. In his own words, 'Breadth and vigour are the main characteristics of a work which, rather surprisingly, is a little lacking in the serenity and lyrical charm discoverable in all the other early pieces. But there is no fault to be found with its architecture, and its downright force makes it an effective showpiece.' Needless to say, he relishes the opportunity to recommend this neglected work, playing it for all it is worth. Urgent *tempi* disguise the four-square rhythms of the more vigorous passages, while an irresistible strain of nobility courses through the more lyrical moments. Only a few tiny lapses in the playing – for once even the normally imperturbable Dennis Brain seems a little ruffled by the taxing horn passages – can be the reason why Beecham decided against publishing this recording along with the others made at the time of the 1946 festival.

Over the Hills and Far Away *orchestra*
LPO. 28 September 1936. Columbia SDX12/13 (78rpm)
RPO. 7 February 1950. Columbia 33C1017 (LP)
RPO. 2 April and 7 October 1957. HMV ALP1697 *mono* ASD329 *stereo* (LP)

Beecham seemed to have a particular fondness for this early (1897) orchestral fantasia and it appeared in his programmes at regular intervals between his first playing of it in 1908 and his last in 1956. There is little to choose between the first two recordings listed above – in both the opening bars with their scanning-of-the-far-horizon-with-shaded-eyes effect are completely magical – while any differences in the way subsequent phrases are turned are equally convincing in either. Not so the last two (*two* because the mono and stereo recordings come from different sessions, the earlier stereo one in London and the mono in Paris). Both are much swifter – a difference of almost 3 minutes over the 1950 version – and while all the hallmarks of Beecham's elegant phrasing are still present in the playing, the ear is not able to assimilate them so easily. One might think that a faster overall view would help in minimising the fragmentary effect of a work that is divided into seven sections, but here it is not so and the sensuousness combined with chivalry that informs Beecham's earlier approach, especially the 1950 one, makes a much stronger case for the music.

Paris (The Song of a Great City)
LPO. 9 April 1934. Columbia SDX1/3 (78rpm)
RPO. August 1955. Walthamstow Town Hall, London. Philips ABL3088 (LP)

It was with this orchestral nocturne that Beecham began his life-long crusade for Delius's music: after his first performance of it in 1908, almost 50 more followed in various parts of the world, and *Paris* became a talisman both for him and for its composer. Although Delius heard that first Beecham performance, and others subsequently (including at the 1929 festival), how he must have longed for the permanent record of it that he knew, in his final weeks, Beecham was making: sadly, it was denied to him. That version was the first of the two shown above, and it has not really been surpassed, by Beecham or anybody else: nobody has quite managed to knit its widely contrasting paragraphs into any semblance of a whole so convincingly, or to invest each new section with the sophisticated beauty of utterance or rhythmic piquancy that each one demands. The LPO was, of course, a marvellous instrument as an ensemble, but the performance owes almost as much to superior passages of solo playing from its leading players, notably Léon Goossens and Reginald Kell; meanwhile, Beecham's fastidious care for balance tempers the rowdier moments so that they do not sound overblown. The 1955 account is remarkably similar in outline, even to running to within a few seconds of the earlier one, and the recorded sound liberates the orchestral texture in a wholly desirable way; but it is not such an individual performance.

Sea Drift *baritone, chorus and orchestra*
Dennis Noble *baritone*, Manchester Beecham Opera Chorus, London Symphony Orchestra. 11 November 1928. Portman Rooms, London. Somm-Beecham 10 (CD)
John Brownlee *baritone*, London Select Choir, LPO. 3 April and 2 November 1936. Columbia SDX8/11 (78rpm)
Gordon Clinton *baritone*, [Unnamed] Chorus, RPO. 22 and 26 January 1951. EMI 7 64386 2 (CD)
Bruce Boyce *baritone*, BBC Chorus, RPO. 28 April and 2–3 December 1954. Walthamstow Town Hall, London. Philips ABL3088 (LP)

All four of Beecham's recordings are of interest in one way or another. Even the earliest, which he suppressed at the time, is at least of historical importance since it gives us the opportunity of hearing Dennis Noble in the solo part that he sang subsequently at the 1929 festival; and, in 1936, the Australian baritone John Brownlee is virile and impassioned in a manner unapproached by any of the English singers with their more contained styles. That style is typified by Gordon Clinton and Bruce Boyce, and nobody could accuse them of hectoring (as Brownlee was, unfairly; his was a powerful voice, but it is more a matter of strong emphases). By the time of his recording – like Noble's, suppressed at the time – Gordon Clinton had a great deal of experience of working with Beecham, but he still sounds a trifle over-awed by the undertaking. He had sung *Sea Drift* at the conductor's 70th birthday concert in 1949, though the truth was that he was always doubtful about his ability to command its highest notes with absolute security. When he had taken his doubts to Beecham, however, they were brushed aside with, 'It will be a new experience for you, my boy.' Clinton said he began to realise something of Beecham's superb self-assurance, 'because he knew he could make me do it; and he did'. The recording became to him the most important souvenir of their association, and the unexpected unearthing of the tape after 30 years gave him the greatest joy. (Always an emotional man, when it was played to him and he heard his first entry, he burst into tears.) His voice was softer-grained than Brownlee's and the 1951 recording of this tautly held together performance does it greater justice than on the *Village Romeo and Juliet* discs of three years before. The best all-round version of *Sea Drift* is undoubtedly the last, where Beecham's powerful commitment to the score is unfettered by the restraints of 4-minute sides, where he has in the BBC Chorus the best vocal group of all, and where Bruce Boyce, capitalising on singing for him in the earlier *Mass of Life* recording, is inspired to perform above himself. The orchestral playing is everywhere of the greatest sensitivity and the recording deals with the dynamic range of the music very capably.

Sleigh Ride *orchestra*
RPO. 5 November 1956. HMV ALP1586 *mono* ASD357 *stereo* (LP)

This is the second of Delius's 'Three Small Tone Poems' of 1889–90, all of which Beecham included in the 1946 festival, though he handed them over to Richard Austin to conduct. Beecham did not himself take up *Sleigh Ride* until as late as 1956, and even then did not perform it in concert until a month or so after he had made his recording. Its subtitle is 'Winter Night', under which it appeared at the festival. In Beecham's hands the snow sparkles and glitters as the sleigh with its jingling harness approaches, and in the central section he lingers romantically over the Grieg-like melody to great effect.

A Song before Sunrise *orchestra*
LPO. 16 October 1945. Somm-Beecham 10 (CD)

RPO. 18 February and 6 April 1949. HMV DB9757/8 (78rpm)
RPO. 5 and 7 November 1956. HMV ALP1586 *mono* ASD357 *stereo* (LP)

The first of these three recordings, fast enough to fit on one side of a 78rpm disc, can be discounted straightaway as untypical, but the second is another matter. The pacing here seems ideal for this cheerful, open-air piece and the more modest size of the orchestra (compared with the later LP version) somehow enables Beecham to realise quite miraculously the mood of freshness that Delius wanted ('Freshly' is the only marking at the head of the score: no *tempo* is given). The stereo LP version is most enjoyably played, though it is slightly slower than the 1949 reading and the sound is naturally ampler. Interestingly, Beecham suggested that if an orchestra for this piece consisted of 10 first and 8 second violins, 6 violas, 4 cellos and 2 double-basses, those forces should be reduced to 12 violins (6 + 6), 4 violas, 4 cellos and 2 double-basses for some of the more lightly scored internal passages.

Songs of Sunset *soloists, chorus and orchestra*
Olga Haley *soprano*, Roy Henderson *baritone*, Leeds Festival Chorus, LPO.
    4 October 1934. Leeds Town Hall. Somm-Beecham 12-2 (CD)*
Nancy Evans *mezzo soprano*, Redvers Llewellyn *baritone*, BBC Chorus, RPO.
    30 November 1946. World Records SHB54 (LP)
Maureen Forrester *mezzo soprano*, John Cameron *baritone*, Beecham Choral
    Society, RPO. 1 April 1957. HMV ALP1983 (LP)

All three of these recordings have a 'history'. The first became legendary and there is no doubt that some of the solo singing is thrilling and much of the orchestral nuancing unrivalled in the later versions. But there can only be speculation as to why it was made at all: the final rehearsal for the concert performance at the 1934 Leeds Festival was scarcely the place to try to capture such an elusive work in any permanent way. Roy Henderson always maintained that when Beecham casually announced, 'Some people are recording this', that he, contracted to another recording company, resolved not to sing at full voice (though it is perfectly obvious that he did), while the Leeds Festival Chorus, though adequate, was unlikely under such circumstances to provide the level of sensitivity that Beecham sought in this of all Delius works. Then again, if Beecham and his recording producer Walter Legge intended it for publication in one of the Delius Society volumes, why did the conductor comment at certain moments between the movements? It would have been difficult to erase such interjections from the wax discs. Whatever the intentions, a single hearing of the resulting test-pressings must have convinced them that the project was a non-starter: despite individual beauties the orchestral part, which is very fully and independently scored, comes and goes most unsatisfactorily and important instrumental passages either do not make their full effect or are lost altogether; the choral tone (at least as recorded) is poorly balanced and not sufficiently refined. Incidentally, the statement which persists on record labels to this day that this chorus was the London Select Choir must surely be erroneous: it is hardly conceivable that Beecham would have been taking the final rehearsal for that evening's concert with a different choir.

The reason for the suppression of the second (1946) version was much more straightforward: it was incomplete. The second number, the duet for the two soloists, 'Cease smiling, dear, a little while be sad', was not recorded: 'To be completed later' appeared on the recording sheets, but it never was. The eventual publication in 1979 of the rest revealed splendid choral singing, a little overprominent at first though later settling into a balanced relationship with the orchestra, but some rather prosaic solo singing; while they are perfectly adequate, Nancy Evans is somewhat plain and Redvers Llewellyn tends to clumsiness in his handling of the intimate phrases.

The 'history' attendant on Beecham's last recording is partly covered in the narrative (see Chapter 5 above). To it may be added that, although the work was recorded in both mono and stereo formats, only the monaural version was issued at first (in 1963); it was 1980 before the stereo finally made its appearance. The monaural sound was disappointingly confined, with many important woodwind solos going for nothing, to the extent that the music quite failed to make its proper impact. Later transfers made from the much superior stereo tape have improved this situation beyond recognition (especially EMI's compact disc issue: 5 75768 2) with the result that it is possible to appreciate just what a fine performance this always was. True, there are occasional roughnesses which presumably contributed to Beecham's decision not to issue it, but with fine solo and choral singing and a splendid orchestra, the insights of the work are revealed as never before. Maureen Forrester's voice may not be to everyone's taste, but she makes a beautiful thing of 'Exceeding sorrow'; John Cameron is the ideal Delius singer, contriving to make the vocal angularities sound entirely natural and responding to Ernest Dowson's words with great sensitivity. The Beecham Choral Society, despite the *mea culpa* issued by its chorus-master, Denis Vaughan (see Chapter 5), is fully up to the mark.

*For years the last of the eight test-pressings, containing the final number, 'They are not long, the weeping and the laughter', was thought to be missing, so that for the recording's first-ever issue (on compact disc in 2000: Somm-Beecham 8) the equivalent side from Beecham's 1946 recording was used in order that the music could be issued complete. Then the missing side from 1934 was located and restored to its rightful place on a second CD issue in 2001 (Somm-Beecham 12-2).

Summer Evening *orchestra*
RPO. 18 February 1949. HMV DB9757/8 (78rpm)
RPO. 31 October 1945. HMV ALP1968 *mono* ASD518 *stereo* (LP)

Summer Evening was the other early Delius work of which Beecham produced his own 'edited and arranged' edition (in 1951, together with *Marche Caprice*). It was first heard at the 1946 Delius Festival, though under the baton of Richard Austin. Beecham did not conduct it himself until 2 January 1949, but shortly afterwards made the first of the recordings listed above. Because of its generally swifter handling and more direct approach, the first version is perhaps preferable, as it seems to judge the scale and stature of this miniature tone-poem, with its simple and straightforward A–B–A structure, rather better. All the same, there is no denying that the extra half-minute taken over the LP performance does allow Beecham to coax even more meaningful phrasing out of his players, notably the woodwind; it is just that then the music's tendency to linger unduly at cadences creates a somewhat inflationary effect.

Summer Night on the River *orchestra*
Royal Philharmonic Society Orchestra. 12 July 1928. Central Hall, Westminster,
    London. Columbia D1638 (78rpm)
LPO. 4 October 1935. Columbia LB44 (78rpm)
RPO. 18 February 1949. HMV DB9757/8 (78rpm)
RPO. 28 March 1957. HMV ALP1586 *mono* ASD357 *stereo* (LP)
'No orchestral work by Delius demands such deep insight and sensitive skill in performance as this; the balance and shading of woodwind timbres in this musical *chiaroscuro* is imperative to a visionary realisation of the score' (Eric Fenby in his sleeve note to the 1957 LP). Despite the difficulties inherent in 'bringing off' this exquisite little tone-poem, Beecham is uniformly successful in all his four recordings. Aided by ultrasensitive string playing that provides the perfect backdrop to Delius's delicate woodwind and horn murmurings, he then finds the ideal *tempo* for this consummate piece of orchestral *pointillism* (which is unique in Delius's output in conjuring up visual aspects as well as the atmosphere of his garden at Grez-sur-Loing). The 1928 recording is now too old to do the music full justice, but in all the others (again in Fenby's words) 'the gnats and dragonflies dart over the waterlilies and the faint white mist hovers over the willow-tressed banks and overhanging trees ...'

The Song of the High Hills *soloists, chorus and orchestra*
Freda Hart *soprano*, Leslie Jones *tenor*, Luton Choral Society, RPO. 22 November
    1946. HMV DB6470/2 (78rpm)

If the mere quartet of concert performances that Beecham gave of this work are anything to go by, this was one score of Delius's that was not a particular favourite of his. Yet his one recording is a complete success, making one regret all the more that the sound is confined by the limitations of old shellac 78s, which are hardly ideal for encompassing the spectacular dynamic effects that Delius employs in his contemplation of nature on the heights of his beloved Norway. These effects range from the quietest as the mountain peaks are attained, until the voices that emerge from the distance grow in power and the whole landscape is ablaze with an ecstatic outpouring of tone. The recording is a superior one of its kind, and easily displays Beecham's completely natural instinct for orchestral balance; he also ensures that the arch-like structure of the work is preserved – not easy when one is working in 4-minute stretches.

A Village Romeo and Juliet, opera in six scenes
Manz Fabian Smith *baritone*
Marti Frederick Sharp *baritone*
Sali (as a child) Sybil Hambleton *soprano*
Sali René Soames *tenor*
Vreli (as a child) Marion Davies *soprano*
Vreli Vera Terry *soprano*
The Dark Fiddler Gordon Clinton *baritone*
BBC Theatre Chorus, RPO. Recording of BBC broadcast of 23 April 1948, BBC
    Studio I, Maida Vale, London. Somm-Beecham 12-2 (CD)
Manz Dennis Dowling *baritone*
Marti Frederick Sharp *baritone*
Sali (as a child) Margaret Ritchie *soprano*
Sali René Soames *tenor*
Vreli (as a child) Dorothy Bond *soprano*
Vreli Lorely Dyer *soprano*
The Dark Fiddler Gordon Clinton *baritone*
[Unnamed] Chorus, RPO. 1, 3, 4, 6, 7 and 21 May, 3 and 20 July 1948. HMV
    DB6751/62 (78rpm)

The unexpected appearance on the commercial market in 2002 of the 1948 broadcast of the opera gave Delius-lovers their first chance to hear a performance which had passed into legend as one of the glories of the early BBC Third Programme. (There were, in fact, two performances: the compact disc issue above is of the first.) Listening to it, even at this distance, one can still get an idea of the impact that listeners must have felt as that magical orchestral opening issued from their radio sets, preluding an opera whose action they could easily follow through it being sung in English. Nowadays, for all technical advances (and perhaps because of some of them) the unrecessed recording with its absence of dynamic range makes listening a trifle hard on the ear; but nothing can detract from the sheer address of Beecham's conducting, the sense of flow he achieves and the lovely orchestral playing he secures everywhere, whether from the strings or the (all-important) woodwind. The mood established in those telling little preludes, notably that to Scene IV, has never been matched, nor the almost tragic solemnity of the wedding sequence or the poignancy of the concluding pages. But everywhere, in both performances, there is ardour, tenderness, beauty and passion. The singers, of course, have never been much praised. At the time, Beecham was criticised because they were not 'stars'; no doubt 'stars' were precisely what he was not looking for, even if his chosen group was never going to be quite equal to the more strenuous passages such as the lovers' ecstatic final duet, 'See the moonbeams kiss the woods'. All the same, René Soames knew from experience just how to use the microphone; Gordon Clinton perhaps did not, and the recording quality did him no favours. As the heroine, Vera Terry in the broadcast has generally been preferred over Lorely Dyer on the commercial discs, but surely the former's voice is too matronly for the still-young girl, and the latter's is more realistic. In the end, however, as always with Delius's music, the performance belongs to Beecham; and the BBC broadcast gives us one incomparable moment that the commercial records do not. He begins *The Walk to the Paradise Garden* at the slowest pace imaginable, heralding a particularly deeply-felt reading which stretches to almost 10'20" and is made even more dramatic by some spectacular roars of encouragement early on and several strangulated yelps at the later emotional climaxes.

The Walk to the Paradise Garden *orchestra*

Royal Philharmonic Society Orchestra. 19–20 December 1927. Fyvie Hall, London. Columbia L2087 (78rpm)

RPO. 20 October 1957. Palazzo Scholastico, Ascona, Switzerland. Ermitage ERM 132 (CD)

Since Beecham gave well over 100 performances of this indestructible piece in the concert hall it is surprising to find that he actually made only one commercial recording of it. That comes from his very first Delius recording sessions and, although the record became famous and enjoyed high status, the performance it enshrines does not now strike us as being truly representative of his customary approach to the music. Principally, this is because it is amazingly swift: 9–10 minutes was Beecham's usual duration, but here it takes just 7'20". One cannot help feeling that the 1957 Ascona concert performance at 9'19" is nearer the mark; and so too are those in the opera recordings, despite their situation in the midst of continuous music. Even here, however, there is a considerable difference in timing: in HMV's commercial recording the music takes 8'38", doubtless influenced by, but in fact well within, the constraints of two 78rpm sides. In the 1948 BBC studio performance, on the other hand, Beecham could indulge himself, and he did (see preceding entry).

The circumstances of the 1927 recording are perhaps worth recalling for the light they shed on Beecham's adaptable recording methods. The first of the two days of sessions began with *The Walk to the Paradise Garden* but, after making the first of the two sides three times, he broke off: it is not difficult perhaps to imagine that the favourable atmosphere so necessary for recording Delius's music successfully was evaporating with the constant repetitions. Whatever it was, he switched to *On hearing the First Cuckoo in Spring*, completing its two sides successfully in two and three 'takes' respectively. Next day, perhaps so as not to begin 'cold' on the second side of the *Paradise Garden*, he warmed the orchestra up with marches from Rimsky-Korsakov's suite *Antar* and Borodin's *Prince Igor* before resuming work on the Delius. If that was the strategy, it worked: while it was the last of the three 'takes' of side one that proved to be the best, it was the first of the second side's three.

III: The Songs *with piano or orchestra*

Autumn
Dora Labbette *soprano*, LPO. 11 February 1938. World Records SHB32 (LP)
Elsie Suddaby *soprano*, RPO. 1 October 1949. World Records SHB54 (LP)

Cradle Song
Dora Labbette *soprano*, Sir Thomas Beecham *piano*. 24 June 1929. Petty France
    Studios, London. Columbia L2344 (78rpm)
Homeward Journey
Marjorie Thomas *mezzo-soprano*, RPO. 6 April 1949. World Records SHB54 (LP)

I-Brasîl
Dora Labbette *soprano*, LPO. 11 February 1938. World Records SHB32 (LP)

Irmelin
Dora Labbette *soprano*, Sir Thomas Beecham *piano*. 24 June 1929. Petty France
    Studios, London. World Records SHB32 (LP)

Le Ciel est, par-dessus le toit
Dora Labbette *soprano*, Sir Thomas Beecham *piano*. 24 June 1929. Petty France
    Studios, London. World Records SHB32 (LP)

The Nightingale
Dora Labbette *soprano*, Sir Thomas Beecham *piano*. 24 June 1929. Petty France
    Studios, London. Columbia L2344 (78rpm)

Twilight Fancies
Dora Labbette *soprano*, Sir Thomas Beecham *piano*. 10 July 1929. Petty France
    Studios, London. Columbia L2344 (78rpm)

Elsie Suddaby *soprano*, RPO. 3 April 1951. World Records SHB54 (LP) (first ever issue was on RCA LHMV1050 (LP) and LVT1020 (LP), in the USA in the 1950s)

The Violet
Dora Labbette *soprano*, Sir Thomas Beecham *piano*. 10 July 1929, Petty France Studios, London. World Records SHB32 (LP)
Dora Labbette *soprano*, LPO. 11 February 1938. World Records SHB32 (LP)
Elsie Suddaby *soprano*, RPO. 1 October 1949. World Records SHB54 (LP)

Young Venevil
Dora Labbette *soprano*, LPO. 11 February 1938. World Records SHB32 (LP)

One can imagine the Columbia Company in 1929 being thrilled at the prospect (not least for their sales) of having Beecham's name on their record labels as a piano accompanist as well as a conductor. But, whatever it may have done for them financially, musically it was something of a mixed blessing. As Beecham himself freely admitted, he was really no pianist, and some of Delius's scores stretched his limited abilities. He played in a manner which might be described as patrician, and only his strong sense of rhythm enabled all but the slowest songs to stay afloat: in the second strain of *Irmelin*, for instance, his firmly delineated downward emphases in the bass are endearing, and his sternly insistent rhythm at the opening of *Cradle Song* is too. It is little wonder that he did not allow *Le Ciel est, par-dessus le toit* or *Irmelin* to be published at the time, and fortunate for us that Dora Labbette repeated them later (1938) with Gerald Moore (included in SHB32).

Nonetheless there is something very affecting about all these performances. In Dora Labbette, of course, Beecham had the perfect, peerless collaborator: her singing is a joy everywhere, so good that one's attention is easily distracted from the accompaniments being attempted in the background. Since the opportunities between them for public performance of the songs with piano was in any case clearly limited, one obvious solution must have seemed to be for some of them to be orchestrated. The songs began to appear in this form at Beecham concerts around the time of the 1929 Delius Festival, and when he took up his baton with a handful of players gathered closely around him the results were very different: the songs recorded with the LPO on 11 February 1938, for instance, are absolutely exquisite, a quartet of little gems. *I-Brasîl* in particular, a wonderfully atmospheric song anyway, is sung, played and conducted in a manner that leaves the listener in no doubt that that is the way to do it; never mind if Labbette smudges 'last stars' at one point, the handling of the rising phrase 'So why should I not listen to the song you sing to me' in a perfectly calculated *crescendo* is unforgettable. This is perfection in the conception and execution of a Delius song. Of *Twilight Fancies*, which was also recorded at that same session, there seems now to be no trace, which is a minor tragedy: Elsie Suddaby sings it attractively in her 1951 version, but Dora Labbette knew the composer and sang his songs to him at Grez-sur-Loing. Two other seemingly complete losses – *To Daffodils* and *So sweet is she*, recorded on 4 December 1934 with Beecham at the piano – are also to be regretted, though a second version of the latter accompanied by Gerald Moore was made in 1938 (also in SHB32). At some point Beecham made orchestrations of these two songs, presumably for Labbette to sing, but so far as is known they were never used. In the four songs recorded with the LPO, Beecham used his own orchestrations of *Autumn* and *Young Venevil* (the latter sung in German as *Klein Venevil*) and Philip Heseltine's for *I-Brasîl*. That of *The Violet* appears to have been the work of Henry Gibson, Beecham's musical secretary at the time some of these orchestral accompaniments began to be heard in 1929; the manuscript score is certainly in his hand.

The four songs taken down in the post-war period with orchestral accompaniment – *Autumn*, *The Violet* and *Homeward Journey* in 1949 and *Twilight Fancies* in 1951 – if lacking the intimacy of Dora Labbette's singing, are nicely done by the singers concerned, while the playing of the orchestral accompaniments again touches perfection. In *Homeward Journey*, sung in German under the title *Heimkehr*, the orchestration is by Robert Sondheimer (1881–1956), a German musicologist of whom Beecham thought so highly that he once described him as 'one of the few genuine musical scholars left in the world'. (Sondheimer also made orchestrations of *Irmelin* and *In the Seraglio Garden*.) That for *Heimkehr* is an especially effective piece of work. *Autumn* and *Twilight Fancies* are heard in Beecham's orchestrations, *The Violet* in Henry Gibson's.

Appendix 2

A Beecham Rehearsal of *Paris*

The BBC Symphony Orchestra's programme conducted by Beecham on 12 April 1937 consisted of a Haydn Symphony, Grieg's Piano Concerto, two of Sibelius's *Lemminkaïnen* Legends and *Paris*. At the rehearsal, as Bernard Shore observed, the Haydn and Delius took up three-quarters of the time spent in preparation:

> Both works he has played time and time again, but he tackles them with a fresh outlook. Where many conductors give the orchestra the impression of stereotyped performances of works continually in their programmes, Beecham sets out on a new journey each time, and is seldom heard to say: 'I generally make an *allargando* here,' or 'In this passage I always like the flute to stand out.' On the contrary, from the opening bar of his first rehearsal he seems to be weaving new patterns in his mind, especially in a work of phantasy like *Paris*.

The passage reproduced below is from *The Orchestra Speaks* by Bernard Shore (Longmans, Green & Co., London, 1938). The score numbers and references relate to the Universal Edition score of Delius's *Paris* (UE6900).

Gazing around the orchestra at his first rehearsal he finds the players placed in an unaccustomed way. 'Gentlemen, you are doubtless – ah – used to the queer positions in which I find you, and in time I shall presumably locate one or two of you. I should like the bass clarinet to give some slight indication of his presence by holding up his hand – thank you! Now perhaps, with the help of the contra-fagotto, you will be kind enough to induct us into the lights and – ah – mysteries of "Paris".' He plays the entire work through, sitting on his usual raised chair, listening most intently, occasionally making curt comments: 'Clarinet – 'cello, a little more please – in six – Basses lighter – fliute' (he always pronounces flute thus – fliute). At the same time he strengthens these comments by a gesture of his stick towards the particular instrument. Stopping only once, for a slight misunderstanding at the *molto adagio* (5 bars before No. 17) – 'In six, please!' – and then once more at the end, when the little pan-pipe call on the piccolo (off-stage) goes awry and leads him to remark, *sotto voce*, to the principal violin – 'Who did that?' The piccolo complains that there is no one to keep the door open for him, and if it is shut he cannot see the beat. Whereupon Beecham – 'My dear fellow, I will see that the entire staff of attendants of the Queen's Hall are put at your disposal tomorrow night, or – if they cannot cope with the matter – I will personally break the door down!'

When he finishes the piece he touches on the various points that have arisen: 'Gentlemen, that was very good on the whole: I have little to suggest in the beginning. But at No. 4, basses, a little more please; something between *mezzo-piano* and *mezzo-forte*; a rather heavy sound is required there. At No. 5, oboe and clarinet, I should like you to play that vulgar tune a little harder – in fact, a demonstration of good vulgar spirits in the early morning, which our friends on the Continent seem to enjoy. Third and fourth bars before No. 7, violas and clarinets, a little more distinct, that phrase, if you please. Second violins, a little quieter when you start your quavers after Fig. 8 – it was too loud for you to make the proper *crescendo*. At the *con moto* before Fig. 12, the gentlemen with the quavers are requested to play lightly. Now, at Fig. 13 I want the following instruments to stand out – 7th and 8th bar, clarinet; 9th bar, oboe; 10th, clarinet again; and the accompanying instruments are to play quietly, if you please. Now let us play once more as far as Fig. 13.'

This time he listens less intently, and begins to direct the playing with more decision, stopping to clear up more details, and taking freer *tempi*. At a stop for further detail he mentions Fig. 6. 'Gentlemen, I do not intend to bother about the passage at No. 6. It has never been heard yet, and I doubt whether it ever will be.' He goes on in the same manner to No. 13, then – 'Violas, not too much *crescendo* in your first bar, and then *diminuendo* to help you to build up your phrase right up to the top. Reserve your transports for that note, if you please, and not before. And at the five semiquavers at the end of your phrase, I should like a shade more tone, and *molto diminuendo*, so that they fade into the next bar – and together, please.' He plays on, continually stopping for corrections.

At the *molto adagio* (5 bars before No. 17) he draws out the first violin phrase and moves on again in each alternate bar. The harp semiquavers have to be fitted in from Beecham's back view, as best they can, for he turns full to the first violins for the whole of this passage. At Fig. 18 he speaks to the 'cello and first horn: ''Cello, in your solo you must listen to the horn, who shares your tune – in this case his sound will travel down to you quicker than yours to him, whatever the acoustical experts may say. Now I want this solo played very free, with a slight quickening of the tempo at the beginning of each bar, and making up for it at the ends. Four bars before No. 20, cymbals, a grand smash of your delightful instrument to help in the general welter of sound, if you please!'

In the next passage he asks for special care over the climax, which should be two bars before Fig. 20, and not at the *prestissimo*. He plays this several times – from the *tranquillo* to Fig. 22 – working up both *tempo* and fire, until he is satisfied that the orchestra will respond to any of his demands, which may never be quite the same. This terrific feeling of stress he keeps up at white heat right into the march theme at Fig. 23. This march, at the first rehearsal, was comparatively subdued, both as to *tempo* and power (at the concert he swung it along with the theme *fff* and considerably quicker), and then he suddenly shuts off the sound, like a sharply shut window, for the solo violin passage in octaves with flute and bassoon.

Momentum is again regained until the *ritenuto* before Fig. 25, and he ends the episode with a terrific crash on the two G flat chords, which he rehearses once or twice for sufficient attack and power.

Three bars after the ensuing *meno mosso* [2 bars after Fig. 25] he stops again. 'Gentlemen in the clarinet department, how can you resist such an impassioned appeal from the second violins? Give them an answer, I beg you!' This three-bar sentence starting in the second violins, followed by the clarinets and concluded by solo violin and first horn, is the kind of thing Beecham creates out of Delius – three entirely separate ideas, woven into an intensely expressive sentence that is full of the tenderest feeling, yet never allowed to become sentimental or sickly. At the *adagio molto* after Fig. 27 he beats eight, giving the oboe the utmost freedom to enjoy a *tenuto* on his top A and B flat, before his descending semiquavers, the whole of the accompaniment being hushed to a whisper. Having rehearsed a clear change of harmony on the last chord before Fig. 28, he bustles on to a similar climax at Fig. 30, marking the top three bars before Fig. 31 and demanding still more force at the bar after Fig. 32. The tempo at Fig. 33 is still kept up to the *allegretto grazioso*, and only subsides gradually. No. 34 he takes in six, in *tempo rubato*, with a good deal of space between the quavers at the end of the bar, but the bassoons and horns have to move in strict tempo in the next bar. The same thing happens, only more quietly, in the strings' next phrase, the following two bars subsiding into the quietest sound from the bassoon and bass-clarinet. After a break, the string chords fade, each one less, into nothing. He makes a point for the oboe at this spot [3 bars after Fig. 36]. 'That tune of yours, oboe, I want it played as if you heard someone whistling, walking away from you in the street, and suddenly turning a corner, when he gets to your second D. I hope the piccolo has now succeeded in opening his door!'

Appendix 3

A Selection of Beecham's Writings on Delius

That Beecham was a distinguished writer, orator and conversationalist needs no elaboration here. Rarely did he have occasion to write about Delius, but some of the articles and conversation pieces dating from various times in his career are included here out of general interest and for the additional light they cast on aspects of his relationship with the composer. One piece of oratory is, however, essential to the record of Beecham's work for Delius: the funeral oration he delivered on the occasion of Delius's reburial in England in May 1935. This was much admired at the time. John Barbirolli was one of many musicians present, later recording this impression: 'The stone of the church was not the best sonority for that music, but T.B. has a lovely feeling for it ... and his very eloquent and dignified oration at the grave-side, I like to think, sums up all that is best in T.B. His love and championship of Delius I am sure is absolutely sincere ...' Beecham's words are here reproduced in full.

Funeral Oration at St Peter's Church, Limpsfield, Surrey on 26 May 1935
(The Archive of Shirley, Lady Beecham)

We are here today to bid farewell for ever to Frederick Delius, a great Englishman and a famous man. You have read that it was his wish to be buried in the soil of his native country. I think it may be said that nowhere in the breadth of this land could a fairer spot be found than this to satisfy his wish, nor a more auspicious occasion than this beautiful day.

It may have struck some of you as requiring a little explanation as to why Frederick Delius, who left these shores as a very young man, a wanderer and almost an exile, has returned to them finally only yesterday. You may like to know why it was he wished to lie here amid the countryside of the land which gave him birth. I think I am able to give you the explanation.

The England that we live in today is not by any means that in which Delius was born, some 75 years ago. He was born in those days which excited and provoked the rage of the sages of the time. Carlyle, Matthew Arnold, Ruskin raged and preached against the brutality, inhumanity, and insensibility of that age. England at that time seemed to be a country given up to the worship of commercial prosperity

169

and little else besides. It was a country that revolted the finer spirits of that time, and in certain cases drove them out of it elsewhere, where they hoped to find, and they did indeed find, a more sympathetic environment.

Delius was born in a part of the world which was particularly odious to him and to the kind of critical intelligence I have mentioned. It was the arid, hard, business North. It was into this environment and these conditions that Delius was born, and among which he grew up – and he grew up a rebel and a dissentient. He strove to escape, and he did escape, and when he left this country as a young man he went to other countries and finally settled in the country which, in the opinion of everyone at that time, provided the outlet for his activities and the fitting soil for the reception of his great gifts, as well as circumstances in which he could work in peace and enjoy the sympathy of those about him.

But he returned to this country about 25 years ago, but for brief visits, and he did not find such a world of difference. War broke out, and something strange happened, which revealed this country in a different light to the entire world. To the astonishment of the world, this country turned its back on the idols of the market and the counting house, and embarked upon the greatest adventure of idealism the world has, perhaps, ever known.

From that moment the eyes of this great musician turned inquiringly and wonderingly towards the shores of his native land. Also, in the meantime, another strange thing happened. His music, which I venture to say is extraordinarily redolent of the soil of this country and characteristic of the finer elements of the national spirit, became known, it became loved, and came to be understood. It had always been respected.

Six years ago, yet another event took place in London. It was without parallel in the musical history of this country. A festival was given of his works at which he was present – blind, paralysed, but none the less present, and able to listen to every note. That also was a revelation to Frederick Delius, our friend. In his departure from England back to France after this festival, he turned to those in charge of him – for you must remember he could not see anything – and said, 'Place my chair so that my eyes may be directed upon the shores of England, which has given me the recognition that I have not obtained anywhere else.'

I am proud to say that the greatest respect and understanding of his works proceed from the people of this land, that it grows daily, and it shows no sign of diminishing – and so far as it is possible to foresee, if there is any music that will remain honoured and immortal in the memory of the people of any one country, it is the music of this composer.

I said we were here to bid farewell for ever to the mortal remains of Frederick Delius. I do so in no spirit of sorrow or regret. The most precious part of this man is the immortal part – his spirit as revealed in his work; and in whatever sphere that spirit is, I should like our greetings to pass beyond the confines of this earthy sphere, and let him know that we are here not in a spirit of vain regret, but rather one of rejoicing with us for evermore.

Delius, the Neglected Genius
(*Evening Standard*, 13 January 1927)

A few weeks ago I was dining at a friend's house, and among the subjects of conversation was the Order of Merit. Of those present most knew nothing and only a few anything at all about it. An eminent politician declared it to be the highest honour the Government could confer on a man who had brought uncommon distinction to his craft or calling, but he was able to remember the name of only one recipient, an ex-Prime Minister. An application to a popular book of reference revealed the curious fact that there were over half-a-dozen vacancies in the Order, which suggested that the advisers of the Government were unacquainted with any outstanding personality to whom it might be offered. At least such was the view of the eminent politician, and clearly he ought to know.

I am not of that optimistic tribe that sees the world of today flooded with genius; but I think that the pessimism of the official outlook would have sent a chill to the heart of Jeremiah himself. And on the way home my mind was haunted by thoughts of a great Englishman, one of the most remarkable of this or any other age, upon whom his country has never bestowed a single mark of recognition. As it is likely that there are millions to whom his name is unknown, I may say that Frederick Delius is not one of those flamboyant figures who contrive to be constantly in the public eye in one fashion or another.

There has rarely existed a man of equal consequence who has so assiduously avoided publicity. To him the arts of advertisement mean no more than to an Arab in the desert. He lives alone and far from the haunts of men. But this has not hindered him from developing into one of the most singular and picturesque figures of our generation, from creating a fair portion of its loveliest music, and from being (in the opinion of many) the greatest musician England has borne since the death of Purcell.

There are few things more reckless than prophecy about the arts or artists, and the annals of criticism overflow with examples of the devout faith of one decade transformed into the irreverent doubt of the next. But I propose to ignore the warning of experience and to assert boldly that when the historian of fifty years hence comes to sift the wheat from the chaff of latter-day music, Delius will be found with a heavier account on the credit side of his artistic balance-sheet than any other living composer. A select company already knows this of a certainty, and each succeeding year adds to the number of those who suspect it. But his popularity is likely to grow more steadily than sensationally, for his music is the very counterpart of the man.

In comparison with that of a great contemporary, Richard Strauss, it is as the voice of Wordsworth when first heard beside that of Byron. The storms and struggles, the joys and sorrows of our everyday life are not its main preoccupation. It has much of the aloof and observing spirit that Goethe admired and coveted above all else, and it is less the spokesman of the passions of humanity than the interpreter of the moods of nature from the oppressive and lonely grandeur of the Scandinavian Fells to the soft and soothing calm of the English countryside. It is this contemplative rather than dramatic strain which has delayed a fuller understanding of him, for even in art it is not easy for a man to make himself heard nowadays above the cackling clamour of mediocrity unless he shouts at the top of his voice all the time.

It has also made him unusually difficult of interpretation, and I cannot think of a composer who has suffered more severely from inadequate or perverted readings. I went to the first hearing in London of one of his later works: it lasted a third of the time longer than intended. The audience was plainly disappointed and bored, and no wonder! But in spite of these disabilities the fame of his music as well as the love of it grows apace, and more quickly in foreign lands than at home. On the Continent he obtains more performances than any other English composer, and in this way he has assisted to rebuild the credit of our music more effectively than a dozen lesser gifted musicians I could mention who could have rendered better service to their country by resisting the dangerous temptation to cross the Channel.

And as my memory recalled and traversed half a dozen of his masterpieces, the picturesque breadth of *Appalachia*, the sombre brilliance of *Paris*, the tender pathos of *Sea Drift* (the finest example in all music of the 'arioso recitativo'), the simple charm of much of the *Village Romeo and Juliet*, the *Mass of Life*, and those exquisite fragments *On hearing the First Cuckoo in Spring* and *Summer Night on the River*, the more I wondered what was the purpose of a bauble such as the Order of Merit if not to be offered in humble thanksgiving to a man who has gladdened the world with this vision of beauty.

But our way of judging and rewarding genius has ever been mysterious, as I was reminded later on that same night when my work of preparation for a concert that was imminent evoked the image of another Master who lived and laboured amongst us two centuries ago. For thirty years the mighty Handel strove to scale the rock of British hostility and indifference, only to fall back at the end exhausted and vanquished. The greatest dynamic force known to musical history was driven to ruin, paralysis, and blindness. The public, when satisfied that the creator of eighty operas and oratorios could write no more, indulged in the luxury of a brief revulsion of feeling and buried him in Westminster Abbey.

But fate, powerless to inflict further injury on the man himself, pursued the children of his brain with unchanging malevolence. Ever since his death the musicians of this country, assisted by the barbarous taste of the public, have done everything imaginable to promote a complete misunderstanding of his works, which today lie buried deep beneath the crushing weight of a tradition that has become the scorn of Europe.

I often read that we live in an age which with all its faults is kinder and more merciful than any that has gone before. Posterity will be a better judge of this than ourselves, but I am willing to admit that we have a different method of dealing with artists who do not instantaneously tickle our superficial palates. The aristocratic society of the eighteenth century persecuted them, which may have been unpleasant: the democratic community of the twentieth ignores them, which is fatal.

Wide apart as the Poles in every other respect, these two composers meet on the common ground of affliction, for the same physical calamities which darkened Handel's declining years have overtaken Frederick Delius. Well over sixty years of age, he, too, lies helpless, paralysed and blind; and unless the gods intervene to restore his sight the voice of this sweet singer will now be mute until the day of his death.

Even the loftiest spirits are not insensible to a token of national regard, and in the hour of tribulation they may be partly solaced by it. An act of grace and justice is within the dispensation of our rulers. May they be minded to accomplish it before the ultimate night descends upon their great countryman.

An Unknown Opera of Delius's Youth
(*The Daily Telegraph* and *Morning Post*, 21 March 1953)

Irmelin, Frederick Delius's first completed opera, was written a little over sixty years ago. What I mean by saying that, is that it was his first 'completed' opera is that during the two years preceding the beginning of his work on *Irmelin* he had experimented, none too successfully, with libretti based on Bulwer Lytton's novel *Zanoni* and Ibsen's historical drama *Emperor and Galilean*.

The composer was just thirty at the time, and had already written a considerable quantity of instrumental, choral and vocal music, hardly any of which has been published. In the case of any other musician this might be surprising: but in that of Delius it may be recalled that after the passage of another ten years, not one of his major works had found its way into print.

For this reason the average musical amateur might be excused for concluding that Delius wrote little of interest before the beginning of the present century. Of those works with which the public is most familiar, such as *Sea Drift*, *Appalachia*, *Brigg Fair*, *A Mass of Life*, *A Village Romeo and Juliet*, together with the two miniatures *On hearing the First Cuckoo in Spring* and *Summer Night on the River*, all were written when their author had run into his fourth decade.

It has been too readily assumed by some commentators on this music that, because most of that portion of it written between 1888 and 1899 has not received the benefit either of performance or publication, it must on that account have defects of immaturity which influenced the composer against its issue or production. But this is by no means the whole truth of the matter. During his later days, when he was incapacitated for further creative work on any sustained level, his thoughts frequently turned to the days of his springtime.

More than once he spoke to me of his two earlier operas, *Irmelin* and *The Magic Fountain*, and when I asked him if he would like to see them produced the answer he gave me ran something like this: 'When you are satisfied that all or most of the works of my best period have been made well-known to the public through performance and publication, I should offer no objection to the appearance of any of those earlier pieces of mine which in your opinion would detract nothing from such prestige as my name may have acquired.'

If we give more than a casual glance at the general body of this composer's work, we shall at once recognise that the theatre never ceased to occupy his thoughts. During something like twenty years he wrote six operas, whose playing time exceeds in duration that of all his other compositions taken together; and nearly his last effort of consequence was also a stage work, *Hassan*, for which he wrote a large amount of incidental music.

For this reason I suggest that it is worth examining, with a closer interest than has yet been given to them, some of his operas which so far have never been heard in this country; and it is to the two earliest of them that our curiosity might usefully be directed and, I venture to say, without disappointment.

The term immature can be justified only if we think of the first twenty-five works of Beethoven as unripe, when compared with those that followed them. The early piano sonatas foreshadowed little of the splendours of the 'Waldstein' or 'Appassionata', nor does the Second Symphony anticipate anywhere the dramatic magnificence of the Third and the Fifth. But we have not ceased to love and to play them; and the same may be said of the youthful flights, symphonic or operatic, of many other composers. To me, in any case, the first Delian period has a very lively interest, and the two operas which I have mentioned are the peak points of it.

Although I intend to bring forward at some time or other *The Magic Fountain* as well as the last opera of all, *Fennimore and Gerda*, it is only *Irmelin* upon which I now ask leave to comment. The libretto, which unites two stories of different origin, was written by the composer himself. The legend of Irmelin, a king's daughter who rejects the marriage offers of a hundred noble suitors, is Northern and early mediaeval. That of the Princess and the Swineherd belongs to the less dateable period of the fairy-tale.

To this alliance Delius has added a new element of the sort to be found in all his other operas – save one. This takes the shape of a force, either in nature or destiny, which tends to make the human actors in the drama of almost secondary importance. Here it is the Silver Stream. Before the curtain rises its course has unhappily been lost by Nils, the Prince-swineherd who consequently has been reduced to a condition of degrading servitude under Rolf, a robber chieftain. Eventually he rediscovers it and is led by its friendly influence to Irmelin, who at once recognises in him the lover of her dreams.

In *The Magic Fountain* is to be found the same subservience of the hero and heroine to powers stronger than their own: in *Koanga* we have the semi-mystical influence of Voodoo, and in both *A Village Romeo and Juliet* and *Fennimore and Gerda* we view the slightly disconcerting spectacle of unfortunate creatures struggling without avail against superior forces unseen. But, although vanquished, the victims do not surrender without some show of resistance. Occasionally it is heroic, more often pathetic; but invariably romantic and poetic.

As for the music, the writing for voices is smoothly singable, and that for the orchestra reveals an easy plasticity and wealth of colour, demonstrating that Delius had nothing here to learn from any other composer living at the time. An appealing freshness permeates the whole piece, the style and content of which are unmistakeably those of the creator of *Sea Drift* and *A Mass of Life*.

Lastly, *Irmelin* is the only one of Delius's six operas which has a satisfactorily happy ending, thus making it suitable for performance at a moment when all of us hope to be taking part in joyful celebrations.

Sir Thomas's Tribute to Delius
(*Daily Telegraph*, 5 July 1934)

Sir Thomas Beecham's speech in memory of Delius, at the performance of 'A Village Romeo and Juliet' at the Royal College of Music on Wednesday, was most felicitous and graceful in its phrasing, and moving in its seriousness. He rather surprised his audience by mentioning that there is reason to think the Delius family to have been originally English. The composer's parents were of German extraction, and their ancestors it is known, were Dutch. Sir Thomas's suggestion was that the family, generations ago, had gone to Holland from England.

'How little, my soul, thou needest to be happy!' These words, from *A Mass of Life*, were, said Sir Thomas, supremely applicable to Delius. A garden in France, a summer holiday in Norway – this was all he asked of life. Sir Thomas described the contrast between Delius's intellect and his essential nature – the one so subtle, so cultivated, the heir of centuries of civilisation, and the latter utterly simple. Delius, he said, looked like a prince of the Roman Church of the Renaissance. He had a mind that might have given him high place in the Church, in the world of banking, at Scotland Yard, or in the profession of economics. He chose a life of simplicity, and the simplicity of that life, and of Delius's pleasures – the sight of sunlight on his flower-beds, and the sound of wind in the leaves – was, Sir Thomas insisted, in his music, 'a music', in the Wordsworthian phrase, 'born of murmuring sounds'.

An Anglo-American Composer
(*The Observer*, 26 May 1935)

At midnight last night the body of Frederick Delius, which has been brought over from France, was re-interred at Limpsfield. A memorial service will be held to-day. Fifteen members of the London Philharmonic Orchestra will play, and a funeral oration will be pronounced by Sir Thomas Beecham, who was a great friend of the composer.

'Delius came from a very ancient European family,' Sir Thomas told a representative of *The Observer* yesterday. 'The name seems to have been originally Delij, but was Latinised in the sixteenth century into Delius.' Another name Latinised at the same period was Erasmus. Members of the family were found scattered over Europe, in Holland, Hungary, and England. A Delius was Chaplain to Edward VI. The composer descended from a branch of the family who lived in Westphalia in the early eighteenth century, a member of whom became a wool merchant in Bradford. 'But Delius himself showed no trace of his Teutonic origin in his character, tastes, or accomplishments. He was peculiar to himself, a composite type of another century. He was a throwback to an earlier strain of his family: he bore no resemblance to his parents or to his sisters.'

Norse Influence

'No one has ever fully examined,' continued Sir Thomas, 'the influence of Scandinavia on the music and culture of the North of England, Scotland and Ireland. After all, the Vikings overran Ireland for 300 years. The name of Dublin is Norwegian. The island of Lewis, off the coast of Scotland, was Norwegian till the eighteenth century. The melancholy of Celtic music probably comes from the Vikings. The Vikings invaded and left their stamp on Russia in the eighth, and Ireland in tenth. There is', he said, 'remarkable resemblance between Russian and Irish melodies. Some of the music of "Prince Igor" can be found note for note, cadence for cadence in Irish tunes. Grieg, whose grandfather came from the East Coast of Scotland, was another inheritor of this tradition.'

Germany and Florida

'Although Delius studied in Germany, lived in France, and visited Italy, he derived nothing from the music of those countries. I have thought of writing a book on Delius,' continued Sir Thomas, 'entitled "An Anglo-American Composer". Delius was never poor, though like Horace his means were exiguous. His parents disliked the idea of his going to the Continent to study music, and to head him off from the Continent of Europe bought him an orange plantation in Florida. Germany and Florida! But his family forgot another Continent! – Africa!

'Among the American Negroes fifty-five years ago, Delius came into contact with the spontaneous music of primitive peoples. The Welsh are an example of such spontaneous music,' Sir Thomas said, 'Wales has always been a back-water of European life. The art, and the history of European music mean nothing to the Welsh. They hear instrumental music with reluctance. But they can sing! Any Welsh gathering has the inherited gift of song; they can improvise their own harmonies.'

His Gift of Harmony

'Delius had latent in him the most delicate and complicated feeling for harmony of any European composer. And contact with African music brought it out. Negro music was not then contaminated by jazz: a vulgar imposition of an over-sophisticated degenerate frivolity on the single rhythm of the Negro. Delius did not use the phraseology of negro music except as an illustration, but contact with it brought out his gifts.'

He eventually deserted his plantation and an emissary of his family finally found him teaching music in a girls' school in Jacksonville. His family now saw he had determined to pursue music, and 'Fred' was sent to study in Leipzig 'in the days when every student went to hear Tristan and the next day would desert their classes en masse to discuss it.' 'After Leipzig,' Sir Thomas said, 'he lived in Paris under the protection of his opulent Uncle Theodore, and in France he married, and died there last year after a long illness which left him blind and paralysed.'

His Dying Wish

'Delius's developments of his gifts of melody and harmony made him one of the great composers of all time. He was a cosmopolitan, like the educated English of a former day, like Thomas More. England's cultural insularity only dates from the long isolation of the Napoleonic wars,' said Sir Thomas. 'The three intellectual influences on Delius were the philosophy of Nietzsche, the literature of Scandinavia, particularly Ibsen, Jakobsen, and Lie, and the French impressionist school of painting, the works of Corot, Claude Monet, Sisley, Gauguin, and Cezanne. All of these he talked about constantly.'

Before he died Delius expressed the wish to be buried in England. His wife's illness made it impossible at the time, but his friends have now arranged for his reinterment in Limpsfield, chosen not for particular associations with Delius but for its beauty and accessibility to his friends. The reasons for his desire to return to England Sir Thomas will speak of in a speech which will be broadcast from the churchyard.

In Conversation with Lord Boothby in 1958
(*High Fidelity Magazine*, October 1958)

Delius was a very unusual person, a very uncommon type of man. He was a rebel, an independent, who described himself as a conservative anarchist. This applied to his life as well as to his art. His music, once he had found himself, was largely underivative. He owed very little to predecessors. His ancestry was lost somewhere in the mist of the past. His period of inspiration lasted for about ten to twelve years, say from 1901 to 1914, just as it did with Debussy.

He was good company, until he became tiresome on the subject of religion and Christianity. He considered it a part of his duty on earth to convert everyone to a deeply anti-Christian point of view, especially young people ... He was, by the way, a first-rate conversationalist and very easily wiped the floor with almost everyone of his time. I have heard him converse with Shaw and Belloc and others and he always held his own. Unlike nearly all English controversialists, he had a deep sense of logic. Having created the central point in any argument he hung on to it like grim death and never let go. Other people could scratch around it, but he would always return to the central point.

Appendix 4

Arrangements and Orchestrations of Delius's music by Beecham

The collected edition of Delius's works issued in conjunction with the Delius Trust incorporates Sir Thomas Beecham's scores as 'revised and edited' by him in preparation for his own performances. The following is a list of the works in which he went further than altering dynamics and adding phrasings and tempo suggestions to Delius's original scores, to produce his own 'edited and arranged' edition of certain pieces.

Orchestral Works

A Village Romeo and Juliet: 'Intermezzo', The Walk to the Paradise Garden
[Scoring: 2 flutes, oboe, cor anglais, 2 clarinets, 2 bassoons, 4 horns, 2 trumpets, three trombones, timpani, harp, strings]
Published 1940 by Hawkes & Son Ltd.

Though it was not actually published until 1940, Beecham had been playing this music separately from the opera at his concerts since 1910, so it is likely that his arrangement existed much earlier than the date of publication.

Hassan: Intermezzo and Serenade
[*Intermezzo*: flute, oboe, cor anglais, clarinet, bassoon, 2 horns, trumpet, timpani, harp, strings. *Serenade*: solo violin, harp, strings]
Published 1940 by Hawkes & Son Ltd.

Beecham's first performance of any of the music that Delius composed for *Hassan* was at a concert on 5 March 1933.

Irmelin: Concert Suite from Act II, 'Scenes from Irmelin'
[3 flutes (3rd doubling piccolo), 2 oboes, cor anglais, 2 clarinets, bass clarinet, 3 bassoons, 4 horns, 2 cornets, 2 trumpets, 3 trombones, tuba, timpani, percussion, harp, strings]
Published 1955 by Boosey & Hawkes Ltd.

First performance 14 October 1953.

Marche Caprice
[2 flutes (2nd doubling piccolo), 2 oboes, 2 clarinets, 2 bassoons, 4 horns, 2
    trumpets, 3 trombones, tuba, timpani, percussion, strings]
Published 1951 by Joseph Williams Ltd (now Stainer & Bell Ltd).

First performance 21 November 1946. The programme of the Delius Festival for
this date did not say so, but this was the first hearing anywhere of this piece: and
although Beecham conducted, no mention was made of any arrangement by him,
and so one concludes that the original score was played. Delius included parts for
3rd flute (doubling piccolo) and 2 cornets, which are omitted (but absorbed) in
Beecham's score.

Summer Evening
[3 flutes (3rd doubling piccolo), 2 oboes, 2 clarinets, 2 bassoons, 4 horns, 2
    trumpets, 3 trombones, tuba, timpani, strings]
Published 1951 by Joseph Williams Ltd (now Stainer & Bell Ltd).

First performance 2 January 1949. This was Beecham's first performance of the
piece: Richard Austin had conducted its actual first performance at the 1946 Delius
Festival, presumably in Delius's original scoring. Beecham's publication follows
Delius's scoring.

Song Orchestrations

Autumn
Scoring: 2 flutes, oboe, cor anglais, 2 clarinets, 2 bassoons, 4 horns, 3 trombones,
    tuba, harp, strings.

Young Venevil
2 flutes, 2 oboes, 2 clarinets, 2 bassoons, 4 horns, strings. Transposed from C major
    into D flat major.

Twilight Fancies
2 flutes, oboe, cor anglais, 2 clarinets, 2 bassoons, 4 horns, harp, strings.
    Transposed from B minor into C minor.

To Daffodils
Flute, oboe, strings.

So sweet is she (original title: 'So white, so soft, so sweet is she')
Strings

Beecham's song orchestrations are completely new scores, sometimes (but not always) involving a pitch transposition. A comparison between his and Delius's version of, say, *Twilight Fancies*, is endlessly fascinating, particularly in respect of Beecham's imaginative use of the harp, which the composer does not even include in his instrumentation (otherwise almost identical). Besides Beecham's and Delius's own, song orchestrations exist by Philip Heseltine and Constant Lambert, among others. There are three by Henry Gibson (*The Violet*, *Cradle Song* and *The Bird's Story*) dating from the time when Gibson was Beecham's musical secretary, some of which have been attributed to Beecham, but the above five are the only ones of which a manuscript score in Beecham's own hand exists. They are undated and it is not possible to determine exactly when they were first heard. The three attributed to Henry Gibson, however, were sung by Dora Labbette in Beecham's broadcast concert on 8 February 1929 (see pp.41–2) when they were referred to by *The Times* reviewer (perhaps with inside knowledge) as 'scored by Sir Thomas Beecham for Miss Dora Labbette'. Unidentified Delius songs also figured in the programmes of several orchestral concerts in which she and Beecham appeared together during the 1929–30 season. Then Dora Labbette sang *Autumn*, *Twilight Fancies* and *Young Venevil* at a Promenade concert conducted by Sir Henry Wood on 17 September 1931, when all three were described as 'Orchestrated by Beecham'. (One surmises that orchestrations by Beecham would not have been Wood's first choice, given their personal antipathy and the fact that at least one of the songs, *Twilight Fancies*, existed in an orchestral version by Delius himself which had been specially requested from him by Wood's wife Olga and sung by her under her husband's baton in 1908. But Beecham's transcriptions transposed *Twilight Fancies* and *Young Venevil* up in pitch to suit Dora Labbette's voice better, and that was perhaps the persuading factor for Wood.) On 9 October 1934 Labbette sang *To Daffodils* and *So sweet is she* to Beecham's piano accompaniment at a concert in Liverpool; his orchestrations were presumably made subsequent to this date, but no performance of them in this form has been traced.

Bibliography

Barjansky, Catherine. *Portraits with Backgrounds*. Geoffrey Bles, London, 1948.

Beecham, Sir Thomas, Bart., CH. *A Mingled Chime*. Hutchinson, London, 1944.

———. *Frederick Delius*. Hutchinson, London, 1959.

The Sir Thomas Beecham Society. *The Sir Thomas Beecham Society 1964–88. Newsletters 1–128 complete*. Ed. D.V. Ford. The Sir Thomas Beecham Society, London, 1989.

———. *Sir Thomas Beecham, Bart. CH. A Calendar of his Concert and Theatrical Performances*. Vol. I (ed. Maurice Parker) 1985; Supplement (ed. Tony Benson) 1998.

Bird, John. *Percy Grainger*. Oxford University Press, Oxford, 1999.

Blackwood, Alan. *Sir Thomas Beecham*. Ebury Press, London, 1994.

Camden, Archie. *Blow by Blow*. Thames Publishing, London, 1982.

Cardus, Neville. *Sir Thomas Beecham: A Memoir*. Collins, London, 1961.

Carley, Lionel. *Delius: A Life in Letters 1862–1935*. 2 vols. Scolar Press, London, 1983 and 1988.

Dean, Basil. *Seven Ages 1888–1927*. Hutchinson, London, 1927.

Delius, Clare. *Frederick Delius: Memories of My Brother*. Ivor Nicholson & Watson, London, 1935.

The Delius Society of Great Britain. *Newsletters* and *Journals*. 1962–2003.

Elkin, Robert. *Royal Philharmonic*. Rider and Company, London, 1946.

Fenby, Eric. *Delius as I Knew Him*. G. Bell & Sons Ltd, London, 1937. Revised edition with additional material: Faber & Faber, London, 1981.

———. *Delius*. 'The Great Composers'. Faber & Faber, London, 1971.

Foreman, Lewis (ed.). *The Percy Grainger Companion*. Thames Publishing, 1981.

——— (ed.). *From Parry to Britten. British Music in Letters 1900–1945*. B.T. Batsford Ltd, London, 1987.

——— (ed.). *Music in England 1885-1920*. Thames Publishing, 1994.

Francis, Anne. *A Guinea a Box*. Robert Hale, London, 1968.

Gilmour, J.D. *Sir Thomas Beecham: The Seattle Years 1941–43*. World Press, Washington, 1978.

———. *Sir Thomas Beecham: The North American Tour 1950*. North Beach Printing Co., Washington, 1979.

———. *Sir Thomas Beecham: 50 Years in the 'New York Times'*. Thames Publishing, London, 1988.

Goossens, Eugene. *Overture and Beginners*. Methuen & Co., London, 1945.

184 *While Spring and Summer Sang*

Gray, Cecil. *Peter Warlock: A Memoir of Philip Heseltine*. Jonathan Cape, London, 1934.

———. *Musical Chairs*. Home & Van Thal, London, 1948.

Gray, Michael. *Beecham: A Centenary Discography*. Duckworth, London, 1979.

Harrison, Beatrice. *The Cello and the Nightingales. The Autobiography of Beatrice Harrison*. Ed. Patricia Cleveland-Peck. John Murray, London, 1985.

Heseltine, Philip. *Frederick Delius*. John Lane The Bodley Head, London, 1923.

Hudson, Derek. *Norman O'Neill: A Life in Music*. Quality Press, London, 1945.

Hutchings, Arthur. *Delius*. Macmillan & Co. Ltd, London, 1948.

Jacobs, Arthur. *Henry J. Wood: Maker of the Proms*. Methuen, London, 1994.

Jefferson, Alan. *Sir Thomas Beecham*. Macdonald & Jane's, London, 1979.

Jones, D. Marblacy. 'Look Back in Envy. Reprints of early Delius concert reviews'. *The Delius Society Newsletter*, 1968–70.

Kenyon, Nicholas. *The BBC Symphony Orchestra*. BBC, London, 1981.

King-Smith, Beresford. *Crescendo! 75 Years of the City of Birmingham Symphony Orchestra*. Methuen, London, 1995.

Lloyd, Stephen. *H. Balfour Gardiner*. Cambridge University Press, Cambridge, 1984.

———. *Sir Dan Godfrey*. Thames Publishing, London, 1995.

——— (ed.). *Fenby on Delius*. Thames Publishing, London, 1996.

Moiseiwitsch, Maurice. *Moiseiwitsch: Biography of a Concert Pianist*. Frederick Muller Ltd, London, 1965.

Pettitt, Stephen. *Philharmonia Orchestra: A Record of Achievement 1945–85*. Robert Hale Ltd, London, 1985.

Procter-Gregg, Humphrey. *Beecham Remembered*. Duckworth, London, 1976.

Redwood, Christopher (ed.). *A Delius Companion*. John Calder, London, 1976.

Redwood, Dawn. *Flecker and Delius: The Making of Hassan*. Thames Publishing, London, 1978.

Reid, Charles. *Thomas Beecham*. Victor Gollancz, London, 1962.

———. *Malcolm Sargent*. Hamish Hamilton, London, 1968.

Rosen, Carole. *The Goossens: A Musical Century*. André Deutsch, London, 1993.

Russell, Thomas. *Philharmonic Decade*. Hutchinson & Co., London, 1945.

Sanders, Alan (ed.). *Walter Legge: Words and Music*. Duckworth, London 1998.

Savage, R. Temple. *A Voice from the Pit*. David & Charles, Newton Abbot, 1988.

Schwarzkopf, Elisabeth (ed.). *On and Off the Record: A Memoir of Walter Legge*. Faber & Faber, London, 1982.

Shore, Bernard. *The Orchestra Speaks*. Longmans, Green & Co., London, 1938.

Smyth, Ethel. *Beecham and Pharaoh*. Chapman & Hall Ltd, London, 1935.

Tertis, Lionel. *My Viola and I*. Elek Books, London, 1974.

Threlfall, Robert. *A Catalogue of the Compositions of Frederick Delius*. The Delius Trust, London, 1977.

———. *A Supplementary Catalogue*. The Delius Trust, London, 1986.

————. *Frederick Delius. Complete Works. Editorial Report*. The Delius Trust, London, 1990.

Wetherell, Eric. *Albert Sammons*. Thames Publishing, London, 1998.

Index

Index of Delius's music

Reference is made only to those works mentioned in this volume.
*Figures in **bold type** refer to the work's entry in 'A Critical Discography'.*

Air and Dance 45, 48, 53
Appalachia (American Rhapsody) 134
Appalachia 2, 3, 4, 5, 7, 16, 17, 26, 34, 43,
    46, 48, 61, 63–5, 76, 82, 83, 90, 93, 98,
    104, 108, 120, 129, 131, **141–2**, 173
Arabesque, An 20, 25, 43, 46, 102, 105,
    106, 127, **142–3**

Brigg Fair 4, 5, 7, 16, 17, 18, 20, 24, 38,
    39, 40, 44, 52–3, 56, 57, 61, 81, 83, 90,
    96, 97, 104, 107, 114, 118, 127, 129,
    143, 173

Calinda, La 82, 105, 106, 127, 131, **150–51**
Caprice and Elegy 28, 74
Concerto for cello and orchestra 34, 35, 51
Concerto for piano and orchestra 2, 4, 16,
    17, 18, 21–22, 25, 28–9, 44, 46, 48, 56,
    70, 76, 81, 83, 90, 92, 97, 98, 101, 102,
    104, 107, 108, 111, 113, 114, 118, 127,
    144
Concerto for violin and orchestra 25, 46,
    56, 104, 107, 108, 115, 118, 119, 121,
    126, 135, **144–5**
Concerto for violin, cello and orchestra 28,
    43, 52, 76, 84–5, 105

Dance of Life, A (*see* Life's Dance) 4, 5
Dance for Harpsichord 46, 48
Dance Rhapsody No. 1, A 12, 16, 17, 18,
    20, 26, 35, 46, 57, 81, 104, 107, 114,
    117, 118, 127, 131, **145**, 148
Dance Rhapsody No.2, A 41, 45, 52, 61,
    62, 98, 100, 104, 107, 108, 115, **145–6**
Danish Songs 5, 26, 114
Double Concerto (*see* Concerto for violin,
    cello and orchestra)

Eventyr 25, 36, 41, 46, 56, 60, 61, 62, 64,
    65, 68, 71, 72, 76, 82, 84, 96, 104, 108,
    117, 127, 129, 131, **146**

Fennimore and Gerda 7, 16, 22, 28, 46,
    174
Fennimore and Gerda, Intermezzo from 28,
    78, 79, 129, **146–7**
Five Piano Pieces 46
Florida suite 80, 81, 82, 129, 130, 131, **147**
Folkeraadet (*see also* Norwegian Suite) 22,
    25, 105, 114

Hassan 32, 38, 50, 52, 61, 62, 68, 71, 74,
    82, 84, 105, 114, 117, 127, 133, **147–9**,
    179

Idyll 65, 99, 102, 104
In a Summer Garden 20, 22, 26, 35, 45, 52,
    56, 70, 78, 79, 82, 98, 100, 104, 116,
    117–8, 119, 129, **149**
Irmelin 82, 123–6, 173–5
Irmelin Prelude 80, 82, 85, 96, 105, 106,
    108, 127, 129, **149**
Irmelin, Scenes from 116, 126, 127, 128,
    141, **149–50**, 179

Koanga 2, 15, 20, 62, 68, 71, 76–8, 82, 84,
    96, 102, 104, 117, 147, 149, **150–51**, 174

Lebenstanz (Life's Dance) 2
Légende 5, 7, 23, 24, 25
Life's Dance 5

Magic Fountain, The 123, 173, 174
Marche Caprice 105, 106, 108, 113, 122,
    129, **150**, 180